Fulbright Papers

PROCEEDINGS OF COLLOQUIA

SPONSORED BY THE
UNITED STATES-UNITED KINGDOM
EDUCATIONAL COMMISSION:
THE
FULBRIGHT COMMISSION
LONDON

Volume 6

The United States Constitution

The Fulbright Programme of Educational Exchanges, which has been in operation since 1946, aims to promote mutual understanding between the United States of America and other nations. It now operates in more than 120 countries, with forty-three bi-national commissions involved in its administration. In the United Kingdom the Commission aims to offer qualified British and American nationals the opportunity to exchange significant knowledge and educational experience in fields of consequence to the two countries, and thereby to contribute to a deeper mutual understanding of Anglo-American relations and to broaden the means by which the two societies can further their understanding of each other's cultures. Among its activities the Commission promotes annual colloquia on topics of Anglo-American interest; the proceedings are published in this series.

The United States Constitution

The first 200 years

Papers delivered at a Bicentennial Colloquium
at the University of Birmingham

edited by

R. C. SIMMONS

MANCHESTER
UNIVERSITY PRESS

IN ASSOCIATION WITH
THE FULBRIGHT COMMISSION, LONDON

DISTRIBUTED EXCLUSIVELY IN THE USA AND CANADA
BY ST. MARTIN'S PRESS

COPYRIGHT © THE US – UK EDUCATIONAL COMMISSION, 1989

Published by MANCHESTER UNIVERSITY PRESS
Oxford Road, Manchester M13 9PL
and Room 400, 175 Fifth Avenue, New York, NY 10010, USA
in association with THE FULBRIGHT COMMISSION,
6 Porter Street, London W1M 2HR

British Library cataloguing in publication data
The United States Constitution: the first 200 years.
—(The Fulbright papers; V. 6).
1. International relations. Ethical aspects
I. Simmons, R. C. II. Series
347.302′2

Library of Congress cataloging in publication data
The United States Constitution: the first 200 years / edited by R. C. Simmons.
p.   cm — (Fulbright paper; v. 6)
Proceedings of the Sixth Fulbright Colloquium held at the University of Birmingham,
Department of American History sponsored by the American Bar Association and
the University of Virginia.
Includes index.
ISBN 0-7190-2923-6
1. United States—Constitutional history—Congresses.
2. Constitutional history—Congresses. I. Simmons, R. C. (Richard C.), 1937–.
II. American Bar Association. III. University of Virginia. IV. Fulbright Colloquium
(6th : 1988 : University of Birmingham, Department of American History) V. Series.
KF4541.A2U55   1989
342.73′029—dc19
[347.30229]   88-39148

ISBN 0-7190-2923-6 *hardback*

Printed and bound in Great Britain by
Courier International Ltd, Tiptree, Essex

Contents

Acknowledgements

The Colloquium was convened by the Fulbright Commission, London, with the assistance of Professor J. R. Pole, Rhodes Professor of American History and Institutions, St Catherine's College, Oxford; Professor Peter Parish, Director, Institute of United States Studies, London; and Richard C. Simmons, Professor of American History, University of Birmingham, for whose advice and help the Commission is particularly grateful. The funding provided by the Commission was supplemented by grants from the University of Virginia and the British Academy; the generous co-operation of these two institutions and, in particular, the assistance in planning given by Professor A. E. Dick Howard, White Burkett Miller Professor of Law and Public Affairs, School of Law, University of Virginia, was much appreciated. The Commission also acknowledges the co-operation of Hofstra University, NY, in connection with the publication of Professor Pole's paper. Finally, it would also like to record its appreciation for the secretarial and other facilities provided by the University of Birmingham both in the planning of the Colloquium and the subsequent editing of the papers presented there.

J. E. F.

Foreword

The Fulbright Colloquium to celebrate the bicentenary of the US Constitution was conceived in collaboration with the American Bar Association and the University of Virginia as part of a series of world-wide activities to mark this significant occasion. The University of Birmingham, American History Department, gave the Colloquium its enthusiastic support and provided the venue for a meeting of distinguished scholars and practitioners in the constitutional field from the United States, France, Germany and the United Kingdom.

The Colloquium is the sixth in the series of conferences sponsored by the Fulbright Commission in London. Such colloquia are held at least once, and possibly twice, a year on topics of Anglo-American interest and importance. They are designed to supplement the traditional exchanges of scholars and students undertaken by the Commission in support of its aim of encouraging Anglo-American cultural relations. Such exchanges between this country and America now exceed 10,000 since the Fulbright programme started in the United Kingdom in 1948.

The Commission was especially pleased to have been instrumental in mounting a Colloquium on the US Constitution in its bicentenary year. This unique document, with its privileged position in history and its continuing significance and relevance today, generated wide interest and stimulated wide-ranging discussions. The present volume records the proceedings of the Colloquium in the form of presented papers; from lack of space, reports on the related discussions have not been included.

The opinions expressed are, of course, personal to the contributors and do not necessarily reflect the views of the Commission. Nevertheless, the Commission believes publication of the proceedings will be welcomed by a wide audience and will provide a valuable addition to US constitutional studies.

John E. Franklin, Executive Director
United States–United Kingdom Educational Commission
The Fulbright Commission, London

Notes on contributors

J. W. BURROW, FBA has been Professor of History at the University of Sussex since 1969. He has also held visiting appointments at the University of California, Berkeley and at the Australian National University. His chief publications are *Evolution and Society* (1966), *A Liberal Descent* – awarded the Wolfson Prize (1981) and *Whigs and Liberals* (1988).

A. E. CAMPBELL is Emeritus Professor of American History at the University of Birmingham. He was a fellow of King's College, Cambridge and then of Keble College, Oxford before moving to Birmingham in 1972. He has taught at several American universities and colleges and is the author of *Great Britain and the United States, 1895-1903,* and of other books and articles.

ARTHUR J. GOLDBERG served as US Secretary of Labor (1961-62) and as Associate Justice of the Supreme Court (1962-65). He was permanent US representative to the United Nations and Ambassador-at-Large (1977-78) and has held a variety of distinguished legal and academic appointments. Among his publications ·s *Equal Justice: The Warren Era of the Supreme Court* (1972).

LOUIS HENKIN is University Professor Emeritus, Columbia University, and has served as law clerk to Judge Learned Hand and to Justice Felix Frankfurter. He was the Chief Reporter of the Restatement of Foreign Relations Law of the United States (1979-87) and Co-Editor-in-Chief of the *American Journal of International Law* (1978-84). His many publications include *Foreign Affairs and the Constitution; The Rights of Man Today* and *How Nations Behave.*

RICHARD HODDER-WILLIAMS graduated from the University of Oxford in 1965. He came to the University of Bristol in 1967, where he is now Reader in Politics. He was a visiting Professor of Political Science at the University of California (Berkeley) in 1984-85 and is the author, among other books, of *The Politics of the US Supreme Court* (1980) and co-editor of *Politics in Britain and the United States* (1986). He is currently writing a book on the relations between the Reagan Administration and the Federal Judiciary.

CATHY MATSON received her PhD from Columbia University in 1985 and has been teaching at the University of Tennessee – Knoxville since then. Her forthcoming book (with Peter Onuf), *A Union of Interests: Politics and Economy in the Revolutionary Era,* will elaborate on themes presented in this collection. A second book, *From Free Trade to Liberty: Dissenting Economic Ideas among New York City Merchants, 1690 to 1790,* will locate some of the roots of American political economy in the pre-revolutionary period.

JOHN HERBERT MCCLUSKEY QC (Scotland) was created a life peer in 1976. Lord McCluskey served as Solicitor-General for Scotland (1974-79) and delivered the BBC Reith lectures in 1986. These were subsequently published as *Law, Justice and Democracy* (1987). He has been a Senator of the College of Justice in Scotland since 1984.

GÜNTER MOLTMANN is Professor of History at the University of Hamburg, Federal Republic of Germany. He is the author of *Amerikas Deutschlandpolitik im Zweiten Weltkrieg* (1958) and *Atlantische Blockpolitik im 19. Jahrhundert* (1973). In recent years he has published widely on German–American migration, including the documentary volume *Aufbruch nach Amerika* (1979). From 1975 to 1978 he was president of the German Association for American Studies.

J. R. POLE, FBA, has been Rhodes Professor of American History and Institutions at the University of Oxford, where he is a fellow of St Catherine's College, since 1979. Among his best known works are *Political Representation and the Origins of the American Republic* (1966) and *The Pursuit of Equality in American Life* (1978). He has lectured and taught widely in the United States and is currently jointly editing *The Blackwell Encyclopedia of the American Revolution*.

DAVID M. RABBAN is Vinson and Elkins Professor at the University of Texas School of Law. He previously served as counsel to the American Association of University Professors. His articles and essays on the history of the Free Speech Clause of the First Amendment have appeared in the *Yale Law Journal*, the *University of Chicago Law Review*, and the *Stanford Law Review*. Assisted by a recent fellowship from the National Endowment for the Humanities, he is currently completing an article on the Free Speech League and the origins of the American Civil Liberties Union.

ODILE RUDELLE works at the Centre National de la Recherche Scientifique (CNRS) and teaches at the Institut d'Etudes Politiques de Paris (IEP). Her main interest is comparative government. She has published *La République absolue* (Publications de la Sorbonne, Paris, 1982) and *Mai 1958: de Gaulle et la République* (Plon, 1988) as well as contributing to books on Jules Ferry, Clemenceau and Pierre Mendès-France, and other works.

JAMES L. SUNDQUIST, Senior Fellow Emeritus at the Brookings Institution, Washington, DC, since 1985, published six books on US politics and government as a senior staff member of the Institution, from 1965 to 1985, most recently *Constitutional Reform and Effective Government* (1986). He has served as Deputy Under-Secretary, US Department of Agriculture; as a staff assistant, US Senate; as Assistant to the Chairman, Democratic National Committee; and on the White House and Bureau of the Budget staffs.

KENNETH W. THOMPSON has taught at the University of Virginia since 1975. He is currently Professor of Religious Studies, White Burkett Miller Professor of Government and Foreign Affairs, and Director of the White Burkett Miller Center of Affairs. Among his many publications are *Christian Ethics and the Dilemmas of Foreign Policy* (1983), *American Diplomacy and Emergent Patterns* (1982) and (with Hans Morgenthau) *Politics among Nations: The struggle for Power and Peace* (sixth edition, 1985).

JOHN ZVESPER, an American living in Britain, teaches in the School of Economic and Social Studies, University of East Anglia. He was Chairman of the UK Political Studies Association American Politics Group in 1985-86 and has contributed several articles to *The Blackwell Encyclopedia of Political Thought, Political Studies, Review of Politics, Western Political Quarterly* and other scholarly journals. He is currently writing books on the American party system and the problems of modern liberal politics. In 1977 he published *Political Philosophy and Rhetoric: A Study of the Origins of American Party Politics*.

R. C. SIMMONS (editor) is Professor of American History at the University of Birmingham. Among his publications are *The American Colonies from Settlement to Independence* (1976) and (with P. D. G. Thomas) *Proceedings and Debates of the British Parliaments respecting North America, 1754-1776* (1982-87).

Editorial introduction

In planning the programme of the Fulbright Colloquium for the bicentennial of the United States Constitution the organisers set out to cover three main themes. Two of these were relevant to the fact that this was a British commemoration: the origins of the Constitution and the Constitution's influence on, or the views held of it, in Britain and other European countries. The third was a more general theme, the 'performance' of the Constitution over a long time scale, but with a natural wish to look at some present-day concerns. Finally, two distinguished jurists were invited to share their thoughts on American constitutionalism and to provide opening and closing sessions of appropriately wide reflectiveness.

These were perhaps ambitious plans for a short colloquium but by and large those attending felt that they were well fulfilled.

Lord McCluskey provided a wide-ranging opening address, reflecting his experience as law officer, parliamentarian and judge, in which he outlined some of the objections to bills of rights. In particular he was not prepared to entrust final decisions to judges. In the British system at least, these were, he believed, because of the very nature of their legal training, experience and careers unlikely to have the breadth of vision and the understanding of contemporary non-legal issues necessary to deal with the majority of social and political cases that would come before them. Parliament should remain sovereign. His robust views drew on a broad acquaintance with the Scottish, English, United States and Canadian legal systems. They also implicitly raised questions of whether a modern Parliament, subject to powerful executive influence, should in fact enjoy any more trust than the judiciary and whether a system could not be evolved to give some entrenched rights to the citizenry.

The first paper to open the discussion of the origins of the Constitution was based on Cathy Matson's intensive scrutiny of New York in the years to 1787 and was a contribution to the study, developed by twentieth-century scholarship, of the political economy of the Constitution. She described the existence of certain ideas of 'radical economic liberalism' expressed in a primary form of 'free tradism'. Although such ideas would not triumph at Philadelphia, they were prevalent in New York. But within the state other imperatives pushed many merchants towards accepting the need for 'state guardianship' over various forms of economic activity, although they also feared the establishment of a central government that would tax the state rapaciously. So Antifederalist strength in New York to this extent reflected the successes of government and economy there. But the Antifederalists were not democrats and were unsympathetic to debtor-insurgents of the Shaysite variety. Federalists who emphasised a federated rather than a consolidated union in 1787-88 were perhaps responding to some of these Antifederalist positions. Whether or not New York was a 'special case' and whether or not merchant opinion was coherent and principled will no doubt be argued more fully in the author's forthcoming publications.

David Rabban's paper also emphasised the Antifederalist contribution to the Constitution. The Bill of Rights was a document that many Federalists at first believed, against Antifederalist arguments, to be redundant. The free speech clause had its origins in the English Radical Whig tradition. Its defenders in the 1790s also drew heavily on this. Against the Sedition Act of 1798 and Federalist defences of it (incorporating Blackstonian argum ...ts for legislative restraint of the press) James Madison argued for a libertarian view of press freedom in a country where 'the people, not the government, possess the absolute sovereignty'. Whether or not the framers of the First Amendment had intended to abolish the common-law crime of seditious libel, the arguments of the 1790s would soon lead on to this.

John Zvesper pointed out that though *The Federalist* was well received, its success had and has had significant limits. Antifederalist complaints that the Constitution threatened to put in place a government that would be monopolised by the wealthy rather than one open to the economically efficient middling sort were later joined by Southern attacks on feared Northern commercial exploitation under its aegis. The arguments of Publius in *The Federalist* were never in fact to be persuasive except among a few lawyers, political scientists and historians. The American popular mind has always venerated the power of 'the voice of the enlightened people, which Jefferson's image represents' rather than the Constitution itself or *The Federalist*, its prime interpreter. Among lawyers, indeed, parts of *The Federalist* were used to attack a nationalist interpretation of the Constitution. Among some political scientists those elements of *The Federalist* seemingly reflecting an economic realism and, later, an appreciation of American pluralism were singled out for praise. Other political scientists have wrongly dismissed the importance of the natural rights beliefs of the writers of *The Federalist*. Among historians, there is current disagreement about the degree of commitment to various assumed sets of eighteenth-century political ideas to be found in it. Zvesper generally supports David Epstein's interpretation of the complete (not merely its first volume) *Federalist* as a work of sober constitutionalism in the Aristotelian tradition but one also emphasising the natural rights of individual human beings. Zvesper's paper usefully helps demonstrate the current state of the argument about early American republicanism and its origins.

A historical view was mixed with a contemporary lawyer's view of rights in Louis Henkin's examination of the Constitution and the Bill of Rights from the point of view of those rights which later generations have found important but which, for various reasons, eighteenth-century Americans did not find so. In a lucid and learned survey, relevant both to themes of 'origins' and of 'performance', he provided an overview of the development of constitutional rights and safeguards from the early national period to the present day, an invaluable introduction and summary which concludes optimistically that human rights – social, economic, civil and political – 'are alive and reasonably well in the United States' today. His paper may be instructively compared with that of Lord McCluskey.

A second group of papers treated the Colloquium's second theme, that of the influence of the United States Constitution outside the United States. The topic is obviously a large one and even in necessarily restricting it to the European experience, it was only possible to consider three countries.

Günter Moltmann, using his own work and that of other German scholars, was able to compress a large time scale into an informative paper, covering the first stirrings of German liberalism and constitutionalism from the late eighteenth century to the post-Second-World-War period. He interestingly demonstrated the importance in Germany not only of written models but of personal contacts, including those with John C. Calhoun and Daniel Webster. The unsuccessful revolutions of 1848/49 demonstrated that there was a lively interest in the American model. Later Bismarck examined and rejected certain aspects of the US Constitution. Indeed, as long as Germany remained aristocratic and monarchical, American republican constitutionalism had offered little that was easily acceptable. But American influence became important after each world war, notably (following Woodrow Wilson's interventions) in the short-lived Weimar Republic, and after the Second World War. Then arguments over the exact power of central over state governments occurred as a federal system with a strong supreme court, drawing strongly on the American model, was established.

One obvious difference between Germany and France was the much earlier commitment to republicanism in the latter country together with the rival claims of French constitutionalism against that of the United States. Odile Rudelle's paper on France shows that, at first influenced by American examples, but soon fearful of enemies within and without, the French came quickly to emphasise the revolutionary sovereignty of the people, one and indivisible, and the necessity of centralisation. The 'American school' traceable through the lives and writings of a number of politicians and intellectuals, of whom Tocqueville was the towering exemplar, was thought to have played an important role in the events of 1848. However, if there were similarities of vocabulary and procedures in the documents of 1787 and of 1848, there were also enormous structural differences. Tocqueville's American sympathies found no response from the heart of French society. The practical weight of the American example was reflected in constitutional discussions in 1875 and was rediscovered after the Second World War. For an American audience at least, Charles De Gaulle argued, in 1948, that his own proposals for French government were for 'an organisation of powers which would largely take into account the example furnished by the United States Constitution' and that he accepted a place in the school of George Washington.

As in France, so in Great Britain, with its entrenched Parliamentary monarchy, the US Constitution was influential mainly in the realm of theory. John Burrow discussed the great complexity and variety of views of the American constitution held in Britain, including early fears of Jacksonian development, followed by the more sophisticated perception that, far from being dangerously democratic, the Constitution was designed to check the popular will. Acton's and Bagehot's responses to the constitutional breakdown of 1861 are discussed, as is the crisis of British constitutional confidence in the 1880s and 1890s, when commentators – Burrow dealt with the views of Sir Henry Maine – 'expressed envy, as distinct from merely respect' for some aspects of the American Constitution. Consideration of Bryce, Brogan and Laski allowed Burrow to show how the shifting background of events in both the United States and Great Britain naturally influenced their views, especially Brogan's, over the short but cataclysmic time scale of 1933-43. After 1945, British views have been less concerned with the domestic workings of the Constitution than with its relevance for the conduct of foreign policy.

A. E. Campbell began the final set of papers on the Colloquium's third theme, the 'performance' of the Constitution, with an examination of attitudes in the years around the first centenary of 1887. While immediately after the Civil War a need was felt to diminish the power of the Federal government, by the end of the nineteenth century the feared object was the large corporation. In its decisions the Supreme Court drifted towards a recognition of the public interest and away from the older idea of liberty as freedom from government interference. Rather than being an obstacle to reform, the Court was a gentle facilitator, accepting enlarged Congressional and Presidential powers. Yet it did not clearly act to enlarge the powers of the Federal government at the expense of those of state governments. The Court also granted powers to government in response to new felt needs arising from American racial feelings and American overseas expansion. What was noteworthy was the ease with which the Court and the nation adapted in these years to a great change in the concept of government.

The modern Supreme Court was the focus of Richard Hodder-William's paper. In it he discussed aspects of the Court's political powers, including the use made of the Court by interest groups and by government itself and the way in which the Court has become a fashioner of policy, mainly because of the failure of other branches of government to act (e.g. in redistricting or public school systems). While a few Supreme Court decisions are not obeyed, most are accepted since they are usually in line with shifting public opinion. The Court also usually finds in line with government in most criminal and habeas corpus cases. It acts to put issues on the public agenda or to recognise that they are already on that agenda by its selection of cases for review. Criticism of Supreme Court Justices for the particular political exercise of power is usually based on a misconception of how the Court works. The 'unprecedented' attack on the Court by members of the Reagan administration reflected real concerns but the Court, by its very nature, has to exercise political power. Its actions are by far and away the best *practical* method of constitutional amendment open to the American people.

James L. Sundquist's paper related to what he saw as a *pattern* of mistrust between Executive and Congress existing over twenty years. Although checks and balances work well in exposing mistakes, the absence of collective responsibility for foreign policy decisions is critical. Similarly in domestic matters – the budget, for example – divisions between Executive and Legislative hinder effective action. The fact that since 1956 Presidency and Congress have been controlled by different parties – though a majority of Americans still vote a straight ticket – has compounded these difficulties. The author outlined some of the salient suggestions for reform but pessimistically, and probably realistically, concludes that it is most likely that only a devastating crisis of government will result in action. Foreign policy divisions between President and Congress were also treated by Kenneth L. Thompson who examined the Founders' concept of government and ethics, the separation of powers that it involved and the practical influences on the Founders. Compromise and co-operation marked the nineteenth and first half of the twentieth centuries. Vietnam destroyed this, as did the growing activism of Congressional and White House staffs. The 1980s have seen calls for constitutional reform, though there are good reasons to question the need for this. Rather, improved communication between White House and Congress based on new structures and legal changes may serve.

J. R. Pole's question, 'What is still vital in the political thought of the Founders?' provided the basis for a wide-ranging consideration of the lawyer's and the historian's approach to the Constitution. The historian, believing that the problems of modern life were not anticipated by the framers or by the Constitution, can rarely argue for strict construction or anti-interpretivism, though may suggest that there are certain constitutional principles which 'would in my opinion have seemed to most of the framers an absolutely indisputable application of their own political rules'. The Founders did not agree among themselves on important questions, though they did agree on certain principles, such as the need to call all power to account. In particular, they were divided over slavery as twentieth-century persons are divided over its residue, race. Yet Federalists and Antifederalists did agree on the protection of individual rights, and with the adoption of the Bill of Rights, the Constitution began with a fair measure of general approval. Moreover, in the move towards the idea of legitimate opposition and party, we see the Founders themselves learning from experience. The Constitution itself changed under the crises produced by slavery and sectional conflict and the transforming effects of monopoly capitalism. Even so, it is still possible to extract from some eighteenth-century concepts strands of thought leading on to valid conclusions for the new circumstances of the later nineteenth and the twentieth centuries – the relevance of liberty and equality and the rule of law, for example, as well as the provision for the amendment of the Constitution. Today, when there are really 'two *systems* of government', presidential and legislative, operating side by the 'real need is to make the President accountable to Congress'.

The contribution by the former US Supreme Court Associate Justice, Arthur Goldberg, testified to a lifetime of devotion to liberal causes and to the liberal interpretation of the Constitution. His measurement of the constitutional faith of the American people therefore used the yardstick of liberty, equality and religious freedom and his strictures on those who in his opinion have acted unconstitutionally did not spare the Supreme Court itself (Dred Scott) or President Lincoln (*Habeas Corpus* suspensions) or powerful contemporaries (Iran–Contra). He also rightly gave refreshing prominence to the Constitution, the Court and religious freedom – something perhaps neglected by other contributors. The Justice's peroration in praise of the Constitution was an understandable personal testimony and a fitting conclusion to the Colloquium.

R. C. Simmons
University of Birmingham

Importing American rights

LORD McCLUSKEY
Edinburgh

It used to be said that if some remarkable social phenomenon occurred in the United States it would only be a matter of time before it happened in the United Kingdom. And that has a certain truth. I should say that we in the United Kingdom are more interested in and influenced by the United States than by any other country, despite our imperial history and our new association with continental Europe. Some American influences are benign. Some are harmless. Occasionally we copy some of the worst models from across the Atlantic; so we followed America into hard drugs, Aids, and recently into a Rambo-style mass shooting – the kind of thing that a few years ago we read about in America while telling ourselves that it couldn't happen here. True, we have not yet elected an actor to our chief political office, but we adopted a presidential style of political campaigning; we sing pop songs with transatlantic accents and watch American football on television.

Most of these influences have come in simply because people make almost unconscious choices, sensing perhaps that Americans have a better capacity to evolve freer, more efficient and more liberating ways of doing things. So it is remarkable that we have not got round to adopting or imitating one of the most remarkable of all American institutions: the Constitutional Bill of Rights with final Judicial Review. It is at once obvious, however, that we could not unconsciously, gradually and by the exercise of individual choice introduce a bill of rights. If that were to be done it would have to be done by the making of a series of deliberate choices, made consciously and thoughtfully, not by the ordinary citizen but by the political and para-political leaders, including lawyers, choices involving a constitutional revolution. I do not shrink from using the word 'revolution'; because, although historically most revolutions are achieved by force or in the wake of huge and bloody social upheavals, it is still appropriate to use the word 'revolution' to describe any large change in constitutional arrangements that results in a shift of a large part of the power to govern, the power to make and change the law, from one body of men selected or elected in a particular way to another body of men selected or elected in a different way. It is my belief that to introduce, if it were possible, an overriding charter or bill of rights which would have the status of a supreme law which Parliament could not alter by the ordinary processes of legislation, a supreme law which the courts would be bound to apply, would be permanently to shift a substantial degree of law-making power from elected representatives to appointed judges, and *that*, I believe, I am entitled to describe as a constitutional revolution.

Now why have we not followed this American example? Why has the American experience of human rights in the courts not persuaded us to follow this notable lead? After all, most Americans claim to be very proud of the Constitution and the Bill of Rights it contains. The American Bill of Rights enjoys a good reputation in Britain. So does the Supreme Court. The names and opinions of Holmes, Brandeis, Cardozo and Frankfurter were known to our students of jurisprudence long before I began my professional career thirty-five years ago. And during my professional life the United States Supreme Court has enjoyed an excellent press in Britain amongst an even wider public. It has been seen as the instrument whereby great liberal achievements have been made possible – in relation, for example, to the previously undemocratic voting system, the sometimes unchecked abuse of police power, the unachieved civil rights of blacks and other disadvantaged groups. Of course, you have to be a liberal to accord unqualified admiration to the achievements of the Warren Court; but you only have to be a realist to recognise that in constitutional terms what the modern court has done has been to aggrandise the legislative power of the judges by a judicial activism which discovered within or behind the Bill of Rights a philosophy that appealed to the judges, a philosophy that they excavated from beneath the written word. So the real lesson is about the power of the judges to make policy by the flexible interpretation of imprecise words and their supposed penumbra.

But to return to the riddle: why, given the reputation of the Court, the quality of its outstanding members, and, above all, the shared admiration felt by so many here for the apparent achievements of the Bill of Rights, why, given our propensity to emulate and adapt American institutions to the British climate, have we let two centuries go by without adopting a Bill of Rights? What is wrong with Rights?

In addressing myself to this theme I am conscious of my own shortcomings. But I can claim to possess a brace of qualifications. First of all I am not an American; and secondly I am not an Englishman.

Whether or not these are *positive* qualifications is a matter for argument. But the advantage of not being American is that I can look at the amended Bill of Rights with a degree of detachment which I suspect is difficult for American constitutional lawyers to achieve. Much American writing on the role of the Supreme Court is, if not in the worst sense partisan, at least committed to one or other side of the argument about the policy-making role of the Court. It is very difficult to look at one's own institutions except through lenses calibrated by history, and political leaning. The advantages of not being an Englishman are perhaps more obvious; but so much of the American legal and political systems was either borrowed from England or deliberately made different from English models that an English lawyer tends to see these systems as cousins conceived on the wrong side of the blanket. A Scots lawyer, on the other hand, is the inheritor of a civilian system of civil law – more dependent upon the application of principle than the citation of precedent and the practitioner of uniquely Scottish system of criminal law. So again his perspective is quite different. Even in constitutional terms the Scot has a different tradition. Neither the Magna Carta nor the English Bill of Rights forms any part of his heritage. We have no common legal tradition before 1707 and have preserved many of our differences since.

In the last twenty years or so many distinguished lawyers and constitutionalists have begun to point to what they describe as the tyrannical potential of Parliament and have invited us to 'trust the judges'. In considering that invitation I begin by asking a childlike question: Where do judges come from? I am, of course, principally concerned with finding an answer that is reasonably accurate in the United Kingdom context. Most of Europe recruits its judges in a quite different way, and then trains, promotes, uses and perhaps even regards the Judiciary in a way which is instructively distinct. In the United States the tradition is different again; personal philosophies and politics are important factors in the recruitment and promotion of the federal Judiciary, especially in the highest reaches. The natural reaction of the British lawyers to the processes of scrutiny and cross-examination of nominees to the Supreme Court is one of distaste, occasionally bordering on disbelief. My own view is, however, that it is a necessary consequence of conferring upon the irremovable Justices a practically unreviewable political power. In the United States, as in Canada, we have also seen the appointment to the highest ranks of the Judiciary of lawyers whose experience has been essentially academic rather than forensic. We have not yet been so bold. In the United Kingdom, on both sides of the Anglo-Scottish border, judges of the superior courts are exclusively appointed from the senior

ranks of the practising Bar. Unusually, the United Kingdom has preserved the division of the legal profession into those, on the one hand,
who practise in, and have exclusive rights of audience in the superior
courts – the barristers, the advocates, and, on the other, the rest, usually
solicitors who, when they do High Court work do so only as solicitors
instructing, i.e., briefing counsel. Success at the Bar in England or in
Scotland depends to a substantial extent upon what the instructing solicitors think of the advocates whose services are on offer. There are, of
course, other factors at work. An advocate might possess such qualities
of mind and personality that he would rise to the top whatever system
was in operation; or, for essentially similar reasons, he might sink without trace even if he has taken the precaution of marrying the daughter of
a High Court judge or of a solicitor's managing clerk. But at the heart of
our system, the solicitors, by observation, by exchange of gossip, and by
applying the standards that experience suggests are the right ones, decide
who has got what it takes; and by feeding them with briefs give the
chosen ones nine-tenths of what they need to build up a good practice.
At the end of the day it is forensic success, or at least forensic competence, that distinguishes the high-fliers from the foot-soldiers. The
primary assessors of such competence are the instructing solicitors. As
the Lord Chancellor, or, in Scotland, the Lord Advocate, chooses the
new judges from among the high-fliers, and the solicitors play a major
role in deciding who flies high, the solicitors have a greater part in the
selection of judges than is generally appreciated. What criteria do solicitors apply when they choose which counsel they will instruct? What
attributes do advocates have to possess in order to survive and prosper in
the Darwinian process that selects winners and losers?

I would suppose that the basic qualification is what is known as a good
legal brain. A good legal brain in our context is one that is analytical,
well calibrated with legal knowledge – knowledge of the law including
especially the precedents – and ingenious, that is to say adept at mould-
ing the principles and selecting the critical facts so that the remedy the
client seeks appears as the only, or at least the best, logical solution to
the particular problem. To draw an analogy with contract bridge, the
good advocate, having been dealt his hand, assesses what bids he can
dare to make, what contract he should end up in and finally the order in
which he should play his cards. He must also bear in mind the words of
Lord Justice-Clerk Thomson in 1962 (*Thomson* v. *Corporation of Glas-
gow,* 1962 S.C. (H.L.) 36 at page 52):

> Judges sometimes flatter themselves by thinking that their function is the
> ascertainment of truth. . . The Judge is at the mercy of contending sides

whose whole object is not to discover the truth but to get his judgment. That judgment must be based only on what he is allowed to hear. . . All litigation is in essence a trial of skill between opposing parties conducted under recognized rules, and the prize is the judge's decision. . . Like referees at boxing contests, Judges see that the rules are kept and count the points.

He must remember that in the marginal cases, and they are usually the ones that are fought to a judicial conclusion, the result is not pre-ordained. Choices have to be made. Alan Paterson in *The Law Lords* discusses fully the differing views of eminent judges. Among those quoted, Lord Macmillan, Lord Devlin, Lord Denning, Lord Cross, and Lord Radcliffe agree in thinking that in most cases which reach the highest level it would be possible to decide the issue either way with reasonable legal justification. There are also many examples of cases in different fields of law including negligence, judicial review and diminished responsibility in crime in which judges have openly declared that the court has had to make a policy choice. So the skilful advocate applies his skills to persuade the judge to buy the product that he is trying to sell. Advocates are often said to be like actors, no doubt because of their reputed capacity to be able to display passion, sincerity or sorrowful indignation as the occasion requires. That particular analogy ignores the fact that advocates, within limitations, write their own scripts, that the answers often precede the questions; the conclusions are supplied, and the advocate then works out the premises. Apart from brains, solicitors are interested in the presentational qualities of counsel. Looks, eloquence, an air of authority, charisma, can all be used to persuade the adjudicator that the worse is really the better cause. And, of course, at the Bar success breeds success. So the successful advocate, unless he is F. E. Smith, must work exceedingly hard. Most of his waking life is spent at his study desk or in court, and the professional pursuit of his clients' causes limits his direct personal contact with the wider, non-litigating world. Like a bat, he develops one skill to a extraordinary degree, but though he is incredibly sensitive to forensic echoes he may not hear the music or see the flowers that for others in a wider world are more important. In the result, whether or not it be the necessary result of such factors, *our* judges tend to have qualities that could be summed up in an acronym. I am always preceded into court by a court officer carrying a mace. He is called, appropriately enough, a macer. It would be a suitable acronym for the typical High Court judge, male, affluent, Caucasian, elderly and remote. So to the general public the High Court judge presents an image of an intelligent, precise, disinterested, articulate, confident, venerable, resolute and dependable sage. And lest his authority should be left in any doubt, he wears an eighteenth-century wig and glorious robes.

Small wonder that the call to 'trust the judges' falls upon such receptive ears. I hasten to say that my ears are no less receptive than anybody else's. If it were possible to answer with a simple 'yes' or 'no' the question 'Would you trust the judges?', I should certainly say, 'yes'. But it is not possible. One is forced to respond to that question by asking another: 'Trust them to do what?' If on Christmas morning I found myself standing at the foot of the Matterhorn wondering if I could make it to the top and back in time for lunch, and a stranger speaking English with a Swiss accent offered to show me the quickest route to the top and back, could I put my trust in him? Not I fear without more information about his qualifications. Would it make any difference if he were wearing lederhosen and a Tyrolean hat, and could yodel? No: I have to say it would not be enough. Would I trust the Lord Chief Justice, the Master of the Rolls, the Lord President of the Court of Session, to guide me up the north face? Alas, no. You don't have to be a skilled mountaineer to climb on to the Bench; and I have no reason to suppose that these worthy distinguished gentlemen have any of the skills required to guide me up a Swiss mountain. If I had to choose, I'd go for the yodeller.

The serious point is that many people in this country who are beguiled by the notion of enacting a bill or charter of rights fail to realise that the questions which are raised by litigation and which fall within the ambit of a charter of fundamental rights and freedoms are not in any real sense legal questions at all. They are social and political questions. And whatever excellent qualities a person must have in order to succeed at the Bar, a profound and sympathetic understanding of social and political questions is not one of them. Of course any very clever lawyer can take an issue which is truly social or political, and describe it, analyse it and render it in the language and cadences of the law so that it looks for all the world like a legal issue; and it is then ripe for what appears to be a impartial legal resolution. When I read the opinions delivered in the Supreme Court, when I study the processes whereby, with the assistance of law clerks, the unpublished opinions are converted into legally reasoned opinions, sometimes buttressed by the citation of what are said to be social or medical facts, I believe I am seeing hunches and political philosophies masquerading as legal logic. Issues such as abortion, free speech, the powers of the police, the rights of persons disadvantaged by sex or ethnic origins, surrogate motherhood, sterilisation of the mentally inadequate, religious observances in public schools, telephone tapping, capital punishment, or positive discrimination, however dispassionately, however knowledgeably they are exposed, analysed and considered by judges, cannot lose their character as issues which pose questions that *precede* the law; questions that must be answered before the law is written. Of course judges, here or elsewhere, faced with a question which necessarily arises in a litigation, cannot refuse to answer that question simply because it is fundamentally one which the political process has not yet addressed or resolved; though the United States Supreme Court has shown some dexterity in avoiding awkward questions, e.g. was the Vietnam War legal or illegal? But the common law abhors a vacuum and the judges will pull enough strands out to the existing law to fill any apparent gap. We can, we must and we should trust the judges to do that. But to give the Judiciary either the first or the last responsibility to provide the answers to such questions is, in my submission, a mistake, unless there is no other preferable solution.

Now, in fact, few people would think of expressly giving the judges the first responsibility for evolving and creating the laws that society needs in order to regulate its social and political problems. Nonetheless it is sometimes done, whether by stealth or neglect or because the political estate shirks its responsibility. Indeed just that happened with the law relating to compensation for persons sustaining injury at work or in hospitals or on the roads. Even now, the basic idea that the judges evolved, namely that compensation depends on proof of fault, has been left largely intact. Large tracts of the ordinary private law have been left to the judges with little interference by legislative bodies despite the fact that judges have evolved and applied concepts which have tended to favour the rich and powerful at the expense of the poor and disorganised. Even in the United States, and in a more public field, Congress largely ignored the injustices perpetrated upon the blacks until the Warren Court shamed Congress into real action by the decision in *Brown* v. *Board of Education,* and its *sequelae.* In modern times the attitude of Parliament to the common law evolved by judges has been essentially reformist: Parliament has stepped in to remedy particular injustices rather than to rewrite the books. But when new and substantial problems arise, such as surrogate motherhood, telephone tapping or affirmative action, the legislature does not generally invite the judges to spend fifty years creeping around the individual problems haphazardly thrown up in order to erect a new common law edifice. Still less does Parliament invite the judges in any way to sit down and create a matrix of rights and duties to govern the new phenomenon.

It is a entirely different matter, however, when it comes to giving judges the last word. Legislatures or constitutional assemblies or colonial powers have shown a remarkable readiness to adopt constitutions, bills or charters of rights containing a supreme law which can not be amended by ordinary legislative procedures. I do not propose here to consider why this fashion has caught on. There are, in any event, many different explanations in different parts of the world; and internationally the movement to create internationally recognised fundamental rights and freedoms owed much to the abuse of exclusive sovereignty by various countries, notably Nazi Germany, in the first half of this century. In the great democracies of North America the need to secure national standards in the states or provinces, which enjoyed substantial legislative freedom and freedom to pursue distinct legal policies, no doubt helped persuade the citizens to subscribe to a supreme and overriding law. Such a law, embodied in some form of constitutional document, and interpreted and developed by a national supreme court, would also help to preserve the unity of the State faced with powerful separatist stresses. But why should anyone suppose that such devices are needed in the United Kingdom? I would respectfully remind you that, for all practical purposes (and leaving aside the very special case of Ireland), the United Kingdom became a unitary state in 1707, eighty years before the Ratification of the Constitution. Since then, the law, whatever its particular merits or features, in so far as it touched upon the fundamental rights and freedoms of the citizens, applied equally throughout England, Scotland and Wales. Nor has it ever been supposed that fundamental civil and political freedoms were at any particular epoch any less well safeguarded in the United Kingdom than they were elsewhere, whether in the other common law countries or in the civil law countries. It would no doubt take a long time to debate it but it would be difficult to persuade most Britons that the ordinary members of British society today enjoy, *at law*, more restricted rights and freedoms than are accorded elsewhere. There are of course in the United Kingdom other subtle social influences which put different groups at serious disadvantage, but the law may be a crude and ineffective instrument for rooting out prejudice, discrimination and privilege. Nor was it imagined by those responsible for the legal framework of the State that any supreme law was needed in order to secure and advance the fundamental rights and freedoms of the citizen. Even when the United Kingdom signed the European Convention in 1950, which it played the major part in drafting, the general belief was that it largely enshrined the good practices that had been written into our law by Parliament and the Judiciary over a very long period of time.

So whatever people might think or say about politicians I think there has been a general belief that our freedoms were reasonably safe in their hands. My own conclusion is that some at least of those who now advocate the introduction of a supreme law – and they do so spasmodically rather than consistently – are motivated by a fear of political changes which they would not like and which might be wrought by the advance of collectivist or socialist ideas. Lord Hailsham in the 1970s gave currency to the notion that a democratically elected Parliament could be a instrument of tyranny (though the notion of the 'tyranny of the majority' goes back at least as far as Alexis de Tocqueville). One detects the same kind of thinking behind the proposals in New Zealand for the introduction of a charter of rights on Canadian lines. If, as I believe, our fundamental rights and freedoms are at present well secured by a system which has endured for 280 years, do we need to pull the edifice down and dig fresh foundations? It was Warren Burger, Chief Justice of the United States Supreme Court, who, in this context, reminded me of Murphy's law: 'If a thing ain't broke, don't fix it'. If, however, the real purpose is to buttress our existing institutions and systems of individual, as opposed to collective rights, so as to be proof against elected parliaments, then we should come out and say so and rewrite our whole constitution.

I fear too that in opting for a supreme law we would have to write it in such vague and imprecise terms that we would consciously be giving the Judiciary the last word. The words in which such rights and freedoms are couched are so vague and imprecise that judges would be set free to create out of their own subjective notions of justice and social values a complex of actual and realisable rights undreamed of by many of those who are now ready, albeit blindly, to trust the judges.

I have described the qualities which we look for in selecting and promoting our higher Judiciary. I have suggested that these are essentially narrow legalistic qualities which do not obviously mark out the possessors of them as men of deep social and political wisdom. But even if I am wrong about that, the most striking thing about the Judiciary, whatever the personal qualities possessed by its membership, is that it is not accountable to the electorate. It may, as can be seen from time to time in the United States, move with the times, though it tends to move slowly and uncertainly. But if you give the last word to a body of elderly men who are not accountable and cannot be dismissed then democracy has abdicated its choices to non-democratic institutions. I have no doubt that many of our institutions and procedures are imperfect, inadequate and that they have had and will continue to have spectacular failures in creating and improving the social framework. But I believe the correct approach is not to deprive our institutions of their competence to attempt to address and resolve the fundamental questions, and to pass that task to unelected judges. The better answer is constantly to review and re-assess the performance of our institutions and to find ways to improve their awareness of the human rights dimension of the State's activities and regulation. So if I were to be asked what I suppose would be the role of the Judiciary my answer would be that it should continue to do that which it has been doing so well for such a long time. The Judiciary has shown a wholly admirable capacity to keep its feet on the ground. We should think long and hard before we take it to the edge of the cliff and invite it to fly.

As I have said, one of the great dangers, as I see it, of introducing a bill of rights on the American or Canadian model is the danger of politicising the judiciary, by requiring the judges to decide essentially political questions, behind the veil of legal language, with the result that those essentially political persons who select and appoint judges would come to think in terms of how the individual's philosophy and track record would govern his resolution of politico-legal issues, such as abor-tion, the closed shop, private medicine, equality, privacy, censorship etc., etc. This, as I see it, is what happens in the United States of America. Now it is at once obvious that it is nonsense to say that Parlia-ment should not be political or party political. The philosophies and track records of politicians are highly relevant. And in a representative demo-cracy we *ought* to know what their philosophical imperatives are. And if we don't like them we can, and should, reject them via the ballot box. Furthermore we can probably force them to reveal and commit them-selves to their philosophies before we put them in positions of power: something we, as voters, cannot hope to do in regard to judges. At least I hope not, though we can again learn from the United States, where the utterances of judges in public lectures, learned articles, in opinions in cases, or even on political platforms (usually *before* appointment to the bench) mark them out as liberals or conservatives, interventionists or restrictionists, so that those who appoint, and promote, the federal judiciary can know what kind of judge they are going to get.

One of the inevitable problems that attends the enactment of funda-mental rights in ringing general terms, and of qualifications thereto or derogations therefrom, in equally vague phrases, is that the precise legal rights and responsibilities of citizens become shrouded in uncertainty. Even the judicial resolution of particular issues only shifts the clouds of uncertainty on to adjacent fields of conflict. By contrast, one of the advantages of the enactment in statutes of particular sets of legal rules is that we can aim for, and often achieve, great precision. I recognise of course that the present form of much of our legislation has many critics. We pay a heavy price for precision, a price measured in length and non-readability. In result, much of statute law is not readily accessible to the public. Acts of Parliament are not as readable as Frederick Forsyth's novels. But the same applies to British Rail timetables – they do not make exciting or easy reading. And most people, even if they attempt the exercise of trying to understand and decipher the text, would seldom be confident that they'd got the right answer. They are likely to end up phoning the station to check the right answer. The simple truth is that verbal certainty in the modern world cannot be achieved except at the price of verbal complexity. The bill of rights equivalent of a British Rail timetable between Edinburgh and Birmingham would read: 'there shall be a reasonable and frequent train service between Edinburgh and Birmingham at convenient times and at fair rates of charge, subject however to the right of British Rail to adapt and vary the actual services in the light of their reasonable assessment of the public's needs and their own resources'. Such a formulation would be of little use to the intending traveller, despite its clarity and excellent sentiments.

Another aspect of judicial decision-making to which I would draw attention is the fact, inescapable under our system of litigation, that the only parties represented before the court are the litigants. Each is trying to win the case. There is no *amicus curiae*. And the legal point arises in a particular and often narrow context. The court, even when dealing with a fundamental point, such as, for example, the recent case about sterilising a seventeen-year-old mentally retarded girl, is slow to lay down a general rule – other than the general rule that each case must be decided on its own facts, *if* that can be described as a general rule! The court did not attempt to lay down any general rule about the sterilising of mentally retarded girls, so that those who have parental or quasi-parental responsibility for other girls of different ages and different degrees of retardation could know how the law would apply to such people. Equally the court said nothing about vasectomies for seventeen-year-old mentally retarded males. The *Gillick* case (relating to the right of a government department to suggest what contraceptive advice should be given by doctors to under-age girls) is another example of a decision relating to a matter of fundamental rights of general interest but where the particular facts were all-important. In practising such restraint the courts are being wise. The reason why it is wise to refrain from general utterance is that the courts are not geared up to make a study of relevant facts which might bear upon the desirability of a general rule. The litigants have usually no interest, certainly no duty and seldom any capacity, to research and present the whole relevant facts. We know nothing in the United Kingdom of the Brandeis Brief. By contrast, Parliament can and commonly does make an effort to enquire into all the relevant facts and indeed consult all the interests that may be affected by any particular formulation of the law. Parliament's better appreciation of the facts stems from the way in which MPs especially have daily contact with real people and real problems. Parliament can also consult the reports of the law commissions, Royal Commissions or departmental committees. The citizens can lobby MPs to bring to their attention and, through them, to Parliament itself as a body their legitimate interests. So Parliament has the opportunity to assess the possible consequences of its law-making. Courts cannot properly calculate the consequences of their actions. Indeed, in proclaiming their role as that of discoverers of what the law is, rather than what it *should* be, courts cannot be swayed by the possible social or economic consequences of their rulings. It is very common for judges when arriving at a particular result to express their alarm and regret at the possible consequences, but to wash their hands of such consequences. When we are deciding what the law ought to be, however, the consequences of enacting such a law are all-important and ought to be studied. The courts cannot do this. Parliament can.

The haphazardness of litigation is another element in the argument. Courts cannot reach out for cases. They must wait until somebody choses to bring the point before them. They sometimes have to wait a long time; and until the opportunity arises, the law can remain clouded by uncertainty. Thus it took nearly sixty years before the United States Supreme Court got, and took, the chance in *Brown* v. *The Board of Education* to reverse the earlier ruling that public facilities could be provided on a 'separate but equal' basis. The very haphazardness that affects and determines what points come before the courts, and in what form they come, and indeed whether or not they come at all, also means that the courts cannot keep an eye on how the law works in practice. Of course some types of cases occur frequently and in such cases it is possible to keep the development of the law under some form of scrutiny: but other types of case are rarely litigated. So there can be no standing committee or select committee of judges, as it were, to study the law in action. Since *Gillick,* have judges given any attention to medical practice or advice by public authorities to teenage girls in relation to contraceptives? Of course not.

If, however, the contrary does occur, and points of law relating to fundamental human rights come to be raised in many cases, then it is worthwhile casting an eye towards the Canadian experience. Despite the existence of many other bodies interested and active in the field of fundamental human rights, the courts are being flooded with 'charter' arguments, often badly prepared and researched, and frequently misconceived. So a result is to increase the cost of litigation, to delay cases, to choke the courts, and to increase the degree of uncertainty about what the law is. In the United States, though there are many other factors at work, the same phenomenon can be seen. It has led to calls for the creation of a new national court to relieve the Supreme Court of its unacceptable burden (see *Harvard Law Review,* 1987, 100, p. 1400). The authors of that article, 'The need for a new National Court', both former acting administrative assistants to Chief Justices of the United States, write: 'The consequences of this virtually unmanageable work-load are fragmented majorities, separate opinions, and sometimes even inadequate analysis, as justices have insufficient time to fulfil their institutional charge of "securing harmony of decision and the appropriate settlement of questions of general importance so that the system of federal justice may be appropriately administered".' The Justices of the Supreme Court select the cases that they will give a full, or plenary, hearing to. They select several hundred each year out of more than 5,000. At the present time the petitions for review, the responses thereto, the replies and the memoranda by law clerks on the cases extend to over 360,000 pages per year. Thus a Supreme Court judge, if he chooses to read the papers, has to read more than 1,000 pages per day for each day of the year before he starts his ordinary work. It is hardly surprising that so many people believe that the opinions are commonly written by the law clerks rather than by the Judges.

May I deal with one specific point about the suitability of our judges to think judicially about human rights. It is not easy to see how judges can become specialists in human rights law in the way that they can become specialists in, say, shipping law, or crime – particularly in England where, as distinct from Scotland, barristers specialise to a considerable degree. I don't really see human rights law as being capable of developing as a specialty in which barristers might develop a practice. Even if they did it would not necessarily be the correct training for a judge whose first concern must always be with the application of the ordinary law in the particular case. Human rights law, by reason of the vagueness of its text and its generality, pervades, underlies and to some extent even undermines the ordinary law in many fields. Thus it is not easy to see how practice at the Bar, which is currently a necessary qualification for judges, could make one an expert on discrimination, on equality or on degrading treatment, or indeed on the restrictions necessary, or justified, in a democratic society for the protection of morals. (These, of course, are all concepts taken from the European Convention on Human Rights.) The alternative to using judges and courts for securing and advancing human rights is to rely on Parliament. The United Kingdom Parliament has a good record – though not an unblemished one – of legislating for the advancement of civil and political rights and even of social and economic rights. It is easy to become blasé or hypercritical about the systems we have for the protection of individual liberty; but try to look for example at the British systems of criminal justice through the eyes of a Russian Jew, a South African black or a South American Indian. Parliament has created our remarkable codes to protect the citizen against unjust conviction or even overbearing investigation.

To an outsider it appears that many Americans tend to admire the man who seeks, and achieves, desirable goals by cutting through or bypassing inconvenient checks and balances, by going, if necessary, outside the law itself to win justice or some other end judged to be worthwhile. In popular culture he is celebrated in some of the characters played by John Wayne or Charles Bronson. I can think of some justices in the history of the Supreme Court with whom a parallel could be drawn with a Charles Bronson hero. If our judges were to turn into legislators – as they are sometimes tempted to do – they would betray the true British judicial tradition. Any British lawyer would claim that the feature which is the most distinctive and essential mark of a true, mature and liberal democracy is the Rule of Law. But that does not mean that law *rules*. On the contrary: in such a democracy we rule *ourselves*, through our elected representatives. The Rule of Law simply means that we are all equal before the law, and that the law is administered and applied dispassionately by impartial judges without fear or favour. The consequences of applying the law should not shake the judges. Judges must start with the law and work out the conclusion, not start with the conclusion and work out the law.

The idea that we can in a bill of rights write laws in crystal words that will secure social justice is, I believe, naïve in any society so far seen. This kind of naïvety is often found in our own history, including our recent history. I suspect it played a part in the framing of the American Bill of Rights two centuries ago. If we act in the belief that we can put our trust in laws and the judges who administer these laws we can too readily deceive ourselves into believing that we have thus won the battle for social justice: we can abdicate responsibility for it with a clear conscience and get on with getting and spending. We can even smile indulgently on our politicians as they go log-rolling and neglect fundamental rights in the pursuit of special interests. In short, placing our trust in fundamental laws and in judges to interpret and apply them tends to move the securing of such rights out of the political arena while tending to drag the justiciary into it.

It is no part of my purpose to suggest that North Americans went the wrong way about trying to secure their rights in their context. My one concern is that before we in the United Kingdom, with our wholly different judicial and political traditions, decide to create for ourselves a supreme law which will change the character of our Judiciary we should study more critically the history of the only bill of rights that can be said to have enjoyed real success over a long period of time; we should study the problems posed to the political process in the United States before we import a device that, in our very different context, could subvert traditions which have served us well.

2

American political economy in the constitutional decade

CATHY MATSON

University of Tennessee, Knoxville

Many recent scholars have returned to the perception of the constitutional decade as a 'critical period', not only because of its social turmoil and economic uncertainties but also because of its intellectual fervour. Ideas were being considered, and modified or rejected, in a cacophony of discussion about liberty and authority. The same scholars are asking: Which of these ideas were old, and which were new, in the synthesis of 1787? How can we associate the activities of Americans living at that time with the particular ideas they espoused? And how shall we weigh the relative impact of different kinds of ideas?

One thing that makes any tentative answers to these questions a complicated project is the existence of at least three intellectual trends in the rich discussion of Americans in the revolutionary generation. One strain of thought, covenant theology and dissenting religious traditions, flourished amidst the erosion of ideal compact communities in the colonies and enjoined colonists to challenge once-perdurable elites for a share in local social and political authority. Dissenters also described the depravity of those who chose an excessively material rather than a spiritual path in life; only individual piety could rejuvenate America. It is unclear how Protestant innerlight theology might have overlapped with popular sovereignty during the 1770s and 1780s, but we can reasonably suppose that it provided a context for discussion and feelings about the precarious balance between moral accountability to the community and self-reliance, thus enriching the experience of newly-empowered popular majorities in the states.[1]

More powerful in discussions of liberty and authority were republican ideas. Republicanism taught Americans the virtues – indeed, the necessity – of vigilance over political power and the passion for material self-interest so that these might not become dangerous to the common good. It forced many Americans to confront sovereignty squarely. How authority was constituted and expected to be exercised; who would wield this authority and for how long; and whether ultimate sovereignty would rest with a single or infinitely varied source, with a supreme executive, a representative legislature, or 'the people' – all these possibilities for shaping sovereignty took inspiration from the republican emphasis upon civic participation. Nevertheless, the republican legacy had no clear formula for widespread civic involvement in a territory as large and diverse as the United States. There were contradictions in the tradition of republicanism as well. It sought to inspire obedience as well as participation in the Commonwealth, and it never promised to free property from traditional, prescriptive rights. Yet Americans like James Madison, John Adams, Thomas Jefferson, and Alexander Hamilton faced the need to retain republican order and elite, propertied rule, while also freeing Americans to pursue property according to natural rights and common law, in a manner which suited the materialism and mobility of expanding Americans.[2]

Liberalism, the third body of ideas influencing the revolutionary generation, rose from the third to first place among the intellectual discourses about the new nation's political economy. Although the terms 'liberty' and 'freedom' had an ambiguous past in Anglo-American thought, especially when mercantilists tried to fuse them with statist authority, by the 1780s their predominant usage in economic matters emphasised political and economic action under the moderately restraining influence of a private moral commitment to act for the common good. In the new American states, economic liberals comprised the majorities of popular government. Natural law and custom commanded duty to the community even as the pursuit of greater political participation and economic opportunity brought tangible satisfactions. This liberal tradition overlapped with the Protestant dissenting sensibilities of the revolutionary generation, and incorporated the moral components of Lockean and Scottish Enlightenment liberalism. It also removed the hesitation Americans felt about republicanism's tendency to validate landed property and to excoriate certain forms of commerce. But it never invited Americans to acquire unlimited goods or to consult only private interests. At every turn of events, but most notably during the non-importation movements of 1765 to 1774 when they attempted to confront the nagging problems of imperial dependency, Americans hesitated to appropriate too much economic freedom. Economic liberalism might create a commercial empire with clear prescriptions for a new political order, but it did not prescribe a daring consuming and producing machine.[3]

There was, however, another dimension to liberalism, less congruous with dissenting and republican tradition. Immortalised in the works of Hobbes and his followers, radical economic liberalism eschewed moral law and an idealised, static social fabric. It celebrated unbridled individualism and became obsessed with a new kind of higher law: the equilibrating, beneficial effects of the impersonal market. Market, rather than moral liberalism promised a brave new world of goods, peace, and an end to poverty. Not a dominant current in Anglo-American thought at this time, such economic liberalism was nevertheless associated with an influential core of 'free traders'. By the 1750s there were free traders of two kinds throughout the European empires. On the one hand, theorists like Josiah Tucker, policy-makers like some West Indies governors, and a vocal group of colonial merchants argued that a self-sufficient empire could not thrive on a mercantilist basis. Energetic competition of merchants would create a flourishing, consuming nation. Some individual merchants stopped at nothing to rid themselves of duties, fees, regulations, and all imperial authority. While sharing Tucker's antipathy to mercantilism, these independent free traders thrived outside diplomacy and national politics, claiming that freedom in commerce rescued them from corrupt politicians, unwarranted mercantile regulations, and the zero-sum effects of moral concerns.[4]

The majority of revolutionary Americans were still republican enough to admit that self-interest, luxury, pride, and ambition needed the restraining hand of government. Flirtation with radical economic freedom during the revolution proved not to be a viable model for the new nation. However, by 1787 liberal ideas were muted in the voices of republican Federalists at Philadelphia, as well as by the moral position taken by many Americans. Yet at a critical intellectual moment for the constitutional generation, radical liberalism did offer Americans far-reaching possibilities for their future political economy. And despite its defeat it would persist in subtle fashion in the early Republic. It was one important source of new – or newly tried – ideas during the period. The initial strength and ultimate demise of this radical economic liberalism, and its primary form as free tradism, has been all but ignored until recently. We can make a small beginning towards rectifying this by considering radical economic liberalism in light of another question already posed: how did the idea correspond to the political economy which emerged in practice? The example of New York is instructive.

Since the mid-seventeenth century a few New Yorkers had argued for more unfettered economic relations. Their calls for free trade referred to easier access to markets, the right to seek the lowest cost in trade, and the greatest private gain, without taxes, fees, and regulations. Their 'libertye of trade' was won, on occasion, in colonial legislative battles; but more frequently they benefited simply from the 'salutary neglect' of imperial officials who did not enforce regulations, or from bribery and smuggling. Individual merchants' practices were also reinforced by theorists who began to doubt whether mercantilism was the best commercial policy. Over the decades this political economy, founded upon 'natural harmonies' among citizens, reciprocal satisfaction of economic desires, individual autonomy in the market-place, and images of international peace, grew in popularity. Middling and rising New Yorkers were attracted to aspects of radical economic liberal discourse because it seemed compatible with local experiments in direct sovereignty, but by their successful practice of forms of extreme economic liberty they instilled confidence about alternatives to classical republican 'virtue', elitist as the latter was. During the final colonial decades radical economic liberals came self-consciously to oppose both the constraints of classical republicanism and the extensive economic regulations and special interest politics of mercantilism. Liberty, said these free traders, was to be found in neither republic prescriptive rights nor mercantilist coercion; it derived from the autonomy of individuals able to pursue continually changing opportunities.[5]

Although radical economic liberals often shared oppositionist Whig desires to eradicate monopoly, corruption, and paternalistic regulation of the poor, they never adopted a sense of natural-law duty to the community as Lockean liberals had. Open ports and open markets, they said, would bring higher farmers' prices, lower import costs, and incentives to expand foreign trade as merchants turned outwards to mingle with new peoples and return with new articles of consumption. Self-interest, they insisted, was a benign force, even a socially useful one, because of the desire it released and the circulation it promoted. The vision was thoroughly secular: it considered only the effects of human, not God's, agency upon the material happiness of society.[6]

By the time of the non-importation movements of 1765 to 1774 New Yorkers faced some of the ambiguities of their economic thinking. On the one hand, these movements called for self-denial and restraint in consumption for political ends. On the other, some New Yorkers assured themselves that temporary restraint would stimulate their own productivity and increase economic liberty. What they no longer imported they might make for themselves. Radical economic liberals at first aligned themselves with non-importation, but they remained sceptical about its moral thrust and limited goal of reforming imperial relations. Self-sufficiency within the empire would not lead to greater productivity, but perhaps to scarcities, since colonists would cut themselves off from world markets. Without continued access to these, capital would grow short, internal trade shrivel, and the spectre of unemployment replace the busy circulation of goods. New York's free traders, among them many West Indies smugglers, agreed with the general challenge to imperial authority and the idea of increasing domestic consumption, but they were not prepared to turn inwards, away from the Atlantic. In the midst of colonists' mutual non-importation accords some free traders returned to smuggling. Thus, even as they reached for greater autonomy before most Americans were ready for it, these free traders also turned their backs on the community's welfare at a highly symbolic moment.[7]

The revolution at first wiped away the problems raised by illegal smuggling and clarified lingering hesitations about economic liberty raised by non-importation. Once the city of New York was occupied by British forces, the new state's markets were forced into the interior. There, merchants and farmers enjoyed new opportunities to trade with the military, extended their networks of debt and paper currency to breaking point, discovered new profits in engrossing supplies or inflating prices, and expanded their horizons from local marketing to commercial farming to meet the bulging demand of the militias. By 1776 the rhetoric of self-restraint and the dream of creating a classically virtuous republic competed with the reality of unfettered private enterprise at all levels of American society. Internal commerce as well as that in the world's oceans was now the means to prosperity. New habits called forth a recognition of a 'universal self-interest' suffused with 'liberty and freedom of the most extreme sort'.[8]

In the first months of the war the Continental Congress itself was not immune to the lure of free trade. An April 1776 resolution endorsed the principle of open ports and of international trade reciprocity; and there were repeated appeals to merchants associated with smuggling and free trade for military supplie. In September some delegates committed themselves to the rudiments of a free trade policy as they began to formulate economic goals for an independent America. Trade, agreed James Wilson and Christopher Gadsden, would 'regulate itself'.[9] Before the war was over John Jay wrote that 'In future the whole world will be open to us, and we shall be at liberty to purchase from those who will sell on the best terms and to sell to those who will give us the best prices.' English protectionists often commented on the 'universal bent of those people [Americans] to entire equality in trade' and some of them felt that had the Treaty of Paris been signed in 1782, 'it is not unlikely that it would have contained a prohibition of all laws in restraint of trade, foreign or domestic'.[10]

Yet the requirements of the revolutionary war also called forth a barrage of economic regulations by the new state governments. By October 1777 they began to formulate their own commercial tax laws and to refuse trade with any foreign nation not offering reciprocity. Leaders in New York and Philadelphia were particularly strong advocates of these measures. New York also passed laws to fix prices and wages, prevent forestalling, limit profits to 25 per cent, embargo exports of necessary foodstuffs, and requisition its citizens for military supplies. New York's new government printed large amounts of paper money to defray rising revolutionary expenses, and it repeatedly attempted to tax the money out of circulation, a currency system known throughout the eighteenth century.[11] Revolutionary economic liberty seemed to be placed ever more under the watchful eye of a political authority which zealously protected the fragile revolutionary experiment against excessive economic freedom.

In the face of these regulations, some of the state's farmers and merchants protested a loss of economic liberty. Their loss of the 'usual channels of trades', they also noted, did not affect the more fortunate public creditors and commissary officials. Farmers who opposed embargoes which deprived them of markets also opposed the commissaries who seized grain to sell to needy troops, and price fixing by insensitive state officials; they joined with New York City exporters, who were alienated from their usual commercial opportunities by wartime embargoes and requisitions, to set the 'price which justice commands the private trader and the public will bear'. Both constituencies grew to distrust taxes even more, and both failed to benefit from the depreciating state and continental certificates received for their services and goods. Open hostility to tax collectors continued through 1778, when the state government gave up trying to make the loathsome levies.[12] Optimists believed that such state regulations would dissolve once Americans secured political independence. But as the revolutionary crisis persisted, others echoed the words of David Hume, who had warned an earlier generation about the ill effects of 'jealousy', the tendency to introduce too many economic regulations through political channels instead of freeing competitors to seek their own interests. Some New York merchants explained how their own 'trading libertye' was stifled by policies first 'bred of a jealousy of the mother country in her commerce', and then maintained by a jealousy among the state's interests after 1776. They asked whether there was not 'too much [republican] *virtue* to support their *liberty*?'[13]

Americans' flirtation with radical economic liberalism persisted in the post-war decade. In 1783, John Adams expressed the hope that England's 'jealousy of American ships, seamen, carrying trade, and naval power' would not result in renewed mercantile restraints on American commerce. But, continued Adams, if Americans were denied complete reciprocity, especially in the West Indies, then Congress must 'attach herself more closely to France'. That country's policy of 'free ports and no odious discriminations' was more compatible with American liberty. James Madison, Benjamin Rush, Pelatiah Webster, Thomas Paine, and others would optimistically add their voices to the idea of obtaining free trade. In New York merchants scurried to re-establish economic liaisons in old and new channels of trade. Among them, a vocal group of West Indies smugglers and re-exporters – the latter faced paying duties twice as they imported and then reshipped to another location – demanded autonomy and free ports. Here and there, farmers of the interior explained how they could recover markets and a decent living only if they were free to seek their own best prices.[14]

But the majority of the Americans quickly withdrew from the tantalising prospects of such extreme economic individualism. Reasons changed quickly over the post-war decade, but they began to clarify in the post-war economic recession. The language of economic freedom had gone from both the *ad hoc* attempts of merchants and farmers to prosper and the only slightly more systematic explanations of anti-mercantilist theorists. But prices would not remain where free traders wanted them – low for merchants and high for exporting farmers of the interior – simply by unfettering economic activity. Private debts did not diminish but grew over the period; so did the inability to pay them without government intervention. Nor would the public debts of state governments go away. And their loans to needy states compelled merchants to grow restive about the future health of the state governments which would repay them. As a result, in the years 1781 to 1785 interests which were united by their need for protection and redress of grievances increasingly refashioned their radical economic liberty into a powerful coalition controlling the political sovereignty of New York.[15]

Other interests felt that the states were too weak. To them, it seemed that an uncontrollable, consuming majority had so overcorrected mercantilist restraints that the whole revolution was endangered. An unmistakably Hobbesian impulse had overwhelmed what was potentially good about the new economic activities. These men gathered in their personal capacities at conventions in various cities beginning in late 1779, with the purpose of stopping states from issuing paper money and introducing more adequate means to pay for military supplies. At a Hartford meeting in November 1780, New York delegates, Alexander Hamilton among them, proposed that since separate state remedies were inadequate to meet revolutionary tasks, they should merge their private economic powers and the states' corporate powers into one Congressional effort to raise revenue by import duties. Under their influence Congress asked the states in 1781 and again in 1783 for a 5 per cent impost on trade, 'a permanent Fund to support the national Credit and cement more effectually the common Interest of the United States'.[16] Presumably the national impost would help defray New York's indebtedness to Congress and obviate the need for real estate taxes which would fall most heavily upon the 'agrarian interest'. But the impost's firmest support in fact came from revolutionary suppliers and commissaries, Congress's main creditors, and from a core of nationalists who would press more and more firmly for overturning the tide of popular sovereignty and economic liberty.[17]

The national impost was rejected repeatedly by the states. As it became clear that federal officers would collect state monies and forward them directly to Congress, the majority of states failed to support the measure since it removed a main source of sovereignty from local to distant authority. However much it had been agreed to accommodate the dream of liberated economic activity to new republican forms of political authority, the states, not the national government, continued to be seen as the proper arenas for this. As one New Yorker saw it, men who favoured the national impost had increased the existing fears about economic liberty; they had transformed the fear which states had of individuals' 'licence' into the fear which certain nationalist interests had of state authority. But if individual economic liberty had to be limited, it should be under the moderate regime of state control over trade and revenue.[18]

The next indications that free trade was doomed came from the American diplomats who had been most hopeful of commercial reciprocity. In England Adams began to despair of negotiating an open commerce with the former mother country. Lord Sheffield's influential pamphlet, *Observations on the Commerce of the United States*, argued two points about the United States which became the foundation of British hardline policies. John Adams stated these succinctly: American economic interests needed English goods and credit to such an extent that 'our commerce has returned to its old channels, and . . . it can follow no other'. And, secondly, the British felt 'sure of the American commerce' for a long time to come because of the fragmented political authority which stood behind it: 'the American States are not, and cannot be united'.[19] By 1786, United States trade with the British West Indies was restricted largely to provisions, tobacco, and naval stores.[20]

Public outrage was immediate, as were proposals in Congress to ban

English imports and exports from American waters. However, in part because the Articles of Confederation prevented Congress from legislating unilaterally in the interests of the sovereign states, and in part because many congressmen preferred patient negotiation to confrontation, the proposals failed.[21] Some of the states now initiated a retaliatory policy, a series of commercial laws similar to the mercantile legislation of the colonial period. On 22 March 1784 the New York legislature passed a law to collect 2½ per cent duty on all imports arriving in New York vessels and intended for New York consumers, and a 5 per cent duty on British goods entering New York City from the West Indies in British vessels. On 18 November 1784 additional duties were levied on goods deemed 'luxuries' and which the British often carried into the city: southern European wines, British West Indies rum, English watches, carriages, and buckles, and, although they were hardly luxuries in New York's agricultural economy, many iron manufactures and tools. This legislation became known as the state impost. Down to the Constitution other states followed New York's example, their lawmakers arguing, as they had about non-importation and revolutionary trade regulation, that retaliation was a temporary expedient, a lesser evil in the face of continuing foreign imperial domination.[22]

Although a few activists continued to praise free trade, most New Yorkers could not deny the usefulness of the state impost, which proved to be the mainstay of state revenues from 1784 to 1789. About 51 per cent of New York's remittances to Congress and a significant portion of its debt repayments to private creditors during that period came from the single source of import duties. Import duties also allowed the popular Clintonian government to retire its citizens' federal notes and securities and issue reliable state securities in their place. Finally, the Clintonians issued large amounts of paper money and instituted a system of moderate taxation to retire it in a timely manner; import duties also provided a specie 'fund' to back up this currency. All these policies earned the trust of those post-revolutionary creditors who were not already committed nationalists, the confidence of commercial interests needing an inflation-proof currency which would not wipe out debts owed to them, and the undying loyalty of the 'agrarian interest' seeking paper money to rebuild the economy of the interior. Here, many New York interests could agree, was a new basis of economic liberty: a state responsive to the needs of its various local interests without catering to any one special interest.[23]

During the recession of 1785-87 it became apparent how important modest Clintonian intervention was. As private indebtedness rose steeply by mid-decade, the Clintonian paper money emissions and reissue of state securities seemed exactly appropriate. As gluts of imported goods and New Yorkers' foreign debts increased, accusing fingers were pointed at British merchants who had over-extended credit and at British ministers who had closed off the West Indies trade. It seemed that while Congress only dallied in international discussions the state decisively retaliated with commercial taxes. At the same time, agriculturalists praised the Clintonian legislature because it did not levy export taxes; they attributed the early recovery of prices for grain and flour to 'being left free' of duties on outgoing state products. Moreover, it was a received wisdom among commercial farmers that if the state's purse were 'drained into a consolidated union' export taxes, or even worse, land taxes, would be imposed by the 'external power' of Congress.[24]

A number of New York City's dry goods merchants, whose commodities and credit tied them to prominent London exporters, also agreed that a state impost provided adequate financial support without unduly prejudicing their interests. Although not normally welcoming taxes on their goods, they discovered that higher import costs could be passed on to the consumer during the 1780s with less public protest than in the colonial period. Furthermore, commercial retaliation worked in their favour. While England would continue 'to supply our wants, and, more, the productions which our own inhabitants see is beyond their industry', American shippers could now import these goods at lower cost than English merchants. New Yorkers received more commodities from England than from any other foreign nation between 1784 and 1787, and they were now quite happy to carry them in their own ships. Besides, local merchants' agreement to pay the state impost was the minimum they had to concede to secure their future against nationalists favouring a Congressional impost. The latter were associated with returning Loyalist merchants, auction sales, and favouritism towards British factors living in the city, all anathema to the recovering American dry goods merchants.[25]

This state guardianship over various forms of local economic self-interest was paralleled in New York's relations which its sister states. Since 1779 the state had kept its own agricultural export prices higher than New Jersey's and Connecticut's by placing temporary embargoes on wheat, flour, and meal – a form of forestalling until market conditions improved – and by requiring satellite states to pay the same discriminatory double duty which foreigners paid. New Jerseyites, whose port facilities were relatively underdeveloped and whose agriculture was devastated by the revolutionary war, felt they had only one recourse. Unless they turned to a policy of absolute free trade, said 'Candidus', they would 'have to divide ourselves between the two great States that overshadow us', New York and Pennsylvania. Free trade would allow them to export more cheaply and attract foreign commerce away from a domineering New York. Connecticut, however, chose to abandon ideas of free trade and to compete with New York in policies of discrimination. Yet New Haven and New London fared little better than New Jersey's ports. Neither state could overcome the strength of New York City, and both continued to move one half to two-thirds of their agricultural exports and imported manufactures through it. Weakened shipping interests in Massachusetts and landlocked Vermont also relied on New York during the Confederation.[26] In all these cases, desires for economic autonomy and the theoretical predilections towards free trade had gradually yielded to the imperatives of interstate competition. However, by 1786 merchants in cities around New York were prepared to turn their attention towards the benefits of a 'higher authority' in the national Congress, in hopes of overcoming their dependency upon the overwhelming sovereignty of New York.[27]

The success of New York's commercial and fiscal policies, coupled with the recovery of agricultural prices and exports by early 1787, marginalised not only radical economic liberals but nationalist republicans as well. Instead, as state guardianship over many economic interests grew and was successful, moderate Lockean economic liberalism seemed ever more compatible with the state's policies. By 1788, it would also be the primary discourse of Antifederalists. They made few references in their writings to the virtuous citizen and orderly hierarchical government in the manner of classical Republicans or Commonwealth Whigs. They did not believe that a 'harmony of interests' would always arise in a competitive, expanding environment like America's, but that certain conditions provided the best opportunities for the largest number of people. One of these conditions was vigilance, the watchful eye of local and state participants in the political economy over the collective welfare. The independent yet accountable individual was the animating spirit of the future. Not merely self-regarding nor self-sufficient, he was 'productive' and 'industrious' within a series of overlapping sets of economic relations connecting him to places near and far. Most economic liberals – and most articulate New York Antifederalists – believed the small producer to be the primary link in this economic chain.[28]

These moderate liberals were optimistic that in the future New Yorkers would have their 'reciprocal wants' satisfied, even as their numbers grew very large. This view was reinforced by gradual economic recovery after 1787. European demand increased for grain from the interior valleys of the north, and prices began to rise. Farmers' private indebtedness began to diminish in New York, though certainly not everywhere. After 1787 New York's exports of grain rose to pre-war levels and then beyond them. Shipbuilding revived and re-exports of New Jersey and Connecticut agricultural products rose steadily through the late 1780s and after. While cataloguing previous rural woes, Phineas Bond, the British Consul in Philadelphia, reported that those who had weathered the war and depression 'seem now to be opened to their true interests'. Another observer remarked that in the interior, where local self-sufficiency was prevalent, recovery was attributable to the 'spirit of emulation, of industry, of improvement, of patriotism, raised throughout the states . . .'. He added 'this is not by the interposition of the legislature, but by . . . interested and enterprising spirit of individuals; perhaps, even by the want of an effective government . . . for it might have meddled, and, as in most similar cases, might have marred'. Nevertheless, most New York observers agreed that even when the state had intervened to guide economic activity it had been consistently modest and fair. As Governor Clinton remarked, 'The Country [side] is in a great measure recovered from the wastes and injuries of War.'[29]

Some optimists reached almost prophetic levels by 1787. John Stevens wrote that an enlightened combination of private self-interest and popular government meant that Americans could now escape the past's downturns of scarcity and depression.[30] A writer in the *New York Journal* focused on the productive capacity to be released with territorial expansion. He saw 'a *new birth* to *glory* and *empire*' as New Yorkers settled the hinterlands; the west would provide the safety valve which would continuously rebalance population and economic interests between city and country. Americans would avoid the crowding which led to corruption in Europe. Sooner, rather than later, American agricultural producers would exchange their goods in international commerce, with the result not only of a favourable balance of trade but of a balance of freely competing producers, merchants, and consumers who together would also adjust the balance of supply and demand. By the late 1780s comments of this nature often included references to the contributions of a new American interest, the manufacturer.[31]

Moderate liberals usually warned that, because of flaws in their moral character, two kinds of Americans were likely to threaten this vision. Some merchants were prone to excessive accumulation and consumption without regard for the general welfare. As 'Federal Farmer' put it, most merchants were to be applauded for their contributions to circulating commodities. Yet some among them would succumb to 'imprudent living, imprudent importations', resulting in a 'despondency and disposition to view everything on the dark side' instead of looking to the future with optimism. Such men would indiscriminately legislate against the wills of all other Americans and 'avariciously grasp at all power and property' in order to preserve their 'aristocratic interests'. This would rob Americans of their economic liberty, for the 'weak and ardent men who always expect to be gainers by revolutions, and whose lot it generally is to get out of one difficulty into another . . . are very little to be regarded; and as to those who designedly avail themselves of this weakness and ardour, they are to be despised.'[32] A writer in the *New York Packet* believed that shopkeepers, Whig merchants, farmers, butchers, and actors could not reasonably meet the demands of creditors because of the special privileges assigned to 'brokers, usurers, constables, and coiners of circulating coppers'.[33] Even lesser but rising merchants singled out men in their own ranks for criticism, among them the West Indies smugglers who were formerly their allies but now figured among the 'dishonest traders' whose allegiances 'are so easily broken' in order to under-sell the law-abiding traders of the city.[34]

But moderate economic liberals were no democrats. The other group scorned by them was 'the little insurgents, men in debt, who want no law, and who want a share of the property of others; these are called levellers, Shayites, etc.'. Farmers and artisans who pushed up prices excessively during the war, and debtor insurgents of 1786 who had 'invaded the rights of others', were not included among 'the honest and substantial people', 'the weight of the community: the men of middling property'.[35]

It was this rising, expectant, middling sector of propertied Americans which had the most to fear from a national impost. Sometimes referred to as the small producer, sometimes as the consumer, this very broad layer coveted a form of 'liberty' which was grounded on a contradiction inherited from moderate economic liberalism. In the first place, New York's Lockeans could agree with radical economic liberals that, if left to the workings of self-interest, 'trade generally finds its own level, and will naturally and necessarily leave off any undue burdens laid upon it'. Merchants would moderate their imports and consumers would shun unnecessary commodities.[36] But once taxes were introduced, however necessary they might be, certain dangers arose. As 'Federal Farmer' argued, the 'uncommon exigencies' of Congress might require either excessively high rates on imports or the imposition of export and real estate taxes. 'Cato' warned that taxes had a tendency to rise over time, and

> you will find that if heavy duties are laid on merchandise . . . the price of the commodities, useful as well as luxurious, must be increased. The consumers will be fewer. The merchants must import less; trade will languish, and . . . if [the merchant] pays more duties, he will sell his commodities at a price proportionably raised . . . the farmer, whose produce will not increase in the ratio with labour, utensils, and clothing . . . must sell at the usual price of labour

until he reaches 'inevitable bankruptcy'. 'Brutus' feared that national fiscal needs would rise to the point where taxes would fall 'on everything we eat, drink, or wear . . . and come home to every man's house and pocket', until they would 'grind the face of the poor' and force 'merchants [to] . . . cease importing or smuggle their goods'. The 'honest self-interest' which energised the new nation's economy ran the risk of being displaced by what 'A Republican' called 'gentlemen . . . of great weight and influence, who have . . . been most largely concerned in the monied transactions of the United States, and whose accounts remain unsettled'.[37]

However, if in avoiding the inevitable abuses of centralised taxation New Yorkers provoked the unvirtuous behaviour of both rapacious merchants and Shays-like levellers, they would be no better off. So radical economic liberty was to be avoided as much as centralisation. Trade, said many Lockean liberals, would never 'regulate itself' as radical economic liberals and free traders believed. The modest restraints of state government were required to correct the effects of improperly channelled economic activities and to realise the potential of Americans who properly consulted their 'true interests' with respect for the wider community. In this, moderate liberal opinion had none of the classical republican's fear of creating a public debt. In fact, the impost was most central to emerging Antifederalist concerns in New York because any symbiosis between country and city, hinterland farmers and powerful urban merchants, required a just system of taxation.[38] Abraham Yates's famous pamphlets in 1785 argued that some power had to 'take care of your poor, . . . and order the laying out roads, and mend them . . . and . . . make laws for blackbirds and crows, yoking and ringing your hogs'. 'The power of raising money gives a tone to every government. It is the main spring in the machine. It is the centre of gravity for it will eventually draw into its vortex all other powers.' But if this power lay in 'distant hands' it might rob New Yorkers of 'the most precious jewel, even [their] sovereignty itself'. Modest state import duties were permissible because 'they may be carried no higher than trade will bear or smuggling permit; in the very nature of commerce, bounds are set to them'. In fact, the present state impost did not 'overburden' New Yorkers at all.[39] As another New Yorker summed up, 'It is *money* and not *power*, that ought to be the object; the former will pay our *debts*, – the latter might destroy our *liberty*.'[40]

New York's Antifederalists did not explain how the state would recognise the 'natural boundaries' of an impost while a national tax plan would not. Nor could they adequately suggest why local or state economic interests but not certain individuals nor a national government would consult the 'true interests of the community'. But they did articulate the economic experiences of a majority of the revolutionary generation. Those experiences taught that radical economic liberalism was too selfish; it could not contribute to a satisfactory collective political expression of the majority's economic vision. Thus, for years after the Constitutional Convention, radical aspirations were progresseively tamed by incremental doses of state intervention. Americans first reached for the limits of economic liberalism, and then retreated away from them. Nationalists watched with dismay as the more moderate political economy became firmly grounded in the states. Ironically, however, Federalists would accommodate *their* vision to the same liberal majority. In the debates of 1787-89 most Federalists would retreat from an emphasis on a 'consolidated' union and speak of a federated one instead. Federalists also borrowed Antifederalist language to speak of the moral failures of extreme individualism. This they linked to the moral failures of sovereign states which exercised their 'jealousies' in mutually discriminatory stances. Only after state activists had groped towards forming the most inclusive policy possible did Federalists articulate a vision of the expansive republic. Only after state leaders had tried to find the formula which released the greatest amount of economic energy and yet avoided serving special interests did Federalists promise to transcend particular interests with union. Federalism was, of course, much more than mimicry on a larger scale of its opponents in the states. But there is a strong belief among Americans of the value of opportunity more than that of custom, of the value of a political economy which frees new energies more than it protects established economic privilege. Surely these values owe much to the liberal economic vision which arose in state experiments, and to the discourse it engendered during the 1780s. Perhaps the Antifederalists in 1787-88 did not really lose at all.

NOTES

1 The best recent study on the dissenting tradition in the revolutionary era is Ruth Block, *Visionary Republic, Millennial Themes in American Thought, 1756-1800*, Cambridge, 1985.

2 Assessments of the vast literature on classical republicanism and its reinterpretation by American revolutionaries include : Linda Kerber, 'The republican ideology of the revolutionary generation', *American Quarterly*, XXXVII, 1985, pp. 474-96; Cathy Matson and Peter Onuf, 'Toward a republican empire: interest and ideology in revolutionary America', *American Quarterly*, XXVII, 1985, pp. 496-531; Robert Shalhope, 'Republicanism and early American historiography', *William and Mary Quarterly*, XXXIX, 1982, pp. 334-56; Lance Banning, 'Jeffersonian ideology revisited: liberal and classical ideas in the new American republic', *William and Mary Quarterly*, XLIII, 1986, pp. 3-19; and Joyce Appleby, 'Repblicanism in old and new contexts', *William and Mary Quarterly*, XLIII, 1986, pp. 20-34. For republicanism in the early national period see Drew McCoy, *The Elusive Republic: Political Economy in Jeffersonian America*, Chapel Hill, 1980, especially chs. 1-3; and Gerald Stourzh, *Alexander Hamilton and the Idea of Republican Government*, Stanford, 1970.

3 On early liberal thought, in both its economic and ethical dimensions, see John Dunn, *Rethinking Modern Political Theory: Essays, 1979-83*, Cambridge 1985; Joyce Appleby, 'Ideology and theory: the tension between political and economic liberalism in seventeenth-century England', *American Historical Review*, LXXXI, 1976, pp. 511-15; James Tully, *A Discourse on Property: John Locke and His Adversaries*, Cambridge, 1980; Istvan Hont and Michael Ignatieff, *Wealth and Virtue, The Shaping of Political Economy in the Scottish Enlightenment*, Cambridge, 1983; and Matson and Onuf, 'Toward a republican empire'.

4 For sources of radical economic liberalism and free trade, see C. B. Macpherson, *The Political Theory of Possessive Individualism*, Oxford, 1962; Joyce Appleby, *Economic Thought and Ideology in Seventeenth-Century England*, Princeton, 1978; and Cathy Matson, 'Fair Trade, Free Trade: Economic Ideas and Opportunities in Eighteenth-Century New York City', PhD dissertation, Columbia University, 1985, chs. 1-2, 6.

5 Matson, 'Fair Trade, Free Trade', chs. 3-7.

6 Joseph Dorfman, *The Economic Mind in American Civilization, 1606-1865*, 4 vols., New York, 1946, I, pp. 280-95.

7 On the non-importation movements see Jacob Crowley, *This Sheba, Self: The Conceptualization of Economic Life in Eighteenth-Century America*, Baltimore, 1974; Arthur Schlesinger, *The Colonial Merchants and the American Revolution 1763-1776*, New York, 1918; and Matson, 'Fair Trade, Free Trade', pp. 402-46.

8 McCoy, *The Elusive Republic*, pp. 86-106; Matson, 'Fair Trade, Free Trade', ch. 7.

9 The free trade resolutions of Congress are to be found in C. Ford Worthington *et al.*(eds.), *Journals of the Continental Congress, 1774-1789*, 34 vols. Washington, DC, 1904-37, V, pp. 768-78 (17 Sept. 1776); V, pp. 576-88 (18 July 1776); and XIII, pp. 231-2 (22 Feb. 1778); hereafter referred to as *Journals of the Continental Congress*.

10 John Jay to Robert R. Livingstone, Paris, 17 Nov. 1782, in Francis Wharton (ed.),

The Revolutionary Diplomatic Correspondence of the United States, 6 vols., Washington, DC, 1889, VI, pp. 11-49, at 31.

11 On prices and wages in New York, see *Laws of the State of New York Comprising the Constitution and the Acts of the Legislature Since the Revolution, from the First to the Fifteenth Session Inclusive*, New York, 1792, 1st sess., ch. 34, p. 36 (June 1778); and 3rd sess., ch. 43, p. 106 (9 Feb. to 13 Mar. 1780), hereafter referred to as *Laws; Journal of the Provincial Congress, Provincial Convention, Committee of Safety and Council of Safety of the State of New-York, 1775-1776-1777*, 2 vols., Albany, 1842, I, p. 299; hereafter *Journal of the Provincial Congress*; and *Journals of the Continental Congress*, IX, pp. 826-7, 827-8, 833, 835, 911; XI, pp. 569; and Richard B. Morris, *Government and Labor in Early America*, New York, 1946, pp. 103-16. On embargoes, *Laws*, 1st sess., ch. 10, p. 10 (June 1778); 3rd sess., ch. 21, p. 82 (4 Sept. to 25 Oct. 1779) 4th sess. ch. 2, p. 149 (1 Sept. to 10 Oct. 1780); 4th sess., ch. 24, p. 173 (2 Feb. to 31 Mar. 1781); George Dangerfield, *Chancellor Robert Livingstone of New York, 1746-1813*, New York, 1960, pp. 114-19; Thomas Cochran, *New York in the Confederation: An Economic Study*, Philadelphia, 1932, pp. 30-4, 46-7, 51-2. On paper money issues, Sept. 1775 to Aug. 1777, see *Journal of the Provincial Congress*, I, pp. 133-4, 239, 435, 560.

12 *New York Journal and General Advertiser*, 14 Feb., 26 July, 2 Aug., 9 Aug. 1779; Cochran, *New York in the Confederation*, pp. 39, 46-7.

13 David Hume, 'Of the jealousy of trade', in Eugene Rotwein, *David Hume: Writings on Economics*, Madison, Wis., 1955, p. 78; and Douglass Adair, 'That politics may be reduced to a science: David Hume, James Madison and the Tenth *Federalist*', *Huntington Library Quarterly*, XX, 1957, pp. 343-60. On free trade during the revolution in New York, see, e.g., 'A Farmer', *New York Journal and General Advertiser*, 4 Jan. 1779, 21 Dec. 1778, 11 Jan. 1779; *Journal of the Provincial Congress*, I, p. 132.

14 John Adams to Robert R. Livingston, 14 July 1783, in Wharton, *The Revolutionary and Diplomatic Correspondence*, VI, pp. 540-2; Foner, *Tom Paine*, ch. 5; and J. P. Brissot de Warville, *New Travels in the United States of America, Performed in 1788*, 2 vols., first pub. New York, 1792; repr. New York 1970, I, pp. 463, 464.

15 *New York Packet*, 21 Nov. 1782; 'Rough Hewer' [Yates], *New York Gazetteer* (Alb.), 6 Oct. 1783; 'A Correspondent', *New York Journal*, 25 Jan. 1787; Cochran, *New York in the Confederation*, p. 38; Morris, *Government and Labor*, pp. 92-119.

16 For the 1781 impost see *Journals of the Continental Congress*, XIX, pp. 102-3, 110, 112-13 (31 Jan., 1 Feb., 3 Feb. 1781); Jonathan Elliott, *The Debates in the Several State Conventions on the Adoption of the Federal Constitution*, 5 vols., Washington, DC 1836-45, II, p. 359; *Laws*, 4th sess., ch. 31, p. 177 (19 Mar. 1781) *Journal of the Senate of the State of New York*, 4th sess., p. 79, (16 Mar. 1781); C. H. Lincoln (ed.), *Messages from the Governors*, 11 vols., Albany, 1909, II, p. 120; *Journal of the Provincial Congress*, VII, p. 267; *Minutes of the Albany Commissioners of Correspondence*, ed. J. Sullivan, Albany, 1923, I, p. 772. The 1783 impost is printed at *Journals of the Continental Congress*, XXIV, pp. 257-62 (18 Apr. 1783); XXIV, pp. 186-92 (18 Mar. 1783); and XXIV, pp. 195-201 (20 Mar. 1783). On emerging nationalists see Merrill Jensen, *The New Nation, A History of the United States During the Confederation, 1781-1789*, New York, 1950, chs. 2-3.

17 *Journal of the Senate*, 6th sess., p. 124, (1 Mar. 1783). See also *New York Packet*, 24 Oct. 1782, 19 July and 7 Aug. 1783, and 21 Apr. 1785; and Cochran, *New York during the Confederation*, pp. 148-9. Congress tied its requests for western land ces-

sions to this bill too. For commissary and speculator support for the impost, Alexander Hamilton, 'The Continentalist', 18 Apr. 1782, in Syrett and Cooke (eds.), *Papers*, III, pp. 75-82, at 79-81; *idem.*, 4 July 1782, III, pp. 99-106; and *idem.*, 'Remarks on appropriating the impost exclusively to the army', III, p. 262, (19 Feb. 1783).

18 On New York's repeal of the impost, see *Laws*, 6th sess., chs. 26-7, pp. 281-2; Cochran, *New York in the Confederation*, p. 148; and E. Wilder Spaulding, *New York in the Critical Period, 1783-1789*, New York, 1932, pp. 170-80.

19 John Lord Sheffield, *Observations on the Commerce of the American States, with Europe and the West Indies*, 6th ed., London, 1784; John Adams to John Jay, 19 July to 21 Oct. 1785, in *Works of John Adams*, VIII, pp. 281-3, 289-91, 322-5, 332.

20 Henry B. Dawson, 'The Motley Letter', *Historical Magazine*, 2nd ser., IX, 1871, pp. 157-201, at 164-9; Bayard–Campbell–Pearsall Correspondence, 1751-1806, New York Public Library; 'Cincinatus', *Independent Journal and General Advertiser*, 10, 14, 21 May 1784; Bryan Edwards, *The History, Civil and Commercial, of the British West Indies*, 5 vols., London, 1819, repr. New York, 1966, II, ch. 4.

21 'Common Sense',*Independent Journal and General Advertiser*, 10, 14, 21 May 1784; *Journals of the Continental Congress*, XX, pp. 218n, 237-8 (30 Apr., 4 May 1782).

22 *Laws*, 7th sess., ch. 10, pp. 11-17 (22 Mar., 1784), ch. 53, p. 77 (4 May 1784); 8th sess., ch. 7, p. 180 (18 Nov. 1784), ch. 53, p. 213 (4 Apr. 1785); and 10th sess., ch. 81, p. 142 (11 Apr. 1787). See also Lincoln (ed.), *Messages from the Governors*, II, p. 201; and *Journals of the Assembly*, 7th sess., pp. 158-60 (3 May 1784).

23 For 1783 revenues see Allan Nevins, *The American States During and After the Revolution, 1775-1789*, New York, 1924, pp. 283-4, 510-11, 556-7; for 1784-87, *Journal of the Assembly*, 10th sess., pp. 31-2 (1 Feb. 1787); and Report on Revenue, 11th sess., pp. 14-26 (16 Jan. 1788); also for 1787, Spaulding, *New York in the Critical Period*, p. 155; for 1788, *New York Packet*, 23 Jan. 1789; and for estimates of annual averages, de Warville, *New Travels*, I, pp. 170-1. For the 1774 comparison, see Governor Tryon to Lord Dartmouth, 1774, *Documents Relative to the Colonial History of the State of New York*, 15 vols., Albany, 1853-87, VIII, pp. 452-4. For the success of the impost see 'Common Sense', *Independent Journal and Daily Advertiser*, 10, 14, 21 May 1784. For amounts paid to Congress against the state's debt, see E. James Ferguson, *The Power of the Purse, A History of American Public Finance, 1776-1790*, Chapel Hill, 1961, pp. 180-1, 209-10, 239-42; *Journals of the Continental Congress*, XXVI, pp. 185-97 (15 April 1784); XXVI, pp. 297-314 (27 Apr. 1784); XXIX, pp. 765-71 (27 Sept. 1785); XXXI, pp. 461-5 (2 Aug. 1786); XXXIII, pp. 649-58 (11 Oct. 1787); XXXIV, pp. 433-42 (20 Aug. 1788). See also Jackson Turner Main, *The Antifederalists: Critics of the Constitution, 1781-1788*, Chapel Hill, 1961, p. 75; Hamilton to George Clinton, 14 May 1783, in *Papers*, ed., Syrett and Cooke, III, pp. 354-5; and E. James Ferguson, 'State assumption of the federal debt during the Confederation', *Mississippi Valley Historical Review*, XXXVIII, 1951, pp. 403-4. For New York's state assumption, *Laws*, 9th sess., ch. 40, p. 283 (18 Apr. 1786); 9th sess., ch. 64, p. 326 (5 May 1786); *New York Daily Advertiser*, 28 Jan., 2, 5 Feb. 1788, reflecting backwards; *Journal of the Senate*, 8th sess., pp. 48, 50 (17 Mar. 1785); and *Journal of the Assembly*, 9th sess., pp. 40-1 (15 Feb. 1786). On paper money see *Laws*, 9th sess., ch. 40, p. 283 (18 Mar. 1786); *New York Packet*, 14 Apr. 1785, 18 Feb., 6 Mar. 1786; Main, *Antifederalists*, pp. 47-50; and Jensen, *The New Nation*, pp. 320-2.

24 On private debts, e.g., 'Petition of Henry Remsen and others, merchants of this city',

Assembly Journal, 10th sess., p. 89 (9 Mar. 1787); *Journals of the Continental Congress*, XXXII, pp. 124-5 (21 Mar. 1786); XXXII, pp. 176-4 (13 Apr. 1786; and *Laws*, 9th sess., ch. 40, p. 283 (18 Apr. 1786. On gluts, David Clarkson Letters, New York Historical Society, and De Warville, *New Travels*, I, p. 128. On bankruptcies, *New York Morning Post*, 10 Mar. 1785; *New York Packet*, 21 Apr. 1785; and *Journal of the Assembly*, 8th sess., p. 32 (11 Feb. 1785), p. 181 (27 Apr. 1785); and 9th sess., pp. 100-1 (24 Mar. 1786), for Lawrence Marston, Cadwallader Colden, Thomas Armstrong, John Turner, Thomas Miller, Henry Sickles, Stephen Crosfield, John and Michael Anthony, Benjamin Cole, and others. On tonnage, Minutes of the Chamber of Commerce of New York City, 3 Mar. 1785, New York Public Library. On feelings of grain exporters, John Williams, *Country Journal* (Poughkeepsie), 4 Mar. 1788; also *New York Journal*, 29 Feb. 1788; Jensen, *New Nation*, pp. 43-53.

25 Bayard, Campell, Pearsall Correspondence, 1751-1806; John Van Schaack Letter Book, Taylor-Cooper Papers, and John Lansing's letters in the Gansevoort–Lansing Papers, all at the New York Public Library; Cochran, *New York in the Confederation*, pp. 163-5, 165 n. 6. State senators Ward, Klock, Webster, Swartwout, Whiting, Paine, Gutherie, Morris, McDougall, Russell, and Stoutenburgh – all merchants – supported the duties on commerce; see *Journal of the Senate*, 8th sess., pp. 48, 50 (17 Mar. 1785). Other major merchants known to support the state impost were Marinus Willet, John Lamb, Isaac Sears, John Rutgers, Jacobus Van Zandt, and Hugh Hughes. See also Hamilton's letters to Governor Clinton, 12 Jan., 24 Feb., 14 May, 1 June 1783, in Syrett and Cooke (eds.), *Papers*, III, pp. 240-1, 268-74, 354-5, 367-72; 'A Correspondent', *New York Journal*, 25 Jan. 1787; 'Rough Hewer' [Abraham Yates], *New York Gazetteer* (Alb.), 6 Oct. 1783. On auctions, see Jerome Paige, 'The Evolution of Mercantile Capitalism and Planter Capitalism and the Development of Economic Ideas', PhD dissertation, American University, 1982, pp. 101-2; and *Laws*, 9th sess., ch. 17, p. 249 (21 Mar. 1786).

26 For New York's discriminatory legislation, see *Laws*, 1st sess., ch. 10, p. 10 (June 1788); 3rd sess., ch. 21, p. 82 (4 Sep.–25 Oct. 1779); 4th sess., ch. 2, p. 149 (1 Sep. 1780); 4th sess., ch. 24, p. 173 (2 Feb.–31 Mar. 1781); 7th sess., ch. 10, p. 11 (22 Mar. 1784); 8th sess., ch. 7, p. 180 (18 Nov. 1784); 10th sess., ch. 81, p. 142 (11 Apr. 1787); *New York Packet*,, 23 Mar. 1786. On interstate rivalry see *New Haven Gazette*, 19 Oct. 1786, 28 June 1787, and 17 Jan. 1788; *Public Papers of George Clinton, First Governor of New York*, ed. Hugh Hastings, 10 vols., Albany, 1911, VI, p. 174; *Connecticut Courant*, 16 Oct. 1786; Hugh Ledlie to General Lamb, 15 Jan. 1788, Lamb Papers, New-York Historical Society; 'An American', *New York Packet, 27 May 1788; and 'Address to the New York Convention', Pennsylvania Gazette*, 11 June 1788.

27 Main, *Antifederalists*, pp. 99-100. For Rhode Island, see H. M. Bishop, 'Why Rhode Island opposed the federal constitution', *Rhode Island History*, VIII, 1949, pp. 1-10, 33-44.

28 Countryman, *People in Revolution*, pp. 260-5; 'Federal Farmer', (Poughkeepsie) *Country Journal*, 31 Dec. 1787; [Anon.], *Hudson Gazette*, 28 June 1787; 'Agrippa' (*Daily Advertiser?*], 14 Jan. 1788.

29 [Anon.], (Poughkeepsie) *Country Journal*, 11 July 1787, 22 Jan. 1788; *New York Packet*, 16 Feb. 1787; Phineas Bond, 'Letters to the Foreign Office of Great Britain, 1787-1789, and 1790-1794', in American Historical Association *Annual Report of the Year 1786*, I, Washington, DC, 1897, pp. 537-657, at 652; Nevins, *American States*,

pp. 556-7; Governor Clinton to the Assembly, *Journal of the Assembly*, 11 Jan. 1788.

30 John Stevens, *Observations on Government*, New York, 1787.

31 *New York Journal*, 16 Feb. 1787. Also, *Journal of the Assembly*, 11th sess., p. 7 (11 Jan. 1788), pp. 94-5 (27 Feb. 1788); Dawson, 'Motley Letter', pp. 167-8. On manufacturers see, for example, 'Petition from John Broome, Alexander Robertson, and others, merchants and manufacturers of New York', New York Public Library; and 'Petition of New York merchants and manufacturers' in Alfred Chandler, Jr. (ed. and intro.), *The New American State Papers, Manufactures*, Wilmington, Del., 1972, I, p. 34. The petition was signed by Anthony Post, Francis Childs, John Campbell, Henry Pope, James Bramble, John Goodeve, Jacob Morton, White Matlack, George Lindsay, William J. Elsworth, and John Swine. On the significance of early protectionism see Nelson, 'Hamilton and manufacturers', pp. 280-9, 290; Paige, 'Evolution of mercantile capitalism', pp. 103-5; Young, *Democratic Republicans*, pp. 207-30; and McCoy, *Elusive Republic*, ch. 6.

32 'Federal Farmer', (Poughkeepsie) *Country Journal*, 8, 15 Oct. 1787, 28 Jan. 1788.

33 [Anon.], *New York Packet*, 12 Feb. 1788.

34 De Warville, *New Travels*, I, pp. 463, 464; Edwards, *History of the British West Indies*, II, ch. 4; Countryman, *People in Revolution*, pp. 109, 114.

35 [Abraham Yates], *Political Papers, Addressed to the Advocates for a Congressional Revenue, in the State of New-York*, New York, 1786, essay for 17 Mar. 1785, p. 8; see also 10 Oct. 1787, pp. 5-6, 18-20.

36 'Federal Farmer' (Poughkeepsie) *Country Journal*, 15 Oct. 1787.

37 'Cato' (George Clinton), *New York Journal*, 22 Nov. 1787; 'Brutus' (Abraham Yates), *New York Journal*, 18 Oct., 13 Dec. 1787, 'A Republican', *New York Daily Advertiser*, 19 Oct. 1786, 27 Dec. 1787; 'Agrippa' [*New York Journal?*], 14 Jan. 1788.

38 'Philo-Patria', *New York Journal*, 28 Sep. 1787, [Yates], *Political Papers*, 17 Mar. 1785, p. 8.

39 [Yates], *Political Papers*, 10 Oct. 1787, pp. 5-6, 14-15, 18-20.

40 'A Republican', *New York Journal*, 12 Oct. 1786,

3

The original meaning of the free speech clause of the First Amendment

DAVID M. RABBAN
University of Texas

The bicentennial of the United States Constitution provides a particularly appropriate occasion to examine the original meaning of the First Amendment's protection for freedom of expression. Ratification of the Constitution depended upon the adoption of the ten amendments that formed the Bill of Rights. Equally important, but less frequently appreciated, the original meaning of the First Amendment must be understood in the context of the structure of the entire Constitution.

Unfortunately, most contemporary legal scholarship and most judicial opinions have rarely explored either the history of the First Amendment or its relationship to the general constitutional scheme. The few historical references that do exist are often cursory and inaccurate.[1] Attempting to understand the original meaning of the First Amendment is thus not only a natural commemoration of the bicentennial; it also helps us address current First Amendment issues. One need not accept the narrow and unrealistic adherence to the 'jurisprudence of original intent' recently popularised by United States Attorney-General Meese to recognise the relevance of original intent to contemporary analysis of a constitutional provision. Even those who would allow the modern judge to depart from the framers' original intent generally concede that compelling reasons – for example, dramatic and obvious shifts in societal values – must justify such departures. Few deny entirely the significance of original intent.

The intrinsic difficulties in reconstructing original intent are compounded for the free speech clause of the First Amendment because the framers themselves did not engage in extensive debate over its meaning. Nor is the actual language of the First Amendment very revealing. It provides that 'Congress shall make no law . . . abridging the freedom of speech, or of the press; or of the right of the people peaceably to assemble, and to petition the Government for a redress of grievances.' This language, while emphasising the limited congressional role in regulating speech, does not define 'the freedom of speech' that is protected. And while this restriction on federal power may itself have been perceived as an important structural means to protect the substantive right of free expression, the First Amendment does not address the extent to which the state may regulate speech.

The diametrically opposed conclusions of two of the most influential twentieth-century commentators on the First Amendment underline its ambiguity. Zechariah Chafee, Jr., the seminal modern scholar of the First Amendment, maintained that the framers 'intended to wipe out the common law of sedition, and make prosecutions for criticism of the government, without any incitement to law-breaking, forever impossible in the United States of America'[2] Yet Leonard Levy, whose pioneering research into the historical background of the First Amendment has dominated the field for a generation, continues to assert that the framers did not intend to abolish the common law of seditious libel.[3]

Despite the difficulty in ascribing a technical legal content to the original understanding of the First Amendment, it is possible to reconstruct the framers' views on freedom of expression by examining the central intellectual traditions that influenced them. Happily, some of the most impressive historical scholarship of the past generation has investigated these traditions.[4] Although this scholarship does not resolve the debate between Chafee and Levy, it clearly supports the conclusion that a substantial libertarian conception of free political expression, tied to the ideology of opposition and dissent that led to the American Revolution, had become part of a mutually reinforcing intellectual tradition in England and North America before the creation of the United States Constitution in 1787 and the ratification of the First Amendment in 1791. The Constitution and the First Amendment represented the political and legal victory of this tradition.

Three generations of English Radical Whigs preserved and transmitted to the American colonists the radical social and political thought of the English Civil War of the 1640s. They transformed Christian liberties into natural rights and political demands. Their publicists and certain opposition politicians stressed the importance of checks on government to the preservation of individual liberties. Their commitment to freedom of conscience translated into support for freedom of speech and of the press. Perhaps most significantly, they recognised the connections among theories of sovereignty, freedom of political expression, and seditious libel.

Blackstone's famous *Commentaries* expressed the dominant English

conceptions that the Radical Whigs challenged. They reflected the prevailing understanding that the Glorious Revolution of 1688, by transfer-
ring absolute sovereignty from the Crown to Parliament, had addressed
the longstanding popular perception that the king and his magistrates
threatened individual liberties. Parliament would protect these liberties
against executive infringement and, because it embodied the will of the
entire population, would not itself present an independent danger. Yet
absolute sovereignty in Parliament, as Blackstone emphasised, meant
that its actions, however arbitrary or unreasonable, had the force of binding and unappealable law.[5]

The discussion of freedom of expression in Blackstone's *Commentaries*
comported with this view of parliamentary sovereignty. Liberty of the
press, in Blackstone's view, is essential to a free state and must preclude
prior restraints on publications. But Blackstone immediately added that
the law did not prevent subsequent punishment of publications having a
tendency to disrupt peace and good order, such as attacks on government
officials and policies. Accordingly, he considered the law of seditious
libel, which applied to criticism of the government to be compatible with
freedom of expression.[6] In order for Parliament to guard the liberties of
the people, the privileges of its members had to include a freedom to
express criticism of the King and his magistrates that would constitute
seditious libel if uttered outside the legislature.[7] Yet Parliament, as absolute sovereign, could and did prosecute speech directed at it.[8] And
because Parliament protected individual liberties, the people themselves
did not need the freedom to criticise either Parliament or the executive
actions that members of Parliament, through their parliamentary
privileges, could freely attack on the people's behalf.

The English Radical Whigs challenged all three of these related
theories. Unlike Blackstone, they viewed the people as the ultimate
source of sovereign power, and Parliament as the agent of the people.

Famous Radical Whigs in England, from John Trenchard and
Thomas Gordon in the 1720s to Joseph Priestley and Richard Price in
the generation that lived through the American Revolution, stressed that
freedom of political expression provided the most effective way for the
people to guard their sovereignty and their liberties against governmental
aggrandisement. Writing as 'Cato', Trenchard and Gordon emphasised
'That Men ought to speak well of their Governors, is true, while their
Governors deserve to be well spoken of; but to do public Mischief, without hearing of it, is only the Prerogative and Felicity of Tyranny; A free
People will be shewing that they are so, by their Freedom of Speech.'
'Freedom of Speech', Cato concluded, 'is the great Bulwark of Liberty;

they prosper and die together.'[9]

In the generation of the American Revolution, Joseph Priestley and Richard Price reiterated the relationship between popular sovereignty and freedom of political expression. Priestley, after calling magistrates *'the servants of the people'*, added that the people should react to official oppression by 'strong remonstrances to those governors who have betrayed their trust'. 'It is essential to the freedom of government', Preistley declared, 'that all public measures should be imputed to persons who may be freely censured, and arraigned at the bar of the public.'[10] In defining 'liberty of discussion', Price included 'the liberty of examining all public measures and publishing on all speculative and doctrinal points'.[11]

Consistent with these views, English Radical Whigs proposed reforms in the law of seditious libel to expand the freedom to criticise government. In addition to advocating truth as a defence to a charge of seditious libel, Cato objected to the judicial reliance on the supposed bad tendency of speech to find seditious intent. Judges, Cato complained, often strained the 'genuine Signification' of words whose 'literal and natural Meaning, import nothing that is criminal'.[12] The conviction of John Wilkes in 1764 for a seditious libel on King George III, combined with the refusal of the House of Commons to seat him following his election, produced major protests, including anonymous pamphlets reiterating and expanding upon Cato's earlier writings.[13] Priestley similarly attacked the English ministry for restricting the freedom of the press, 'that great security for every other branch of our liberty, and the scourge of their arbitrary proceedings, by construing all censures upon them, and their measures, into *libels*, and procuring the authors of them to be severely punished'.[14]

Thomas Erskine's famous defence of Tom Paine, who in 1792 was convicted of seditious libel for publishing Part Two of *Rights of Man*, underlined the interdependence of popular sovereignty, freedom of political expression, and seditious libel.

> I have insisted at great length on the origin of government . . . because I consider it to be not only an essential support, but the very foundation of the liberty of the press. . . . If the people have, without possible recall, delegated all their authorities, they have no jurisdiction to act, and therefore none to think or write upon such subjects; and it would be a libel to arraign government or any of its acts, before those who have no jurisdiction to correct them. But . . . no legal argument can shake the freedom of the press in my sense of it, if I am supported in my doctrines concerning the great unalienable right of the people to reform or change their govern-

ments. It is because the liberty of the press resolves itself into this great issue, that it has been in every country the last liberty which subjects have been able to wrest from power. Other liberties are held *under* government, but the liberty of opinion keeps governments themselves in due subjection to their duties.[15]

Both defenders and opponents of eighteenth-century English orthodoxies recognised that the law of seditious libel and broader theories of freedom of political expression ultimately depended on the fundamental issue of sovereignty. Blackstone's limitation of freedom of the press to the prohibition against prior restraints reflected his view that absolute sovereignty rests within Parliament. The Radical Whigs, by contrast, located absolute sovereignty in the people. The efforts of Radical Whigs to restrict the crime of seditious libel derived from their basic premise that the effective exercise of popular sovereignty as a check on the powers of government required substantially greater freedom of political expression than the common law allowed.

Although the English Radical Whigs had little impact in their own country, they were enormously influential and popular in the American colonies. They linked the English struggle against tyranny with the American movement for independence. Actual developments in the American colonies, especially popular influence in colonial assemblies, provided practical illustrations of their theories.[16] Many provisions of the United States Constitution incorporate devices they sought in vain to establish in England.[17]

These English Radicals had close religious and cultural ties with the American colonists.[18] Their academies maintained associations with American universities throughout the eighteenth century.[19] Trenchard and Gordon were the Englishmen who most clearly influenced the thought of the American colonists. Americans modelled their own writings on Cato, and often quoted from and plagarised Cato's letters and journal. The lawyers for John Peter Zenger, whose popular acquittal in 1735 limited further colonial prosecutions for seditious libel, naturally cited Cato as theoretical authority in their attack on the traditional law.[20] Wilkes, himself raised and educated as a Radical Whig, became a hero in America after his conviction for seditious libel.[21]

Richard Price and Joseph Priestley were among the most influential contemporary English writers during the generation of the American Revolution.[22] Personal friendships during this period between English Radical Whigs and important American leaders reinforced their intellectual affinities.[23] The legacy of the English Radical Whigs influenced Americans throughout the 1790s and provided much of the intellectual opposition to the Sedition Act of 1798.[24]

Disagreement over the meaning of sovereignty was the crucial intellectual issue of the American Revolution. Not content simply to gain political independence from Great Britain, the Americans implemented a theory of government that rejected Blackstone's view of sovereignty as the binding command of a legislature. Instead, they maintained that sovereignty derived from the people's continuous assent.[25] As the first significant successful assertion of this principle, the American Revolution represented a major victory of Radical Whig thought.[26]

In several major respects, the Americans transformed the conception of sovereignty they had inherited from the English Radical Whigs. Perhaps without appreciating the distinctiveness of their emerging views, some commentators began to conceive of the executive as well as the legislature as the representative of the people. As a result, they weakened the English theory that a constitution is a contract in which the people delegated power to the executive as long as it respected individual rights and promoted the public welfare. Of equal importance, was the extension of the Radical Whig mistrust of the executive to legislative authority. Throughout the 1780s, as state legislatures, which theoretically embodied the will of the people, seemed to abuse their power, Americans increasingly transferred their fear of government authority, originally concentrated on the British Crown and its agents, to their own legislatures.[27]

The emerging American conception of the constituent convention, upon which the legitimacy of the United States Constitution ultimately depended, developed from this increasing mistrust of even the most representative legislatures. Conventions of the people were a traditional means in England and America of petitioning government for redress of grievances. As the crisis with England deepened in the early 1770s, Americans began to view the convention as replacing rather than as petitioning the existing government. In reaction to the perceived despotism of the state legislatures in the 1780s, Americans further transformed the conception of a convention into the embodiment of the sovereignty of the people. The convention thus became a superior authority to any legislature.[28]

The Constitution of the United States reflected what were becoming distinctively American conceptions of popular sovereignty and constituent conventions. Europeans had never conceived of the people as actually creating a government through a written constitution. The Constitution of the United States was both antecedent and superior to the actual structure of government. It provided a written model for government against which the actual performance of the institutions it created would be measured.[29]

This new conception of sovereignty suggests why many Federalists initially considered a bill of rights to be redundant. Because the people did not contract with the government to obtain their liberties, but retained whatever power they did not delegate to either state or federal authorities, the very structure of the Constitution secured these liberties from governmental encroachment.[30] Some Federalists worried that a written bill of rights would actually jeopardise the fundamental liberties of the people by implying, contrary to the theory of the new Constitution, that the government legitimately could impair any right not specifically enumerated.[31]

The Antifederalists feared that the strengthening of the federal government contemplated by the Constitution would threaten the personal liberties which the American Revolutionary War was fought to protect. They may have agitated for a written bill of rights as a springboard for attacks on the Constitution itself, but this broader strategy does not detract from their concern over potential abridgements of the liberties eventually enumerated in the Bill of Rights. The extent of this concern was underlined by the strong popular support for a bill of rights by many Americans who did not share the Antifederalists' more general objections to the relationship between federal and state power in the proposed Constitution.[32]

Federalists, moreover, readily acceded to a written bill of rights despite the initial misgivings some of them had expressed. Most Federalists came to realise that a bill of rights, though perhaps a redundancy, would not harm the constitutional scheme whose ratification its inclusion was likely to assure.[33] In addition, once the ratification debate began, many Federalists came to believe that a written bill of rights would provide additional protection for fundamental liberties. Jefferson eventually acknowledged that the Antifederalist agitation for a bill of rights provoked 'further guards to liberty without touching the energy of government'.[34] And Madison, who drafted the Bill of Rights despite his initial opposition to the idea, soon maintained that these written guarantees might create a standard to 'counteract the impulses of interest and passion' and to provide an 'appeal to the sense of the community'.[35] In introducing the Bill of Rights in Congress in 1789, Madison pointed out that the Magna Carta, while restricting the power of the Crown, did not affect the authority of Parliament. Under the new American constitutional scheme based on popular sovereignty, by contrast, the people wanted 'to raise barriers against power in all forms and departments of

Governments'.[36] During the subsequent congressional debate over the Bill of Rights, Madison identified freedom of speech and of the press as among 'the most valuable on the whole list'.[37]

American attitudes to freedom of political expression had changed significantly between the colonial period and the framing of the Constitution. During the colonial period, Americans viewed the press as a fundamental device for unifying the people in the struggle against the threat posed by the British Crown. As did the English Parliament, colonial assemblies used the doctrine of parliamentary privilege to restrain criticism of legislators by citizens and the press.[38] Americans demanded freedom of the press at the same time that they suppressed loyalist opinions, believing that the overriding need for popular unity justified silencing opposing views. Not surprisingly, this position intensified as the crisis with England led to war. American independence removed the major justification for suppression, and the disappointing experience under the popularly elected state legislatures of the 1780s led most Americans to abandon the notion that the people could be a unified force. Increasingly, Americans stressed the protection of individual rights, including freedom of expression, from encroachment by any branch of government.[39]

The ratification of the Constitution and the Bill of Rights, however, did not end debate over the role of freedom of political expression in the United States. The emergence of the competing Federalist and Republican political parties produced major disagreements over the role of public opinion in a republic. Republicans believed that public opinion should influence government, and, more pragmatically, that a well-informed public would support the policies of their party. Writing in 1791, Madison identified public opinion as 'the real sovereign', the force that must scrutinise and, if necessary, challenge the operations of government. In order to perform this responsibility, the public required 'a free press, and particularly a circulation of newspapers throughout the entire body of the people' in addition to the 'Constitutional Declaration of Rights'.[40] Federalists, on the other hand, believed that government ought to retain substantial independence from public opinion.[41]

The activities of the Democratic Societies that had organised throughout the country in 1793 produced a concrete controversy over which to debate these opposing views of freedom of political expression. Relying heavily on Radical Whig ideology, the Democratic Societies justified their organisation by emphasising the tendency of government to abuse power and the necessity of popular vigilance to check this. Claiming that isolated individuals are unlikely to be able to perform this function, the

Societies took it upon themselves to monitor the government, pledging to warn the general public in times of actual danger to its liberties.[42]

Republicans generally supported the activities of these societies, but Federalists expressed concern that they would lead to a 'simple democracy' dominated by demagogues. Even in a republic, Federalists asserted, an effective legislature must retain some distance from popular influences. Significantly, Federalists did not question the doctrine of popular sovereignty itself, which had become so broadly accepted in the United States that any challenge to it seemed to assure political defeat. Rather, they declared that the Democratic Societies threatened popular sovereignty by interposing themselves between the people and their elected representatives in government. Contrasting the 'self-created' societies with the mass of citizens, Federalists accused the societies of trying to obtain disproportionate political influence for a minority in the guise of acting for the people.[43]

The Whiskey Rebellion in western Pennsylvania in 1794 intensified existing divisions over the Democratic Societies. Federalists claimed that local Democratic Societies had instigated the rebellion and cited it as confirmation that all Democratic Societies threatened the new Constitution and government. Because the Whiskey Rebellion coincided with the most violent period of the French Revolution, Federalists found it relatively easy to equate the American Democratic Societies with the Jacobin clubs that allegedly had destroyed the French Constitution. President Washington's annual message to Congress attributed responsibility for the Whiskey Rebellion to certain Democratic Societies. A Federalist member of the House subsequently moved to censure these societies for 'misrepresenting the conduct of Government, and disturbing the operation of the laws'.[44]

The Democratic Societies and their Republican defenders in Congress responded to this Federalist assault by emphasising the natural and constitutional right of association and expression. They often invoked the ideology and language of the English Radical Whigs, relying particularly on Cato's identification of freedom of expression as the 'Bulwark of Liberty'.[45] Madison's comments in Congress stressed the fundamental relationship between popular sovereignty and freedom of political expression. 'If we advert to the nature of Republican Government,' he declared, 'we shall find that the censorial power is in the people over the Government and not in the Government over the people.'[46] In a letter to Jefferson, Madison called Washington's criticism of the Democratic Societies an attack 'on the essential and constitutional right of the citizen'.[47] While largely a rehearsal for the more intense controversy over the Sedition Act of 1798, this debate provoked by the Whiskey Rebellion of 1794 demonstrates the substantial extent to which libertarian views of the freedom of expression protected by the First Amendment had already been articulated by the mid-1790s.

The divisions between Federalists and Republicans over the Sedition Act brought into sharp focus ideological differences that had been developing throughout the 1790s.[48] Unsuccessful diplomatic negotiations with France provided the immediate background for the Sedition Act. Outraged at the revelation of French claims that France could divide the American people from their government, Federalists in Congress determined to prepare for war and to insure a united front at home. When the Republicans, who had opposed Federalist domestic and foreign policies for a decade, refused to co-operate, the Federalists passed the Sedition Act, which was used primarily to silence the Republican press.[49]

In their effort to justify the Sedition Act to a republic whose Constitution explicitly protected freedom of the press, the Federalists cleverly attempted to graft concepts that had supported legislative sovereignty in England on to the American ideology of popular sovereignty. The Federalists argued that excesses of the Republican press had weakened popular sovereignty. Although Federalists agreed that the government derived all of its power from the people, they maintained that the people delegated power to their representatives at periodic elections. Once elected, these officials had to be protected from unjust criticism in order to govern effectively. Indeed, attacks on public officials constituted attacks on the people, whose interests the officials were elected to represent.[50]

A number of Federalists added that the danger of press licentiousness was greater in a republic than in a monarchy because monarchs possessed stronger weapons to combat the press. In a republic, by contrast, government depended on public opinion. 'To mislead the judgment of the people, where they have no power', one Federalist observed, 'may produce no mischief. To mislead the judgment of the people where they have *all* power, must produce the greatest possible mischief.' Another Federalist added that 'the publication of false, scandalous, and malicious matter against the Government . . . tends to produce insurrection and total disrespect for its authority, and that, without the power of preventing these, no Government can exist'.[51] Not surprisingly, Federalists often supported these arguments by the contention that the First Amendment did nothing more than incorporate the English common law of freedom of expression as set forth by Blackstone's *Commentaries*.[52]

Republicans, elaborating arguments they had advanced throughout the 1790s, vigorously rebutted this Federalist defence of the Sedition Act. The most significant Republican attack on this legislation was written by James Madison, who had drafted the First Amendment. In his famous Virginia Report of 1800, Madison expanded upon his congressional statements of 1789 and 1794. He explained why the crucial differences between American and English conceptions of sovereignty demonstrate that the protection for freedom of expression in the First Amendment goes beyond Blackstone's prohibition against prior restraints. Madison's language merits extensive quotation because it captures better than any other single source the relationship between American constitutional theory, derived from the ideology of the English Radical Whigs, and the First Amendment.

> In the British government, the danger of encroachment on the rights of the people, is understood to be confined to the executive magistrate. The representatives of the people in the legislature, are not only exempt themselves, from distrust, but are considered as sufficient guardians of the rights of their constituents against the danger from the executive. Hence, too, all the ramparts for protecting the rights of the people, such as their magna charta, their bill of rights, &c., are not reared against the parliament, but against the royal prerogative. They are merely legislative precautions against executive usurpations. Under such a government as this, an exemption of the press from previous restraint by licensers appointed by the king, is all the freedom that can be secured to it.
>
> In the United States, the case is altogether different. The people, not the government, possess the absolute sovereignty. The legislature, no less than the executive, is under limitations of power. Encroachments are regarded as possible from the one, as well as from the other. Hence, in the United States, the great and essential rights of the people are secured against legislative as well as against executive ambition. They are secured, not by laws paramount to [royal] prerogative, but by constitutions paramount to laws. This security of the freedom of the press requires, that it should be exempt, not only from previous restraint by the executive, as in Great Britain, but from legislative restraint also; and this exemption, to be effectual, must be an exemption not only from the previous inspection of licensers, but from the subsequent penalty of laws.[53]

Significantly, St George Tucker, the editor of the tremendously influential 1803 American edition of Blackstone's *Commentaries*, added a lengthy Appendix explaining why Blackstone's exposition of freedom of expression was inconsistent with the American system of government and the First Amendment. Tucker's Appendix incorporated almost verbatim this passage from Madison's Virginia Report of 1800.[54]

In one major respect, the experience under the Sedition Act led to an important advance in libertarian analysis of freedom of political expression. According to many libertarian thinkers of the eighteenth century, the vague definition of seditious libel at common law allowed liability to depend on arbitrary and unpredictable determinations by judges that criticism of government had gone too far.[55] The Sedition Act incorporated the major reforms in the law of seditious libel that English and American libertarians had been advocating throughout the eighteenth century. This legislation gave the jury the power to decide whether a defendant's language constituted seditious libel, allowed truth as a defence, and required proof of a defendant's criminal intent. Yet these reforms did not prevent the successful prosecution of political opinions that offended the Federalist administration. As a result, several Republican theorists, including Madison, soon reached the conclusion that the necessary protection for freedom of political expression in a republic founded on popular sovereignty was incompatible with punishment for seditious libel.[56]

It may be, as Leonard Levy claims, that the framers of the First Amendment did not intend to abolish the common-law crime of seditious libel. Certainly, Chafee's undocumented assertion to the contrary cannot be demonstrated. No contemporaneous crisis focused their attention on this issue. Yet the attack on the crime of seditious libel generated by the debate over the Sedition Act of 1798 should not prevent recognition of the significant extent to which libertarian views about freedom of expression had already been incorporated into the United States Constitution. A new conception of sovereignty, derived from the Radical Whig tradition in England, arose during the American Revolution and developed under the impact of the French Revolution on the Anglo-American world. Because the people retain absolute sovereignty in the Republic created by the Constitution, they have the power to criticise all branches of government, whose officials are their servants. This popular power helps avert the perpetual danger that government will infringe individual liberties. The freedom of expression guaranteed in the First Amendment thus reinforces the fundamental principle of popular sovereignty that underlies the Constitution of the United States. This relationship between freedom of expression and popular sovereignty, which too often has been obscured throughout American history, should remain at the core of contemporary interpretations of the First Amendment.

NOTES

I have adopted much of this essay from D. Rabban, 'The ahistorical historian: Leonard Levy on freedom of expression in early American history', *Stanford Law Review*, XXXVII, 1985, p. 795.

1 The major exception is D. Anderson, 'The origins of the press clause', *UCLA Law Review*, XXX, 1983, p. 455. In his extensive review of the legislative history of the First Amendment's protection for free speech and the press, Anderson concedes that it is impossible to determine the meaning ascribed to the constitutional language by either the framers or the ratifying legislatures. Yet he convincingly maintains that this language reflected widespread commitment to the importance of free expression in the new republican form of government that followed independence.

2 Chafee, 'Freedom of speech in war time', *Harvard Law Review*, XXXII, 1919, p. 947; reprinted in Z. Chafee, *Free Speech in the United States*, Cambridge, Mass., 1941, p. 21.

3 L. W. Levy, *Emergence of a Free Press*, New York, 1985, pp. 220, 281; L. W. Levy *Freedom of Speech and Press in Early America: Legacy of Suppression*, New York, 1960, pp. 214, 248.

4 *See especially* B. Bailyn, *The Ideological Origins of the American Revolution*, Cambridge, Mass., 1967; J. R. Pole, *Political Representation in England and the Origins of the American Republic*, London, 1966; G. S. Wood, *The Creation of the American Republic, 1776-1787*, Chapel Hill, N.Y., 1969.

5 W. Blackstone, *Commentaries*, ed. S. Tucker, Philadelphia, PA, 1803, I, pp. 90-1, 146-7; Bailyn, *Ideological Origins*, pp. 202-2; Wood, *Creation of the American Republic*, p. 265.

6 Blackstone, *Commentaries*, IV, pp. 123, 150-3.

7 Blackstone, *Commentaries*, I, pp. 164-7.

8 Levy, *Emergence*, p. 14; F. Siebert, *Freedom of the Press in England 1476-1776*, Urbana, Ill., 1952, pp. 368-74.

9 *Cato's Letters* (6th ed. 1755), No. 15, 4 Feb. 1720.

10 J. Priestley, *The Present State of Liberty in Great Britain and Her Colonies*, London, 1769, pp. 384, 386-7, reprinted in *The Theological and Miscellaneous Works*, ed. J. Rutt, XXII, London, 1823.

11 R. Price, *Observations on the Importance of the American Revolution*, London, 1784, p. 20.

12 *Cato's Letters*, No. 101, 3 Nov. 1722.

13 Levy, *Emergence*, pp. 145-52; Pole, *Political Representation*, pp. 426-7.

14 Priestley, *The Present State*, pp. 389-90.

15 *Rex* v. *Paine*, Howell, 22 State Trials 437 (1792).

16 Pole, *Political Representation*, pp. 514-15 and *passim*.

17 C. Robbins, *The Eighteenth-Century Commonwealthman*, Cambridge, Mass., 1959, pp. 4, 385-6.

18 A. H. Lincoln, *Some Political & Social Ideas of English Dissent, 1763-1800*, Cambridge, 1938 (reprinted 1971), p. 25.

19 A. Goodwin, *The Friends of Liberty*, London, 1979, pp. 39-40.

20 Bailyn, *Ideological Origins*, pp. 35, 45, 52.

21 Bailyn, *Ideological Origins*, pp. 110-12; P. Maier, 'John Wilkes and American disillu-

sionment with Britain', *William and Mary Quarterly*, XX, 1963, p. 373.

22 Bailyn, *Ideological Origins*, pp. 41, 132-3; R. R. Palmer, *The Age of the Democratic Revolutions*, Princeton, N.J., 1959, I, p. 235.

23 Goodwin, *Friends of Liberty*, p. 66; S. Lynd, *Intellectual Origins of American Radicalism*, New York, 1968, pp. 26-7; N. Hans, 'Franklin, Jefferson, and the English Radicals at the end of the eighteenth century', *Proceedings of the American Philosophical Society*, LXXXXVIII, 1954, p. 406.

24 R. Buel, 'Freedom of the press in revolutionary America: the evolution of libertarianism, 1760-1790', in *The Press and the American Revolution*, ed. B. Bailyn and J. Hench, Worcester, Mass., 1980, pp. 91-2.

25 Bailyn, *Ideological Origins*, pp. 174, 198, 201-2, 228; Palmer, *Democratic Revolutions*, p. 235.

26 Palmer, *Democratic Revolutions*, p. 185.

27 Pole, *Political Representation*, pp. 171, 345, 379, 510-11; Wood, *Creation of the American Republic*, pp., 282, 328, 340, 409, 450, 453.

28 Wood, *Creation of the American Republic*, pp. 306-43.

29 Bailyn, *Ideological Origins*, p. 185; Palmer, *Democratic Revolutions*, pp. 214-15; Wood, *Creation of the American Republic*, pp. 266-7, 288, 600-1.

30 Palmer, *Democratic Revolutions*, pp. 228-9; Wood, *Creation of the American Republic*, pp. 539-43. Wood, appropriately, entitles his discussion 'The irrelevance of a bill of rights'.

31 R. A. Rutland, *The Birth of the Bill of Rights, 1776-1791*, Chapel Hill, N.Y., 1955, pp. 132-3, 140; Wood, *Creation of the American Republic*, p. 540.

32 R. A. Rutland, *The Ordeal of the Constitution,* Norman, Okla., 1965, pp. 213, 301; Wood, *Creation of the American Republic*, pp., 540-3.

33 Rutland, *Bill of Rights*, pp. 171-2; Wood, *Creation of the American Republic*, p. 542.

34 Letter from Thomas Jefferson to John P. Jones, 23 March 1789, quoted in Rutland, *Bill of Rights*, p. 197.

35 Letter from James Madison to Thomas Jefferson, 27 Oct. 1788, quoted in Rutland, *Bill of Rights*, p. 193.

36 *The Debates and Proceedings in the Congress of the United States*, I, 1789, p. 454, ed. J. Gales, Washington, DC, 1834.

37 *Debates and Proceedings*, p. 755.

38 Levy, *Emergence*, pp. 16-61, 82-4, 119-22; Pole, *Political Representation*, p. 505.

39 Buel, 'Press in revolutionary America', pp. 63, 71-5, 81-2; Wood, *Creation of the American Republic*, pp. 608-9.

40 J. Madison, *The Writings of James Madison*, VI, p. 70, ed. G. Hunt, New York, 1910.

41 R. Buel, *Securing the Revolution*, Ithaca, NY, London, 1972, pp. 91-2.

42 Buel, *Securing the Revolution*, pp. 103-4; E. P. Link, *Democratic–Republican Societies 1790-1800*, New York, 1942, pp. 6, 211.

43 Buel, *Securing the Revolution*, pp. 99-101.

44 Buel, *Securing the Revolution*, pp. 127-33.

45 See generally *The Democratic–Republican Societies, 1790-1800. A Documentary Sourcebook of Constitutions, Declarations, Addresses, Resolutions, and Toasts,* ed. P. S. Foner, Westport, Conn., 1976.

46 *Debates and Proceedings*, 3rd Congress, p. 912.

47 Foner, 'The Democratic–Republic societies: and introduction', in *Democratic–Republican Societies*, p. 35.

48 Buel, *Securing the Revolution,* p. 243.
49 J. M. Smith, *Freedom's Fetters: The Alien and Sedition Laws and American Civil Liberties,* Ithaca, NY, 1956, pp. 5-14, 176-7, 385.
50 Buel, *Securing the Revolution,* pp. 244-6; Smith, *Freedom's Fetters,* pp. xii, 420.
51 Buel, *Securing the Revolution,* pp. 256-7.
52 Smith, *Freedom's Fetters,* pp. 424-5.
53 J. Madison, *The Virginia Report of 1789-1800,* in *Freedom of the Press from Zenger to Jefferson,* pp. 213-14, ed. L. W. Levy, Cambridge, Mass., 1966.
54 S. Tucker, 'Note G, of the right of conscience; and of the freedom of speech, and of the press,' in Blackstone, *Commentaries,* II, pp. 19-20.
55 Levy, *Emergence,* pp. 126, 149.
56 Levy, *Emergence,* pp. 301-7; Madison, *Virginia Report,* 224.

4

Interpreting *The Federalist*

JOHN ZVESPER
University of East Anglia

THE UNPOPULARITY OF PUBLIUS

Many a modern academic could testify how much better it is to have written and published a book than an article (to say nothing of a paper contributed to a conference). In this, if in little else, the authors of *The Federalist* would probably concur with modern academic opinion. Alexander Hamilton, the author of the first several numbers of this series of papers, did his best to ensure that it became well known in New York by saturating the New York press. Four out of the five newspapers in New York City carried at least some numbers of *The Federalist*. He also encouraged reprinting of the series by newspapers in other states, so that *The Federalist* would immediately become the best known defence and explanation of the new Constitution. He arranged to have the papers 'published and republished as no other series was." Moreover, and more decisively for the future success of *The Federalist,* as well as appearing in the press (from October 1787 to August 1788), the series was published as a book, in two volumes, in March and May 1788 (the whole series thus being published in time to be sent down to Virginia to serve as a debaters' handbook in the ratification convention there).

The Federalist was meant to be very comprehensive. The plan of the series was outlined by Hamilton in the first paper, and consisted of two major tasks: first, to discuss the utility of the Union, the insufficiency of the Confederation to preserve it, and the 'necessity of a government at least equally energetic with the one proposed' to do so (this occupied nos. 1-36, published as Volume One); and then to display the republican character and tendencies of the proposed Constitution (nos. 37-85, or Volume Two), all the while giving 'a satisfactory answer to all the objections which shall have made their appearance, that may seem to have any claim to your attention'. No wonder that the series turned out to be three times as long as its authors had originally planned, and no wonder that abridged editions have always been popular; but less wonder, as well, that this series of articles should have come to be a book, and a book receiving much attention. It was well conceived and well promoted. It was favourably received in Europe and Latin America as well as in the United States.[2]

Yet the success of *The Federalist* has had significant limits. That these limits were foreseen by at least one of the authors (Hamilton) is indicated by his choice of pseudonym, a choice that was the first interpretation of *The Federalist*. According to Plutarch, Publius Valerius – the Roman statesman who was the source of our Publius's name – was marked out for success when Rome became a democracy, because he always employed his eloquence 'with integrity and boldness in the service of justice', while with his wealth 'he gave liberal and kindly aid to the poor and needy'; yet he was at first passed over, feared and envied by the people, and it was not until he democratised both his own lifestyle and the customs of the government that he became securely popular, and received the name Publicola (people-cherisher), by which he was thenceforth known.[3] Hamilton's choice of the pseudonym Publius thus suggests, among other things, some doubt as to the political acceptability of *The Federalist*, or at least some recognition of the uphill battle that the American Publius faces in establishing his views and acquiring popularity. This was in part caused by the very ambitious scope and attention to detail in Publius's writing. 'The dry trash of Publius in 150 numbers' was one contemporary putdown published in the *New-York Journal*.[4] But the unpopularity of Publius runs deeper than that. We can see this if we consider an objection made by several contemporary opponents of Publius – the speakers and writers who somewhat misleadingly came to be known as Antifederalists – who complained, and to some extent rightly complained, that proponents of the new Constitution were (consciously or unconsciously) favouring a system of government that would be run by a political elite and would encourage the formation of a new business elite. For example, in the New York ratifying convention, Melancton Smith – himself a prosperous merchant – noticed that agriculture, manufactures, and commerce, although naturally hindered in many places by the burdens of the war for independence, were already improving throughout the country, without the assistance of a new central government. He argued that the proposed constitution would set up a government that would be incompetent to preside over a continuation of this economic revival, because it would exclude men of the 'middling class', with their invaluable 'knowledge of the circumstances and ability of the people in general', and their more direct involvement in the interests of the poor as well as those of the rich.[5] This fear, widespread among Antifederalists across the country, sometimes seemed to arise from a populistic resentment against all elites; Amos Singletary complained to the Massachusetts ratifying convention that

> These lawyers, and men of learning, and moneyed men, that talk so finely, and gloss over matters so smoothly, to make us poor illiterate people swallow down the pill, expect to get into Congress themselves; they expect to be the managers of this Constitution, and get all the power and all the money into their own hands, and then they will swallow up all us little folks, like the great *Leviathan*. . . .[6]

But more characteristically, this fear resulted not so much from the resentment of the 'little folks' as from the anticipation of the more comfortable (including, of course, many rich Southerners anticipating Northern commercial exploitation) that their and their country's continued prosperity would be undermined by a monopoly capitalism allied to the new government, with its too greatly enlarged commercial and fiscal powers and its too greatly restricted representation.

From the beginning, then, the arguments of Publius were suspected (perhaps even by Publius himself) of being too exclusive and high-toned for the American republic. That is one of the main reasons that Federalists came unstuck in the 1790s and had to relinquish the management of their constitution to the Jeffersonian Republicans.[7] It also explains why one could not so easily write a book on what history has made of *The Federalist* as one could 'a book on what history made of Thomas Jefferson', as Merrill Peterson did in a volume of more than 500 pages. *The Federalist* 'image in the American mind' seems much less deeply embedded than 'the Jefferson image'. Not simply, I think, because Publius's active career was considerably shorter, nor because his personality was less public. But rather, I believe, because for all their venerability, and for all their being venerated, the Constitution of 1787 and its prime interpreter, *The Federalist,* remain less authoritative than the idea of the rightful power of the voice of the enlightened people, which Jefferson's image represents. Institutional structures and constituted rights command much loyalty among Americans, but, rightly or wrongly – rightly and necessarily in a republican government, I think it can be shown – popular sovereignty and public opinion ultimately command more. As Professor Peterson has noted, American conservatives have had no counter-symbol as useful and durable as Jefferson. Neither Publius nor the Constitution has served that function. In fact, so powerful have been the popular, Jeffersonian images in the American mind that they have even been able to absorb from their conservative opponents 'the impersonal symbol of the Constitution' itself,[8] if not the thunder – or is it only lightning? – of Publius.

Ironically, Publius has proved most serviceable in popular and effective political rhetoric mainly when opponents of energetic central government have seized on Publius's assurances that the central government would not be so energetic that it would usurp the functions of the individual states. Antebellum Southern proponents of state sovereignty and nullification, when they did not dismiss *The Federalist* as wrongheaded and outdated, cited only those few passages emphasising the modesty of the Constitution's innovations in respect to states' rights. This very partial use of Publius, for purposes opposite to those of Publius, was made possible, perhaps even inevitable, by Publius's rhetorical position, that is by the fact that he was addressing primarily not those who already favoured ratification, but those who needed such reassurances.[9] Therefore, this selective use of Publius, in a spirit opposite to that of Publius's arguments in favour of energetic government and firm union, hardly constitutes a successful influence by Publius on public opinion. Indeed, in the 1830s, one of the authors of *The Federalist*, James Madison, spent much time and energy refuting the arguments of the nullifiers, showing how not even the Virginia and Kentucky Resolutions of 1798 and 1799, and certainly not *The Federalist* essays of 1787 and 1788, could properly be used to support their arguments.

One can trace *The Federalist* image through American history, but it is more exclusively in judicial and academic history that this image, as opposed to the Jeffersonian image, is to be found. Publius has been less at home in the court of public opinion than in the literature emerging from the courts of law and from the pens of political scientists and intellectual historians. One cannot readily see a popular Publius, but one can see a constitutional lawyers' Publius, a realistic political scientists' Publius, and an intellectual historians' Publius.

THE LAWYERS' PUBLIUS

The earliest history of the use of *The Federalist* in American courts of law makes it clear that even here Publius was not guaranteed a fair hearing. Selective use of *The Federalist* in the manner of the antebellum states' rights politicians was common in opinions of antebellum federal courts. The influence of this use or misuse was checked during the period that John Marshall dominated the judiciary. But Marshall himself was not quick to turn to Publius for support. Even when such support seemed easy to find (for example, in the case of the establishment of judicial review, in *Marbury* v. *Madison*), Marshall appeared reluctant to resort to citations of *The Federalist*. Not until 1819 did he cite *The*

Federalist in an opinion (*McCulloch* v. *Maryland*), and then only because the arguments of the wrong (anti-nationalist) side had tried to claim Publius for their own. In fact, Marshall's lack of dependence on Publius was based in part on his recognition of Publius's rhetorical position, which made it possible for opponents of Marshall's nationalism to quote *The Federalist* in their briefs and opinions. According to Marshall, this made it more appropriate for judges to defer to Publius only when he was frankly avowing and defending the grant of a power to the central government, rather than when he was issuing a soothing reassurance to Antifederalist fears of national domination.[10] So *The Federalist* was occasionally useful in court, in a way that was faithful to the original spirit of Publius. But it was also recognised as a two-edged sword.

Moreover, consider John C. Calhoun's rule for construing *The Federalist*. In his *Discourse on the Constitution*, Calhoun argues that, having failed to obtain 'their own scheme of a national government' at the Constitutional convention, the authors of *The Federalist*, although they 'acquiesced in the decision' of the convention (which Calhoun argued was for a wholly federal constitution), did not surrender their preference, and wrote *The Federalist* under the 'strong influence' of this preference. Therefore 'on all questions connected with the character of the government, due allowance should be made for the force of the bias, under which their opinions were formed'.[11] This rule of construction is the opposite to Marshall's. Both Marshall and Calhoun acknowledged Publius's nationalism, but Marshall also recognised that a less constrained case could be made for that nationalism (and for the power of the judiciary)[12] in courts of law than in *The Federalist*, and Calhoun simply dismissed the nationalistic elements in *The Federalist* as 'radical and dangerous' errors. Publius's description of the Constitution as an intricate compound, 'partly federal and partly national', eventually satisfied neither of the extremes in the debates over constitutional interpretation preceding the Civil War. Furthermore, even if one is satisfied that such anti-Southern interpretations as James Kent's *Commentaries on American Law* (1830) and Joseph Story's *Commentaries on the Constitution of the United States* (1833) are more or less accurate reflections of Publius's arguments in favour of union – as I believe they are – this legalistic interpretation of Publius can be undermined by a rejection of Publius's political science, as the arguments of Calhoun will again illustrate.

The usefulness of Publius as a legal authority is substantial, but – as Madison and Hamilton themselves seem to have realised – it is vitiated by three things: by the fact that Publius was an advocate, and recognised as such; by the intricacy of that advocacy on a question that was much debated in the first decades of the republic (and 'partly federal and partly national' is still not an easy theory for courts to apply); and by the dependence of Publius's argument on a prior agreement with the principles of the political science of American republicanism. The relevance of Publius as constitutional lawyer is dependent on the relevance of Publius as political scientist.

THE POLITICAL SCIENTISTS' PUBLIUS

Even before Story's *Commentaries* brought Publius firmly into American legal education (at least in the North), *The Federalist* had been recommended or required reading in many American universities, and it continued to be so throughout the nineteenth century.[13] American political science in the twentieth century continues to devote attention to Publius; however, there occurred in the late nineteenth and early twentieth centuries an important change in the way that Publius was read by students of politics. This change can be summarised briefly as a turn towards realism and behaviouralism, and a turn towards progressivism, evolutionism, and statism.

Realism. The turn towards realism was a conscious rejection of the formalism and legalism that allegedly dominated the study of politics, political history and law in nineteenth-century America. Some of the founders of the American discipline of political science were lawyers, but the profession quickly found its proper work to begin with a rejection of the fictions of constitutional law that were too often mistaken for accurate descriptions of the actual process of government. The impatience of this new discipline with its forerunners is perhaps nowhere more visible than in Arthur Bentley's concise portrait of the 'dead political science' that his own pioneering classic, *The Process of Government*, was intended to supersede. Bentley condemned both the 'barren formalism' of the 'formal study of the most external characteristics of governing institutions' and the apparently more substantive study of practising politicians: '. . . the boss himself is almost as formal an element in a political science as is the president or governor. When you state him you have not stated the living society. You must still go behind to find what are the real interests that are playing on each other through his agency.'[14] To Bentley, and to countless political scientists ever since, this search for 'real interests' meant a search for the sub-political groups and the pressures emerging from them, which determine and explain the political process. For many of these political scientists – although not for Bentley – it has meant a search for the economic interests involved in any given political organisation or activity.

It was only some years after Bentley's book was first published that it gained wide professional recognition. However, one of the political scientists who reviewed it (favourably) when it first appeared in 1908 was Charles Beard. Beard praised Bentley's realism and his 'attempt to get below formalism'.[15] And Beard's own most famous work, *An Economic Interpretation of the Constitution*, was inspired by a similar 'hope that a few of this generation of historical scholars may be encouraged to turn away from barren "political" history to a study of the real economic forces which condition great movements in politics'.[16] The relatively realistic views of the origins of America's Constitution and political parties that were available in contemporary commentaries regrettably 'had been largely submerged in abstract discussions of states' rights and national sovereignty and in formal, logical, and discriminative analyses of judicial opinions'.[17] Among the contemporary commentaries that Beard found most revealing was *The Federalist*. Emerging from twentieth-century political science from its origins is Publius not in the guise of constitutional lawyer but in the guise of realistic political theorist and practitioner.

Beard described Publius's political science as a 'theory of economic determinism'.[18] He picked put Madison's tenth *Federalist* paper for special attention, as Publius's 'most philosophical examination of the foundations of political science'.[19] However, Beard was not attracted to *Federalist* 10 by its basic argument – that the larger number of interests and the more refined political representation that are possible in a larger country provide a better basis for republican government than is provided in a small country. What Beard found attractive was simply Madison's description of the irrepressible role of economic interest groups in politics. This was 'the underlying political science of the Constitution', 'the principle that the first and elemental concern of every government is economic'.[20] He briefly quoted from both the tenth and the fifty-first *Federalist* papers Madison's argument about the importance of an extensive size and a concomitantly 'greater variety of parties and interests' for healthy republican government,[21] but was unimpressed by this, and devoted all of his attention to Publius's discussion of the machinery of representation and none to the underlying social pluralism of the extended republic (which he attributed not to 'the new Constitution', which his book set out to interpret, but simply to 'the Union').[22]

Political scientists after Beard have been more faithful to Bentley's original, more pluralistic notion of the group basis of politics, and have included in their own political sciences and in their reconstructions of

Publius's political science a wider range of groups than Beard's political science and Beard's Publius. However, while later, pluralistic political scientists have not been so obsessed by the economic basis of politics, and not invariably so concerned to prove the compatibility of their own political science with that of Publius, they have accepted from Beard the centrality in Publius's political science of the analysis of factions that appears in the tenth (and again in the fifty-first) *Federalist*. This analysis was written by Madison – although Hamilton evidently made space for it in his outline of *The Federalist* – and political scientists in our century have tended to follow Beard in crediting to Madison's essays the most fundamental reflections that appear in *The Federalist*. It is likely that many political scientists today think of Madison as the main author of *The Federalist*, and that most think of the argument of *Federalist* 10 as the most notable argument of the whole series. As Douglass Adair pointed out in his well-known critique of Beard's Publius, there was, before Beard's *Economic Interpretation* was published, practically no emphasis on the special importance of *Federalist* 10, although early biographers such as John Quincy Adams and William Rives had briefly noted the 'power of analysis' of the 'abstract reasoning' of that paper; whereas after Beard's work, *Federalist* 10 'became the most frequently quoted and most regularly anthologized essay of Publius'. In his own rather left-handed way, Beard thus contributed significantly to the revival of the reputation of James Madison, who had become subordinate to Hamilton in most commentaries on *The Federalist* between the Civil War and the Populist and Progressive challenges to industrialism that Beard himself was participating in.[23]

Political scientists in the second half of the twentieth century have been more favourably impressed than was Beard with the actual argument of *Federalist* 10. They reject Beard's assumption that without the force of the Constitution's separation of powers (in particular, the force of judicial review) there would be a more openly class-based and more successfully democratic politics in America. However, many of them share Beard's uneasiness with Madisonian politics, precisely because they give more credit to Publius's prediction that a socio-economic pluralism, rather than a war of rich against poor, would characterise the politics of the extended republic. Thus we find political scientists such as E. E. Schattschneider,[24] Robert Dahl,[25] and James MacGregor Burns,[26] all admiring the beauty of Publius's appreciation of American pluralism but deploring the tendency of that pluralism to prevent actions favoured by a majority of the American people, even without the operation of the separation of powers. Much of the political science that distances itself from Beard's Progressive conviction that the Constitution as defended by Publius, however adequate it was in the eighteenth century, was no longer an appropriate or just method of organising American politics.

Evolutionism. This Progressive impulse in twentieth-century political science is associated with an evolutionist critique of the assumptions of the arguments of both Publius and his Antifederalist opponents. Just as the realism of the twentieth-century political science has questioned the relevance of the fictions of constitutional law, its evolutionism has questioned the relevance of what it alleges are the fictions of natural law. Its realism turns it away from legal formalism; but its evolutionism turns it towards historicist formalism (the emptiness of historical progress) by turning it away from the substance of the law of nature. This substantive 'higher law background' to the Constitution – which Publius clearly recognised and depended upon[27] – came to be somewhat dogmatically rejected by twentieth-century political science. Writing *A History of American Political Theories* in 1903, Charles Merriam described the 'more systematic and scientific' type of political scientist who was becoming dominant in the profession. Many 'were trained in German schools, and all. . . had acquired a scientific method of discussing political phenomena' that led them to repudiate 'ideas of the "natural right" school of political theory'; 'the idea that men possess inherent and inalienable rights of a political or quasi-political character which are independent of the state, has been generally given up', claimed Merriam, although he had to admit 'that the political scientists are more agreed upon this point than is the general public'. Merriam also noticed the related tendency of scientific political science to 'drift away' from the eighteenth-century principle of separation of powers, and to replace this with the modern distinction between politics and administration, which emphasised the inevitability and the advantages of the centralisation of political power.[28]

From these points of view, Merriam himself indicated how *The Federalist* could be interpreted so as to show Publius seemingly pointing in the direction of these 'scientific' advances, particularly in his arguments against a bill of rights and against 'the whole scheme of securing liberty by mere constitutional restraints', as opposed to the 'general genius' of the government. In this interpretation, we can see one of the less sound versions of the Progressive contrast between the Revolution and Declaration of Independence on the one hand and the reactionary Constitution and Federalist movement on the other. Merriam had to admit that 'the "natural right" philosophy lies at the basis of [*The Federalist's*] system', but he also argued that Publius's main argument

. . . rests in no way on these ideas, and is but little related to the political theory embodied in them'.[29] In other words, according to Merriam, Publius showed an admirable detachment from the abstract natural right theories that later became so discredited. A similar approach was taken by Woodrow Wilson in a brief discussion in his *Constitutional Government* (1908). Having unfavourably contrasted the dead Newtonian mechanics of the Constitution with the living, Darwinian 'theory of government' that recognises the necessity of 'intimate, almost instinctive, coordination of the organs of life and action' in government, Wilson excused the authors of *The Federalist* and the framers of the Constitution for their 'Newtonian principle' on account of their more effective 'practical sagacity in respect of the actual structure of government', which produced a 'thoroughly workable model' in spite of the rigid theories that they proclaimed in their less sagacious moments.[30] Wilson actually had serious doubts about the superiority of Publius's Constitution to a more 'efficient', more centralised administrative state that he saw in practice in Europe and that he hoped to see established in the United States,[31] but here he tries to get Publius on his side, by denying that the authors of *The Federalist* applied their rigid theories in a rigid way.

Merriam's *History* points out that the improved science of politics of the twentieth century was actually discovered in principle before the Civil War, by 'Calhoun and his school', who already repudiated the idea of the natural liberty and equality of all humans (although their 'mistaken application' of their opposite idea, that 'liberty was not the natural right of all men, but only the reward of the races or individuals properly qualified for its possession', 'had the effect of delaying recognition of the truth' in this idea).[32] There is a deep though seldom acknowledged affinity between the twentieth-century political evolutionism that would discard the natural right basis of Publius and the nineteenth-century rejection of Publius in the name of the rights of separate states or in the name of the master race. The Progressivism characteristic of twentieth-century political science agrees with the conservative rejection of natural right, and therefore either distances itself from the political science of *The Federalist*, or distorts in order to embrace it. As Douglass Adair reminded us, Gladstone's famous description of the American Constitution as 'the most wonderful work ever struck off at a given time by the hand and purpose of man' was actually expressing this conservative and ethnocentric view that this Constitution, like the English one, 'proceeded from the womb and long gestation of progressive history', a good example of Anglo-American 'ordered liberty', rather than a product of abstract theory.[33] Merriam, without apparent embarrassment, tells us that the repudiation of natural right doctrine by the founders of modern American political science, coupled with a study of the actual historical development of constitutional government, led them to 'the conclusion . . . that the Teutonic nations are particularly endowed with political capacity. Their mission in the world is the political civilization of mankind.'[34]

The natural right basis of Publius's political science, which basis many current political scientists would deny to Publius as well as to themselves, prevented Publius from embracing such 'radical and dangerous' errors. Although this particular kind of nonsense is no longer common among political scientists, those neo-conservatives who praise *The Federalist* for its retreat from the abstract theorising characteristic of the Revolution sometimes come very close to repeating it. And although such racism and nationalism is no longer such a scientific commonplace, modern, evolutionist political science remains inherently more exposed if not more prone to such ideas, and more defenceless against them, than the natural right political science of Publius. Political scientists who regularly class Madison's political thought with Calhoun's obviously have little understanding of the principles that kept Madison's and Calhoun's thought apart. Far better to have a Calhoun openly rejecting Publius's doctrines of natural human equality and liberty than a modern political scientist collapsing their differences, at Publius's expense, by quietly agreeing with Calhoun on these fundamental issues.

THE HISTORIANS' PUBLIUS

Historians of the intellectual and ideological side of political history have been very busy correcting the political scientists' interpretation of Publius for the past four decades. They have opposed the historiographical 'realism' that would direct our attention to deeds and away from words. However, they have not always been quick to liberate themselves from the political 'realism' of the political scientists that makes them concentrate especially on the argument of *Federalist* 10. Even when they freed themselves from that preoccupation, they very often did so by assuming the truth of the evolutionism of modern political science, in so far as they interpreted *The Federalist* as a relic from the past with no possible relevance to us today.

These two themes of modern political science have recurred within the two dominant historical interpretations of early American political thought. The first of these interpretations, well stated in the 1940s and

1950s by Richard Hofstadter and Louis Hartz and recently restated by John Diggins, emphasises the Lockean or even Hobbesian realism of the founding fathers.[35] In a major variation on this theme, the Scottish Enlightenment and in particular David Hume have been singled out as decisive influences on the composition of *The Federalist*.[36] Of course, Publius's realistic distrust of certain Revolutionary enthusiasms has frequently been noticed. The stronger, more specific thesis of this interpretation is that the realism of *The Federalist* amounted to a rejection of the classical connection between republican politics and popular virtue, and that the realistic interest-group politics of the tenth *Federalist* offers a replacement for the classical reliance on republican virtue.

The second main line of historical interpretation is the one associated with Bernard Bailyn, J. G. A. Pocock, Gordon Wood, and others who have emphasised the influence of civic humanism and 'classical republicanism' on early American political thought.[37] Some of these historians have remarked upon the extent to which the authors of *The Federalist* still voice concerns that are part of that pattern of thought. Especially Madison in his proper voice (at least in 1787 and 1788), but also in his Publius essays, relies, it is claimed, on the 'classical republican' virtue of the American people, or at least on their agrarian virtue – a political asset undiscussed but, so it is claimed, assumed even in the apparently realistic arguments of *Federalist* 10.[38] However, more frequently *The Federalist* has been viewed by these historians as a departure from the classical republican school of thought, and as an expression of that more realistic thought analysed by Hartz, Hoftstadter, and the others who dwell on the Lockean liberal character of American politics and political thought; thus there is some shared perception of the text if not of the context of *The Federalist* in these two schools of history. Just as Louis Hartz noticed that the Federalists often failed to fit into his scheme of Lockean liberalism, many of the 'classical republican' historians have noticed that the Federalists – and *The Federalist* – fail to fit their paradigm of civic humanism.[39]

On this showing, *The Federalist* does not easily fit either the interest group liberalism paradigm or the civic humanism paradigm. Perhaps the fault is not in our text but in our paradigms. The 'Lockean' liberalism of the first paradigm is more libertarian than liberal, depressing the public interest far below the private; whereas the opposite extreme characterises the 'classical republican' paradigm. Neither extreme really captures the politics of Publius.

David Epstein's recent study, *The Political Theory of* The Federalist, has successfully pursued the thesis that Publius's thinking transcends

the dichotomy between Lockean liberalism's provision of security ᴜᴏ
private rights and traditional republicanism's cultivation of civic virtue
and the public good. In Epstein's careful interpretation, the fundamental
political thought of *The Federalist* – as it appears in the whole book, not
just in the tenth paper and not just in the first volume – is compared not
to modern pluralism nor to 'classical republicanism' but to the Aristotelian view that humans' 'political nature consists fundamentally . . . in
a capacity to think and speak, i.e., to express and act upon disputable
opinions about good and bad, just and unjust'. In Epstein's view, Publius maintains this moderate, Aristotelian idealism even in the context of
necessary and desirable changes in political life in the modern world: in
Publius's 'representative republic a man can be both a private citizen
spared the vexing and perhaps risky task of continually making political
decisions, and a political partisan, entitled to take his own opinions
seriously because of their equal share in the ultimate authority of a
republican regime'.[40] With due allowances for important changes in
circumstances between ancient Greece and modern America, Epstein's
view seems plausible; one can see great similarities between the sober
constitutionalism of Aristotle and that of Publius. (Constitutionalism
rather than republicanism is probably the less misleading term of comparison.) One may doubt that Publius's political thinking is as far
removed as this may imply from Locke's liberalism; however, Locke's
own politics (if not his epistemology) could perhaps best be interpreted
as an attempt to adapt Aristotelian constitutionalism to the modern
world.

Superficially, especially in the context of the political scientists' 'realistic' Publius, this quasi-Aristotelian Publius seems closer to the 'classical
republican' tradition than to the liberal tradition. There is no attempt by
this Publius to follow the 'realistic' strategy of dispensing with the need
for political virtues both in the people and in their representatives; there
is no reduction of the citizen to the bourgeois.[41] But there is a crucial
difference between this Publius and what is generally called the tradition
of 'classical republicanism' or 'civic humanism'. Like Calhoun and the
founders of twentieth-century American political science, this tradition,
as reported by its historians, elevates the state above the individual, and
defines liberty as a product of the well-developed political community,
rather than as a natural right. (The civic humanism paradigm is thus not
as remote from twentieth-century thinking as it is usually made to
appear.) Although Publius presents arguments in favour of 'energetic'
government, he does not forget that the purpose of government is
defined by nature so as to secure the natural rights of individual human

beings. Nature is not regarded, as it is by 'civic humanists' in the Machiavellian tradition, 'as a moral void from which man must be rescued'.[42]

Once more we come to that fundamental feature of Publius's politics, recurrence to the law of nature. It is this feature as much as or more than the element of 'civic humanism' in Publius's thought that makes this thought seem remote and irrelevant to constitutional and political thought today. It is that feature above all that needs to be reconsidered if we are to assess George Washington's tribute to *The Federalist*:

> When the transient circumstances and fugitive performances which attended this Crisis shall have disappeared; That Work will merit the Notice of Posterity; because in it are candidly and ably discussed the principles of freedom and the topics of government, which will be always interesting to mankind so long as they shall be connected in Civil Society.[43]

NOTES

1 Albert Furtwangler, *The Authority of Publius: A Reading of the Federalist Papers*, Ithaca, NY and London, 1984, p. 53.

2 Gottfried Dietze, *The Federalist: A Classic on Federalism and Free Government*, Baltimore, Md. 1960, pp. 7-16.

3 Plutarch, *Lives*, tr. cans B. Perrin, 11 vols., London, and Cambridge, Mass., 1967, I, pp. 503-31.

4 16 May 1788, quoted in Furtwangler, *Authority*, p. 21.

5 Speeches of 21 June 1788 and 27 June 1788, in J. R. Pole ed., *The American Constitution: For and Against*, New York, 1987, pp. 101-14; see also the editors' Introduction, p. 17, and the writings collected in W. B. Allen and Gordon Lloyd eds., *The Essential Antifederalist*, Lanham, Md., New York, and London, University Press of America, 1985, pp. 225-74. Gordon Wood goes too far, I think, in his recent attempt to portray the Federalists as the backward-looking civic humanists, opposed to the Antifederalists' acceptance of a 'liberal, pluralistic, interest-ridden . . . democracy'. (This departs from his own earlier interpretation in *The Creation of the American Republic, 1776-1787*, Chapel Hill, NC, 1969, pp. 418f., 467, 475, 524.) The execution of this portrait requires him to argue implausibly that such non-populistic Antifederalists as Gerry, Mason and Lee were not 'real Antifederalists', and to understate both the republican idealism that was voiced by Antifederalists – even by his model 'pluralist' Antifederalist, William Findley – and the commercialism and pluralism of Federalists. However, he rightly draws our attention to the unrealistic exclusiveness of Federalist politics and economics. Gordon S. Wood, 'Interests and disinterestedness in the making of the Constitution', in Richard Beeman, Stephen Botein and Edward C. Carter III, eds., *Beyond Confederation: Origins of the Constitution and American National Identity*, Chapel Hill, NC, and London, 1987, pp. 69-109.

6 Quoted in Furtwangler, *Authority*, p. 98.

7 John Zvesper, *Political Philosophy and Rhetoric: A Study of the Origins of American*

Party Politics, Cambridge, 1977, pp. 129-31.

8 Merrill D. Peterson, *The Jefferson Image in the American Mind,* New York, 1960, pp. 98f., 200f., 226.

9 Jack N. Rakove, 'Early uses of *The Federalist,'* in Charles R. Kesler ed., *Saving the Revolution:* The Federalist Papers *and the American Founding,* New York, 1987, pp. 239, 243-5, 248.

10 *Cohens* v. *Virginia,* 6 Wheaton 418 (1821); Rakove, 'Early uses', pp. 240-43.

11 *A Discourse on the Constitution and Government of the United States,* in *The Works of John C. Calhoun,* ed. Richard K. Cralle, 6 vols., New York, 1851-56, I, pp. 150-61.

12 On the greater independence of the judiciary in Marshall's opinion in *Marbury* v. *Madison,* as opposed to Hamilton's arguments in *Federalist* 78, see John Agresto, *The Supreme Court and Constitutional Democracy,* Ithaca, NY and London, 1984, pp. 71-2.

13 Anna Haddow, *Political Science in American Colleges and Universities 1636-1900,* New York and London, 57, 61, 63, 72, 127, 131, 135, 177f., 201.

14 Arthur F. Bentley, *The Process of Government: A Study of Social Pressures,* Chicago, 1908, pp. 162-3.

15 Review in *Political Science Quarterly,* XXIII, 1908, pp. 739-41, quoted in Richard Hofstadter, *The Progressive Historians: Turner, Beard, Parrington,* London, 1969, p. 186 n. 5.

16 Charles A. Beard, *An Economic Interpretation of the Constitution of the United States,* New York, 1956, p. xix (Preface to first edition, 1913).

17 Beard, *Economic Interpretation,* p. vi (Preface to second edition, 1935).

18 Beard, *Economic Interpretation,* p.15.

19 Beard, *Economic Interpretation,* p. 156.

20 Beard, *Economic Interpretation,* pp. 156-8.

21 Beard, *Economic Interpretation* pp. 158, 160.

22 Beard, *Economic Interpretation,* pp. 158-68.

23 Douglass Adair, 'The Tenth Federalist revisited', *William and Mary Quarterly,* 3rd Series, VIII, 1951, pp. 48-53, 61.

24 *Party Government,* New York, 1942.

25 *A Preface to Democratic Theory,* Chicago, 1956.

26 *The Deadlock of Democracy: Four Party Politics in America,* Englewood Cliffs, NJ, 1967.

27 For example, in the fortieth paper, Publius quotes from the Declaration of Independence regarding the natural right of humans to institute government directed to the end of their 'safety and happiness'. The epistemological scepticism of the thirty-seventh paper is thus an invitation to moderation, not to moral relativism or historicism.

28 Charles Edward Merriam, *A History of American Political Theories,* reprinted New York and London, 1968 (1903), pp. 305-27.

29 Merriam, *History,* pp. 100-22.

30 Woodrow Wilson, *Constitutional Government in the United States,* reprinted New York, 1961 (1908), pp. 56f.

31 Charles R. Kesler, 'Woodrow Wilson and the statesmanship of progress', in Thomas B. Silver and Peter W. Schramm eds., *Natural Right and Political Right,* Durham, NC, 1984, pp. 103-27; Dennis J. Mahoney, 'A newer science of politics: *The Federalist* and American political science in the progressive era', in Kesler ed.,

Saving, pp. 258-61.

32 Merriam, *History*, pp. 307, 312; cf. pp. 250f. See also Harry Elmer Barnes, 'Some contributions of sociology to modern political theory', *American Political Science Review*, XV, 1921, pp. 506, 511f., 518f., 532f.

33 Adair, 'Tenth Federalist', pp. 54-5.

34 Merriam, *History*, pp. 313-18.

35 Richard Hofstadter, *The American Political Tradition and the Men Who Made It*, New York, 1948, pp. 16f.; Louis Hartz, *The Liberal Tradition in America; An Interpretation of American Political Thought since the Revolution*, New York, 1955; John Patrick Diggins, *The Lost Soul of American Politics: Virtue, Self-Interest, and the Foundations of Liberalism*, New York, 1984, pp. 74-105.

36 Douglass Adair, '"That Politics May Be Reduced to a Science": David Hume, James Madison, and the tenth *Federalist*', *Huntington Library Quarterly*, XX, 1957, pp. 343-60.

37 Bernard Bailyn, *The Ideological Origins of the American Revolution*, Cambridge, Mass., 1967; J. G. A. Pocock, *The Machiavellian Moment: Florentine Political Thought and the Atlantic Tradition*, Princeton, NJ, 1975; Wood, *Creation*.

38 Douglass G. Adair, 'The Intellectual Origins of Jeffersonian Democracy: Republicanism, the Class Struggle, and the Virtuous Farmer', PhD thesis, Yale University, 1943, pp. 272f., Wood, 'Interests' (n. 5 above), pp. 81-93; Paul F. Bourke, 'The pluralist reading of James Madison's tenth *Federalist*', *Perspectives in American History*, IX, 1975, pp. 294f.; Lance Banning, *The Jeffersonian Persuasion: Evolution of a Party Ideology*, Ithaca, NY and London, 1978, pp. 83-90.

39 Bailyn, *Ideological Origins*, p. 301; Wood, *Creation*, chs. 10-13; Pocock, *Machiavellian Moment*, p. 522.

40 David F. Epstein, *The Political Theory of* The Federalist, Chicago and London 1984, pp. 124f.; see also Charles R. Kesler, '*Federalist* 10 and American Republicanism', in Kesler ed., *Saving*, pp. 13-39.

41 It is still possible to see important differences between the politics of *The Federalist* and the politics of the Republican partisans of the 1790s – differences that help to explain the relative unpopularity of Publius. The politics of Epstein's Publius remains rather high-toned, perhaps even a little too Machiavellian in its recognition of the gulf between 'those who are more and those who are less political' (Epstein, *Political Theory*, p. 197). On the question of the differences between Madison as Publius and Madison as Republican partisan, see my 'The Madisonian systems', *Western Political Quarterly*, XXXVII, 1984, pp. 236-56; Lance Banning, 'The practicable sphere of a republic: James Madison, the constitutional convention and the emergence of revolutionary federalism', and Jack N. Rakove, 'The structure of politics at the accession of George Washington', in Beeman *et al.*, eds., *Beyond Confederation*, pp. 186, 292-4; and William B. Allen, 'Justice and the general good: *Federalist* 51', in Kesler ed., *Saving*, pp. 131-49.

42 Diggins, *Lost Soul*, p. 373 n. 39.

43 Letter to Alexander Hamilton, 28 August 1788, *The Writings of George Washington*, ed. John C. Fitzpatrick, 39 vols., Washington, DC 1931-44, XXX, p. 66.

5

Constitutional rights 200 years later

LOUIS HENKIN
Columbia University

The United States is commonly acknowledged to be a country in which individual rights – human rights – are effectively safeguarded against abuse by government, and the United States Constitution is commonly exalted as the instrument of that protection. Yet one who reads the Constitution which was celebrated in 1987, certainly the foreign reader, might be hard put to find the source and the basis of that reputation.

In this essay I suggest, in brief compass, how the Constitution became the instrument of rights we know today. I venture a explanation of the 'defective' condition of the constitutional text; describe the constitutional idea of rights and its jurisprudential consequences; trace the development of its content, and of the institutions that give it effect; and appraise their strengths and deficiencies to the contemporary eye.

RIGHTS AND ORIGINS OF THE CONSTITUTION

The instrument that was signed in Philadelphia in September 1787 contained no reference to the idea of rights, and mentions hardly any of the human rights recognised and valued today. A bill of rights was added by amendment in 1791 but it suffered glaring deficiencies. Additional amendments during the intervening centuries added some guarantees for rights, but on its face the Constitution today still has serious inadequacies by contemporary human rights standards. Neither the Philadelphia text nor the amendments appear to provide for institutions and procedures designed particularly to ensure respect for individual rights, and even the acute reader is not likely to perceive whether and how such respect is ensured.

I have offered one explanation for inadequacies in the constitutional text as it relates to rights, part of a larger observation about the 'genetic defects' of the Constitution due to its origins, purpose and design.[1]

In 1776, independence from Great Britain brought two related but different developments. With independence, the thirteen colonies became thirteen states, created in the spirit and pursuant to the political theory articulated in the Declaration of Independence. Each state had a constitution, some of which included, indeed commonly began with, a bill of rights. Those constitutions authentically represent American constitutionalism.

The states might have remained thirteen independent states, but from the beginning they saw themselves as constituting 'the American nation' and they contemplated political union of some kind. The first attempt, represented by the Articles of Confederation, proved less than satisfactory. Delegates came to Philadelphia in 1787 to amend the Articles so as to improve the Union. Instead of amending the Articles, they produced the Constitution of the United States. The Constitution replaced the confederation of states with a single federal state by erecting a small superstructure of national government above the state governments.

Unlike the state constitutions, then, the Constitution was not the direct descendant of the Declaration of Independence, but of the Articles of Confederation. The purpose of the Constitution was to form 'a more perfect Union'. The dispositions of the Constitution addressed problems of union not of governance generally. The new superstructure was given power to address problems of union, of interstate and foreign relations; internal governance, and the relation of government to the individual, were to remain the province of the states. The new union was to have a 'government', but it was not to be a complete government, or even the principal government on the American continent, but a small, partial, supplementary segment of government. Therefore the Constitution did not contain or clearly reflect a theory of government, or even attach itself clearly and firmly to the theory of constitutional government expressed in the Declaration and in the constitutions of the 'real' governments, those of the states. So the Constitution did not address individual rights.

Two hundred years later, the same United States Constitution serves what has become a real government, for many purposes *the* real government in the country, enjoying large, dominant, supreme power. But the Constitution has not been replaced, enlarged or even significantly amended for that new role. A bill of rights was added by constitutional amendment, as had been promised in order to achieve ratification, but those amendments did not include a theory of government, or even a theory of rights. And it was hardly a complete bill: it included a few rights which the colonists had enjoyed as Englishmen and which they wished to secure against the new government; it guaranteed a few rights which the colonists had not had under English rule but which they now wished to secure. The amendments did not include many basic personal and civil rights; even its principal preoccupation, the guarantee of fair criminal process, was incomplete and some of the provisions included were ambiguous.

Some of the genetic defects were corrected by later amendments; most of them were not. In the course of history, additional rights were recognised, some rights were extended, some narrowed, by construction and interpretation. A theory of rights was not developed, and theory has remained largely irrelevant to constitutional jurisprudence.

THE AMERICAN IDEA OF RIGHTS

Those who framed the United States Constitution were committed to the idea of rights as expressed in the Declaration of Independence of 1776 and in early state constitutions. I restate the familiar words, adding some gloss:

> All men – human beings, female as well as male – are equally endowed by their Creator with certain inalienable rights, among them life, liberty and the pursuit of happiness. Human beings come together in society and institute government to secure those rights. Government derives its legitimacy from the sovereignty of the people and maintains legitimacy by the consent of the governed. The legitimacy of a government and the conditions under which it governs are best confirmed by a written constitution, a social contract ordained and established by the people.
>
> The people delegate to their government the authority it needs for the purpose of governing, but the people – and every individual – retain rights which government must respect. The idea of rights implies limitations on government, even on the people's representatives. The rights retained include a right to continuing self-government – to be governed by representatives chosen by popular suffrage and accountable through periodic elections. The Constitution can be terminated or replaced by the people, but it, and the rights it protects, cannot be suspended. Only the privilege of the writ of habeas corpus can be suspended, and only in case of rebellion or invasion, and – it is accepted – only by Congress.

That idea of rights was first expressed and given effect in the constitutions of some of the states established in 1776 and thereafter. The United States Constitution, as drafted in 1787, did not include a bill of rights. (It forbids bills of attainder and *ex post facto* laws, Article 1, section 9, but does not refer to any of the prominent freedoms most valued then or now.) The dominant view at the Constitutional Convention was that a bill of rights was not necessary. The new federal government to be created pursuant to the Constitution would not have powers that might impinge on individual rights. The individual would continue to have his principal relations with the state in which he resided, and his endowed rights would be protected by the state constitution and by state institutions. Some of the Framers also thought, apparently, that bills of rights were not necessary or desirable generally: individual rights would be safeguarded by the institutions and the arrangements which the Constitution established.[2]

The arguments against including a bill of rights proved not to be persuasive and, as a condition of ratifying the Constitution, strong sentiment demanded a promise that a bill of rights would be added. A series of constitutional amendments, which came to be known as the Bill of Rights, was adopted in 1791. Those amendments do not express, but clearly reflect, the idea of rights expressed in the Declaration of Independence. The Bill of Rights did not grant rights; it took them as granted. 'Congress shall make no law abridging *the* [pre-existing] *freedom*' of religion, speech, press, assembly. '*The* [pre-existing] *right* of the people to be secure' against unreasonable searches and seizures shall not be violated. The Ninth Amendment made clear that rights were antecedent to and independent of the Constitution: 'The enumeration in the Constitution of certain rights shall not be construed to deny or disparage others retained by the people.'

In principle, then, an individual's rights do not derive from the Constitution, do not depend on their enumeration in the Constitution and are not limited to those enumerated there. But 200 years have brought the conception of 'constitutional rights' – rights rooted in and guaranteed by the Constitution – with attendant consequences. Rights are constitutional in the sense that the Constitution and the Bill of Rights confirm the idea of rights and enumerate some of them. The people of the generation that established the Constitution exercised and confirmed *their* endowed rights as they instituted government to secure those rights. For those who were born or who came later, their rights preceded the Constitution only in a theoretical sense: the Constitution already existed and it confirmed their antecedent rights.

Rights are constitutional also in the sense that the Constitution gave them new applications. Before the Constitution, there was no federal government and, of course, an individual's rights could not be claims against such a government. Under the Constitution, a federal government was established, and the Constitution and the Bill of Rights recognised and guaranteed the individual's endowed rights as limitations on the authority of that government. On the other hand, rights against one's neighbour, or – with minor exceptions – against state and local governments or officials, remained outside the purview of the United States

Constitution.

The constitutional character of rights was confirmed when the courts became the principal guardians of individual rights. The jurisdiction of the federal courts is limited, for our purposes, to cases and controversies 'arising under the Constitution' (US Constitution, Article III). The courts have seen their responsibility as that of safeguarding only rights referred to in the Constitution; the courts have been reluctant to enforce natural rights ('endowed by their Creator') not cited in the Constitution. They have been unwilling even to identify and give effect to the retained rights reserved by the Ninth Amendment. Even enumerated rights are protected by the courts only to the extent provided or contemplated by the Constitution, *i.e.* against violation by the government ('state action'), not by private persons. However, the courts have found and protected (against state action) rights implied in a broad conception of 'liberty' of which a person may not be deprived without 'due process of law'.

The 'constitutionalisation' of rights may have brought also some modification in the conception of rights as they relate to the public interest. Under Jefferson's principles, the people give up some of their antecedent rights to the government for the purposes for which it is instituted; all other rights are retained. Even rights that are subjected to the authority of government are sacrificed only to the extent necessary for legitimate governmental purposes. It has been suggested that, originally, some rights, such as freedom of speech or the free exercise of religion, were narrowly defined and as so defined were absolute. Today, surely, rights under the Constitution are generally seen as not absolute.[3] Even the fundamental freedoms of speech, press, religion, and assembly guaranteed by the First Amendment might be sacrificed to compelling public interests. Some balancing of individual right and public interest is also clearly implied in so far as life, liberty or property is subject to be taken by 'due' process of law, as search and seizure is permitted if it is not 'unreasonable', or punishment if it is not 'cruel and unusual'.

RIGHTS GUARANTEED BY THE CONSTITUTION

The Bill of Rights guarantees the freedoms of speech, press, religion and assembly (Amendment I), and the security of the person and his home, papers, and effects against unreasonable search and seizure (Amendment IV). The federal government may not deprive a person of life, liberty or property without due process of law, or take a person's property for public use without just compensation (Amendment V). A person accused of crime by federal authorities is guaranteed a speedy public trial by jury, with counsel. The accused enjoys a privilege against self-incrimination, and a right to be confronted with witnesses against him and to have compulsory process for obtaining witnesses in his favour (Amendments V and VI). Excessive bail may not be required, and a convicted person may not be subjected to excessive fines or to cruel and unusual punishment (Amendment VIII).

The Bill of Rights had notorious lacunae. It did not abolish slavery or guarantee freedom from slavery or from involuntary servitude in the future. It did not forbid the federal government to practice racial or other invidious discrimination: the commitment to equality, prominent in the Declaration of Independence, was not in the Constitution of 1787 and was not in the Bill of Rights. The Bill of Rights did not guarantee the right fundamental to the Jeffersonian conception, the right to vote. There is not even a constitutional right, surely not an enforceable right, to have government secure the individual's life, liberty or pursuit of happiness, the purposes for which, Jefferson said, government is instituted: a person cannot make a constitutional claim that he has not been provided adequate police protection or security against oppression by an external enemy. By today's standards the Bill of Rights was deficient in that it safeguarded only 'negative' rights – 'freedom from, freedom to' – the rights of man as they existed 'in the state of nature', before government. There was no right to social or economic benefits – no guarantee of a person's basic human needs, no right to education, to social security, to health care.

Even the safeguards against arbitrary detention and police abuse and the guarantees of fair criminal process were insufficient. The Constitution provides that the privilege of the writ of habeas corpus may not be suspended except in limited circumstances, but the uses of the writ are not otherwise guaranteed, and the grounds that permit detention are not indicated in the Constitution. The Bill of Rights does not declare the presumption of innocence or require that a jury determine guilt beyond a reasonable doubt. The Fourth Amendment forbids unreasonable search and seizure but does not declare the consequences of such illegal police activity. The Fifth Amendment provides that a person shall not be compelled to be a witness against himself, and the Eighth Amendment bars cruel and unusual punishment, but nothing in those amendments (or elsewhere in the Constitution) prohibits torture or other inhuman treatment by the police other than as punishment or for the purpose of inducing a confession. An accused enjoys the right to have the assistance of counsel for his defence, but it is not clear that the Framers contemplated that counsel must be provided to those who cannot provide their own.

With minor exceptions (attainder, *ex post facto* law, impairment of contracts), the original Constitution did not protect against violations of rights by the states; the Bill of Rights, too, when adopted, applied only to the federal government.[4] And Congress had no authority to provide protection against state infringement of individual rights by legislation. State constitutions and state laws protected rights against infringement by state officials, but those rights were not governed by the United States Constitution, and were not enforced by federal law or monitored by the federal courts.

Constitutional protection for individual rights was increased in major respects following the Civil War. The 'peace treaty' of that war took the form of three constitutional amendments. The Thirteenth Amendment outlawed slavery. The Fourteenth Amendment established the right to United States citizenship, and provided that no state shall abridge the privileges and immunities of such citizenship, or deprive any person of life, liberty, or property without due process of law, or deny any person the equal protection of the laws. By the Fifteenth Amendment the right to vote cannot be denied on account of race. The principal provisions of the Fourteenth Amendment provide national protection for individual rights against their violation by the states: the federal courts could monitor state compliance with those provisions; Congress was given power to enact laws to enforce them.

During more than 100 years since that time, there have been no further amendments to extend Constitutional safeguards for individual rights, except as regards suffrage. Three Amendments (in 1920, 1960, and 1971) forbid denying the right to vote on account of sex or age (for persons over eighteen) or for failure to pay a tax. For the rest, the Constitution reads today in respect of rights as it did in 1870. And since the principal clauses of the Fourteenth Amendment apply only to the states, as regards the federal government – except for the slavery and the voting amendments, and the clause defining citizenship in the Fourteenth Amendment – the Constitutional text has not been changed since the Bill of Rights was adopted in the eighteenth century.

And yet, constitutional rights in the United States have been transformed, and might be unrecognisable to those who framed the Bill of Rights, even to those who framed the Civil War Amendments. The development of rights reflects transformations in the life and character of the United States, and the influence of ideas, both indigenous and foreign. A major influence for the development of rights, and an impetus to other forces promoting rights, has been the growth of the role of the courts in interpreting, sometimes reinterpreting, the constitutional text. Under judicial aegis, individual rights in the United States have developed directly and indirectly, gradually as well as in quantum leaps, but little of that judicial support for rights and little of the growth of rights occurred before the middle of the twentieth century.

CONSTITUTIONAL RIGHTS BEFORE THE SECOND WORLD WAR

Constitutional rights before the Civil War were not a significant constitutional preoccupation, and the federal courts gave them little support. Towards the end of the eighteenth century, Congress had enacted the Alien and Sedition Laws, which were challenged both as being beyond the powers delegated to Congress and as violating rights under the First Amendment, but those laws were short-lived and the Supreme Court did not consider their validity.[5] Those laws apart, Congress exercised little legislative power during that period, and few federal laws impinged on the individual. Of the few Constitutional provisions that guaranteed rights against violation by the states, only the clause forbidding impairment of the obligation of contracts was frequently invoked, and commonly by corporations rather than by individuals.[6] For the principal outrage to rights, slavery, the Constitution provided neither remedy nor right. The Constitution maintained slavery; it even required fugitive slaves to be returned. Indeed in *Dred Scott*,[7] the Supreme Court, invoking the Fifth Amendment, held that an act of Congress that liberated a slave if he had been brought to a 'free state' deprived the owner of his property without due process of law. (There were some positive developments during those years. Public education burgeoned and spread under the authority of the states, though it was not conceived as involving rights, surely not rights under the United States Constitution. Congress also developed early a broad conception of 'the general welfare' for which it could spend federal funds (Article I, section 8); a century later that conception supported the emergence of the United States as a welfare state, affording what came to be considered by the international community as 'economic and social rights'.)

A leap in constitutional rights followed the Civil War. The Civil War Amendments were a second bill of rights, some would say a second Constitution. Those amendments abolished slavery, established the right to citizenship, forbade the states to deprive any person of life, liberty or property without due process of law, or to deny him equal protection of the laws, and forbade denial of the right to vote on account of race. In their effect, the amendments nationalised individual rights, subjecting the actions of the states, of the Northern victors as much as the vanquished Southerners, to federal constitutional limitations, to scrutiny by the federal judiciary, and to protection by act of Congress.

The Civil War Amendments, however, did not do all that some desired. They did not clearly incorporate the Bill of Rights and make it applicable to the states. They did not guarantee other civil rights against invasion by the states, or require the states to provide political or economic and social rights. (Strictly speaking, the Fifteenth Amendment did not even guarantee the right to vote to blacks. It forbade discrimination against blacks on account of race. But neither blacks nor whites had to be given the right to vote; blacks, like whites, could be denied the right to vote on other grounds. For almost 100 years, both whites and blacks could be denied the right to vote if they did not meet property requirements, or failed to pay a poll tax, or were illiterate (see p. 79 below).) Nor did the principal positions apply to the federal government so as to supply some of the deficiencies of the Bill of Rights.

Even what the amendments promised, moreover, was less than fully realised. Narrow interpretations reduced their safeguards, as well as the powers of Congress to enforce them. The Supreme Court's construction of the privileges and immunities clause of the Fourteenth Amendment reduced that clause to very little.[8] As a result of other narrow constructions of that Amendment, principal provisions of the Civil Rights Acts adopted between 1866 and 1875 were held invalid as beyond the powers of Congress.[9]

The end of Reconstruction in 1876 terminated congressional concern with the rights of blacks, and emboldened states, particularly Southern ones, to establish new patterns of violations of rights. During the next half-century the Supreme Court invalidated a few blatant racial discriminations, but accepted many subtle ones.[10] In 1896, it held that racial segregation – separate but equal – did not deny the equal protection of the laws,[11] a principle that remained constitutional doctrine for more than half a century. What is more, neither Congress nor the courts took steps to assure that 'separate' was in fact 'equal'. Equality suffered, too, as the courts legitimated other traditional, 'natural' inequalities, upholding, for example, the authority of the states to exclude women from the practice of law.[12] Efforts to promote what are now called economic and social rights by regulation of wages, hours, and labour relations were held to be beyond the powers of Congress and forbidden to both federal and state governments, because they were not within the proper purposes of government, because they constituted deprivations of property and infringements of liberty of contract.[13] During and after the First World War, narrow readings of the Bill of Rights led the courts to accept stringent limitations on freedom of speech.[14]

CONSTITUTIONAL RIGHTS TODAY

The rapid growth of human rights in the United States came with the New Deal (1933-39), and accelerated after the Second World War. Perhaps under the influence of world events that transformed the United States in many respects, and of a new *Zeitgeist* including the international human rights movement, constitutional rights in the United States were radically modified both in general and in detail.

The Constitution still retains the same words with which the United States began, the Bill of Rights has not been formally amended, and even the Fourteenth Amendment seems to promise only a little. But rights today are not what they were, and it is easy today to overlook the limited conception of individual rights held by the Framers – of 1787 as well as 1868 – and the radical transformation in that conception in the latter half of this century.[15]

Originally, the rights declared in the Bill of Rights were essentially political, protecting, it has been said, not the rights of man but the rights of gentlemen. The freedoms put in first place – speech, press, assembly – were seen primarily as political liberties with political purposes; it is open to question whether they sought to safeguard individual 'self-expression', or even radical political heresy. Even the guarantee of the free exercise of religion may have reflected a desire to avoid religious hostility more than concern for individual conscience. The 'right of the people to be secure' against unreasonable search and seizure, the guarantee of 'due process of law', the protection of property against confiscation, the catalogue of safeguards for those who might be accused of crime, were couched as rights of every person, but they seem to have reflected a desire to safeguard the established, respectable citizenry against various known forms of repression by tyrannical governments, rather than tenderness and respect for any individual, even the least worthy. The Civil War Amendments, too, were probably not designed to realise radical advances in human rights generally, but only to abolish slavery (as some of the states and other countries had done earlier), establish the citizenship of the former slaves, and remove disabilities and other 'badges' of slavery for black citizens.

Today, the conception of rights and the constitutional jurisprudence of rights ring very differently. By radical reinterpretation the Supreme Court held that the Fourteenth Amendment had effectively incorporated, and rendered applicable to the states, the principal provisions of the Bill of Rights, the freedom of speech, press, assembly, religion, the security of the home and the person, and virtually every safeguard for persons accused of crime.[16] Incorporation also 'homogenised' rights against the federal and state governments, rendering them essentially the same in every state as they were against the increasingly interventionist federal government.[17] Now, every state law impinging on important freedoms, and every state criminal trial, is subject to scrutiny by the federal courts. And Congress has the power to protect rights against violation and provide remedies for violations by state legislatures, by state or federal courts or officials.[18]

Even more radical, perhaps, was the expansion of eighteenth-century political rights to civil and personal rights, rooted in conceptions of the stitution has been read to protect new rights and old rights newly conceived. The Constitution has been opened to every man and woman, to the least and worst of them. Constitutional protection has moved beyond political rights to civil and personal rights, rooted in conceptions of essential dignity and worth of the individual. The Constitution safeguards not only political freedom but, in principle, also social, sexual, and other personal freedoms, and individual privacy, autonomy, and idiosyncrasy. Notably:

— Freedom of speech and press now protects advocacy even of radical ideas or expressions that are deeply disturbing or offensive. It protects not only political and religious expression, but also economic speech and publication, e.g., labour picketing and commercial advertising, as well as 'self-expression', even if it involves 'obscenity'.[19] Speech is protected even when it is 'symbolic', as in wearing an armband to protest a war; one's money, too, may talk, without ready limits, as by contributions to political campaigns.[20] The press enjoys freedom far beyond its relevance to the political process. The freedom to publish is now associated with the reader's 'right to know'; prior restraint on publication as by censorship, requirement of licence, or by injunction is virtually excluded. (The *New York Times* could not be enjoined from publishing confidential official documents relating to the Vietnam War because the government could not persuade the Supreme Court that there was a compelling need for such prior restraint on publication.[21]) The right to publish and the right to know may outweigh also the right of an official or of another 'public' person to be free from libel, or the privacy rights of private persons.[22] Freedom of speech and press includes a right of access to a public forum.[23] It includes also the freedom *not* to speak or publish, to speak and publish anonymously, to be free of governmental inquiry into what one thinks and says.[24] Out of these rights and the right of assembly, the courts have made a right of association, of anonymous association, of non-association.[25]

— Freedom of religion means not only that there must be no interference with, but also no burden on, the free exercise of religion. The
prohibition on establishing religion requires a wall of separation between
church and state. Neither the federal nor the state governments may
give financial aid to religious institutions or permit Bible reading or
prayer in public schools. Government must not advance or inhibit
religion or be excessively entangled with religion.[26]

— Freedom from unreasonable search and seizure applies – though
perhaps differently – not only to the home but also to the office and the
automobile; not only to physical but also to technological intrusion, e.g.,
telephone tapping; not only to incursions by the police, but also to visits
by health and fire inspectors.[27]

— Perhaps the greatest expansion has been in the rights of those
accused of crime. Old laws and accepted official practices, and legislative
delegations that lend themselves to official abuse, are no longer toler-
ated: e.g., crimes such as loitering or vagrancy are now void for vagueness, because the activities are essentially inoffensive and give too much
power and discretion to officials, too little warning to the putative offen-
der. Over-broad laws are invalidated or narrowed to prevent them from
'chilling' and discouraging the exercise of important freedoms. Penolo-
gical assumptions and practices have acquired a constitutional dimension: a person cannot be punished for a condition – being intoxicated or
under the influence of drugs – that he or she was unable to resist; punishment that is excessive in relation to the crime is forbidden as 'cruel and
unusual'; the death penalty, in particular, may not be imposed lightly,
and not to protect values other than life, e.g., for rape.[28] The Bill of
Rights – its principal provisions applicable also to the states – protects
not only the respectable and innocent against the governmental oppres-
sor; even criminals have rights to a fair trial (without improperly
obtained evidence), to counsel (provided by the government if the defendant cannot provide his own), to freedom from self-incrimination and
from comment on their failure to testify.[29]

— The equal protection of the laws has also acquired new ramifica-
tions. By new interpretation of the due process clause of the Fifth
Amendment, the Constitution now effectively requires of the federal
government the same equal protection of the laws that the Fourteenth
Amendment expressly commanded to the states.[30] All racial classifica-
tions – by state or federal government – are suspect and invidious discrimination on account of race, 'whether accomplished ingeniously or
ingenuously', is readily rejected.[31] Official separation of the races, even

'separate but equal', is outlawed.[32]

— There has been a fundamental and, I believe, irreversible transformation in the constitutional status of women. Discriminations against
women on the basis of generalisations reflecting stereotyped and outdated sociological assumptions no longer seem 'natural' and inevitable and
are invalid. And the new equality of the genders entitles males also to
freedom from irrational discrimination.[33]

— The poor, too, have rights to equal protection. The state cannot
offer important benefits for pay – a criminal appeal, a divorce – without
making them available gratis to those who cannot pay.[34]

— Other once-axiomatic inequalities are no longer acceptable. The
states cannot deny to aliens welfare benefits, general public employment,
or admission to the professions; they cannot maintain irrelevant distinctions between legitimate and illegitimate children.[35] Other once-excluded
categories are now included: prisoners have rights, as do military
personnel, mental patients, pupils in the schools; children have rights
independently of their parents.[36]

— In the Constitution now are new rights, for example a right to
travel, abroad as well as interstate; a local residence requirement as a
condition of enjoying rights or benefits is invalid because it burdens the
right to travel.[37]

— In what can be seen as a reversion to the eighteenth-century principle of antecedent natural rights to individual autonomy and liberty,
the courts have found an area of fundamental individual autonomy
('privacy'). Hence, the state may not forbid the use of contraceptives,
the resort to abortion in the first term of pregnancy, or indulgence in
obscene materials in private.[38] Parents may send their children to private
schools; they may even refuse to send their children to high school at all
when to do so would offend their religious scruples.[39]

— Finally, the United States has become a democracy. The indirect
election of the President through an electoral college remains in the
Constitution (Article II, section I; Amendment XII), but has been
largely reduced to a formality, and the presidency is now generally
responsive to popular suffrage. The Constitution seemed to leave voting
qualifications to the states, but later amendments forbidding the denial
of the vote on invidious grounds (race, sex, age, poverty) have supported
voting rights legislation that has rendered suffrage virtually universal, in
fact. In effect, the Supreme Court has built a constitutional right to
vote, and a right to a vote of equal weight, out of a few straws, including
the right to the equal protection of the laws.[40]

The explosion of rights I have described confirms the essentially open character of the Constitution, and constitutional rights as the fruit of a continuing synthesis of immutable principle with contemporary values, both home-grown and imported. Old assumptions are re-examined, stereotypes are penetrated, and rights are accepted today that a few decades ago were not even conceived of. On the horizon may be rights undreamed of – a right to be born and a right to die, and rights for the dead and the unborn.

Perhaps the inevitable consequence of expanding the proliferating rights was the clear emergence of the principle of 'balancing' individual liberty and public interest to determine the limits of each.[41] The courts do not now attend seriously to objections that economic and social regulation limits individual autonomy or liberty, but in principle all governmental action must justify itself as a means rationally linked to some public purpose.[42] Rights are not absolute, however, and virtually every right might, in some times and circumstances, give way to some other public good. Some individual rights and freedoms, however, such as speech, press, assembly, religion, old and new privacy, freedom from racial discrimination, are fundamental, preferred; invasions are suspect, will be sharply scrutinised, and will be sustained only for a compelling state interest. But the Supreme Court has not done well in justifying the weight it gives to particular rights and has done virtually nothing to explain the weights assigned to different public interests.

In the second half of the twentieth century, one constitutional blessing is noteworthy: the constitutional theory of the framers, the institutions they established, the availability of the judiciary to adapt and develop the general principles of the Constitution and to arbitrate political controversy (as well, no doubt, as great good fortune) have saved the United States from extra-constitutional government. There have been no emergency suspensions of the Constitution or of particular rights, such as have bedevilled human rights in other countries. The Constitution does not provide for its own suspension, and that has never been attempted, even in time of war. Habeas corpus was suspended during the Civil War and on two or three other occasions; other rights have been curtailed during war: the relocation of Americans of Japanese ancestry during the Second World War was an inglorious chapter, held by the courts at the time to be constitutionally permissible.[43] But there have not otherwise been mass detentions or other major derogations from rights.

I have been discussing constitutional rights – the rights Americans enjoy as higher law, regardless of the will of majorities and of their representatives and officials. But by interpreting the constitutional powers of Congress broadly, the courts have unleashed and encouraged Congress to expand individual rights. The extension of federal power, notably the Commerce Power, has enabled Congress to legislate against private discriminations (e.g., on account of race) and other private infringements.[44] Expansive interpretations of the Civil War Amendments have permitted sophisticated legislation to protect the right to vote and to safeguard the exercise of other rights from official or private interference.[45] Imaginative lawyers and sympathetic courts have found that old civil rights acts give protections against invasions of newly-conceived rights, prohibiting, for example, private discrimination in the sale or rental of housing or in admission to private school.[46] Congress has also created the 'right to know' by freedom of information acts. It has extended the right of conscientious objection to military service. It has created rights to a more healthful environment. Federal example has encouraged emulation by the states, and some states have taken such rights further.

By contemporary human rights standards, perhaps the most significant legislative extension of rights has been that which, beginning some fifty years ago, brought economic and social 'rights' to the inhabitants of the United States. These rights did not come easily. Except for public education provided by the states early, the welfare state began slowly. The United States has become a welfare state not by constitutional imperative or encouragement but, indeed, over strong constitutional resistance. Welfare programmes had to overcome resistance to governmental intervention and 'activism', resistance that flew the flag of individual autonomy and limited conceptions of government; resistance to various economic regulations, flying the flag of economic liberty; resistance to strong federal government, flying the flag of states' rights; resistance to massive governmental spending based on heavy progressive taxation, flying flags of property, liberty and equality; the Sixteenth Amendment was required to permit a federal progressive income tax, on which the welfare state depends.[47] Only after deep economic depression did traditional fear of government begin to give way to demands upon government – for intensive regulation of business and labour relations, for minimum wages and maximum hours, social security, expanding government employment and government work programmes – with constitutional reinterpretations to make them acceptable.

A second world war, decades of technological, political, and social change, and ideas and examples from abroad proliferated welfare programmes and magnified them manyfold. Economic and social benefits have effectively established equal entitlement as regards minimum basic needs; they have even moved United States society a few steps from equal opportunity to somewhat less inequality in fact. But not being constitutional rights, economic and social entitlements are subject to political and budgetary restraints, sometimes also to recurrent ideological resistance. In the 1980s, the drive for lower taxes and higher defence expenditures, some ideological commitment to 'market forces', and some resistance to the welfare state in principle, significantly weakened economic–social 'rights' in the United States. But the United States remains a welfare state and welfare programmes are likely to increase again.

The 1980s have also seen some regression in Constitutional rights. Since the scope and content of rights are ultimately decided by the Supreme Court, they will fluctuate with changes in judicial interpretation. After the luxuriant growth I have described, the Supreme Court entered a period of consolidation and retrenchment, perhaps of reaction. There have been more restrained readings of the Constitution, greater reluctance to increase individual protection, a tendency to give greater scope and weight to public authority, particularly in the criminal process. There are suggestions of greater judicial toleration of state 'accommodation' rather than 'neutrality' in its relation to religion; the right of privacy has been held not to include the right of adults to engage in private homosexual activity.[48] Some fear that the case upholding the right of a woman to have an abortion may be restricted if not overruled. New fears – increasing crime, spreading AIDS – bring proposals that threaten established Constitutional guarantees, and some of these proposals may be upheld.[49] But whatever the years ahead bring in detail they are not likely to weaken the commitment to individual rights which is now more than 200 years old.

The rights of man in the United States, it need hardly be said, are far from perfect. Past sins are grievous and notorious: genocide and lesser violations of the Indian; slavery, racial segregation, and other badges of slavery for blacks; other racial, ethnic, and religious discriminations, including relocations and concentrations of citizens of Japanese ancestry in time of war; Chinese exclusion and other racist immigration laws; post-war anti-communist hunts, which also 'chilled' political freedoms of others; and many more.

If these are for the largest part happily past, there are still racial discriminations and inequalities, at least *de facto*, and debatable acceptance of instances of private discrimination. Valued freedoms are sometimes empty for those unable or afraid to exercise them, or who are denied access to media that will make them effective or competitive. There is poverty, unemployment (which falls particularly heavily on blacks and other minorities), inadequate housing and health care, even hunger, and

there are wider economic inequities and inequalities. Immigration, exclusion, and deportation laws are built on outdated conceptions, such as
the absolute right of Congress to exclude and deport.[50] Some object to
balancing away rights in principle or to the balance struck in particular
instances, say, the preference of the right to know over the right of
privacy.[51] Some see violations of rights in laws against obscenity, in other
limitations on newspapers and newspapermen, in regulation of other
communications media; some have objected to toleration of laws against
group libel.[52] Some see retrogression in 'affirmative action' discriminat-
ing in favour of the once-oppressed to the disadvantage of others.[53] Some
see failures of rights in excessive toleration, in respecting freedom for
those who abuse it, in too much 'legalism' at the expense of order, in
failing generally to provide freedom from fear. Even where principles
are unexceptionable, there are ever-present instances where practice
deviates from principle and is not readily remedied; at various times, in
various places, there have been accusations and some evidence of 'political justice' – denial of due process and equal protection to 'leftists', to
Blacks, to 'longhairs', to the deviant, or the stranger. Police abuses are
too frequent and notorious, and new technology available to government
threatens essential privacy.

But in all, I conclude, human rights – civil–political as well as
economic–social rights – are alive and reasonably well in the United
States.

THE ENFORCEMENT OF RIGHTS: CONGRESS AND THE COURTS

The Framers of the Constitution, including those who appended the Bill
of Rights, expected that tyranny and oppression would be avoided by
preventing the concentration of political authority.[54] Individual rights
would be safeguarded by dividing authority between the federal government and the states, by the separation of powers and by checks and
balances among the branches of the federal government. Secondarily,
perhaps, the framers expected that Congress might have power to enact
some laws against some abuses of rights, and that the courts would
monitor governmental respect for rights in some measure and by some
means.

It is difficult to determine to what extent these original expectations
have in fact been realised, and how much United States constitutionalism has moved beyond all expectations. Federalism and the
separation of powers, though transformed during 200 years, doubtless
continue to prevent the concentration of power and some of the abuses

that concentrated power brings. But today, Constitutional guarantees rather than institutional arrangements are perceived as the principal safeguards of rights, and the courts are seen as their primary guardians, with Congress in a supporting role. During the eighty years before the Civil War, Congress enacted little that could be characterised as civil rights legislation, perhaps because Congress did not seem to have the power to do so. In the wake of the Civil War, under new powers granted to Congress by the Civil War Amendments, Congressional civil rights acts loomed large, but they were largely nullified by the courts,[55] and Congress did not enact significant civil rights legislation again for 100 years, until the 1960s.

Today, civil rights laws are important safeguards against executive and police violations. But only the courts can protect against violations by Congress, and the courts monitor and enforce constitutional rights also, indeed principally, against violation by the states, including state legislatures, state executives, state courts. It is not incorrect to conclude that against the bureaucracy, whether state or federal, against state legislation, and to a lesser extent against acts of Congress, individual rights are safeguarded in the United States by an alert, independent judiciary, activated by individuals, public interest groups and energetic legal professionals.

In enforcing constitutional rights, the courts have also determined their scope and content. The Supreme Court decided that the Fourteenth Amendment incorporated most of the Bill of Rights,[56] giving the courts a major role in monitoring the state criminal process as well as state regulation of religion, expression and assembly. The courts read the due process clauses as including substantive as well as procedural limitations, and the rise and fall – and rise – of substantive due process determined the ebb and flow of judicial enforcement. Periodically, judicial activism encouraged legislative activism, and new, as well as old, civil rights acts in turn gave the courts new opportunities to determine the limits of rights by (or in the guise of) statutory interpretation. Congress has rarely 'corrected' judicial interpretation.

Judicial supremacy is established in constitutional jurisprudence and is commonly seen as the hallmark and the linchpin of United State constitutionalism. But to credit the courts with the radical growth of rights in the United States is too simple. Often the courts have merely acquiesced and legitimated what political authority (both state and federal) had done. The influence of the courts, moreover, has not been constant and linear. During the course of United States history, courts have sometimes construed constitutional safeguards narrowly, reducing the scope of constitutional protection of rights or denying to state or federal legislatures the power to safeguard or promote rights.[57] At different periods, courts have been more activist or more self-restrained, more liberal or more conservative, in their readings and application of the Constitution. But, after 200 years, the principle of judicial review, and the central part of the courts in the protection of rights, are deeply entrenched. The United States has become a democracy with universal suffrage, but a democracy subject to individual rights; and the courts determine the scope and content of those rights and calibrate the balance between representative government and individual rights.

In the United States, the judicial role in rights enforcement has often been, and in the 1980s is again, a focus of controversy. At the beginning of the twentieth century, the Supreme Court earned condemnation for developing substantive due process and equating it with *laissez-faire*, for frustrating representative government and becoming a super-legislature. Retreat during the 1930s was followed after the Second World War by resurgent activism in support of political freedom, self-expression, separation of Church and State, safeguards for those accused of crime, racial desegregation, a new zone of autonomy in personal matters such as the freedom of women to seek abortion. In the last decade of the second century under the Constitution, voices are again heard to challenge 'government by judiciary', this time voices of a different ideology, the voices of 'law and order', and 'traditional' values.

CONCLUSION

The United States is sometimes described as a rights-ridden society. Surely, even as its democracy has improved, the rights of the individual have increased. The mix of democratic republicanism and individualism is not universally commended or understood. But it remains, I think, an important if idiosyncratic expression in the United States of eighteenth-century ideas adapted to this country's place in the twentieth century. The United States regime of rights is envied and emulated, not always with success, as our idiosyncrasies flourish less well in less hospitable cultures, in less fortunate, less stable societies.

The United States, with France, can lay claim to having taken the idea of rights and given it political expression in national constitutions and in international instruments. The use of courts to monitor the tensions between individual autonomy and public good has been emulated in unlikely places. Several European countries have established constitutional courts; France has something like it; the United Kingdom is seriously talking about it. International human rights courts and near-courts flourish. The eighteenth-century authors of the Declaration of Independence and the Framers of the Constitution, and Thomas Paine, and even John Locke, might not recognise their offspring, but they would not be uncomfortable at this two-hundredth birthday celebration.

NOTES

1 See L. Henkin, 'Constitutional fathers, constitutional sons', 60 *Minn. L. Rev.* 1113 (1976).
2 See, e.g., *The Federalist Papers,* Nos. 47, 48, 51, 84 (Madison); G. S. Wood, *The Creation of the American Republic,* Chapel Hill, NC, 1969, pp. 539-40, 547-53; Brandeis, J. dissenting in *Myers* v. *U.S.,* 272 U.S. 52, 293 (1926); 'The Bill of Rights and the Constitution', address by Justice John M. Harlan at the dedication of Bill of Rights Room, US Sub-Treasury Building, New York, 9 August 1964.
3 See L. Henkin, 'Infallibility under law: constitutional balancing',78 *Colum. L. Rev.* 1022 (1978).
4 *Barron* v. *City of Baltimore,* 32 U.S. (7 Pet.) 243 (1833).
5 See generally J. M. Smith, *Freedom's Fetters,* Ithaca, NY, 1956.
6 *See e.g., Dartmouth College* v. *Woodward,* 17 U.S. (4 Wheat.) 518 (1819); *Charles River Bridge* v. *Warren Bridge,* 36 U.S. (11 Pet.) 420 (1837). In the twentieth century, too, the Contract Clause is commonly invoked by companies, e.g., *Home Building & Loan Ass'n* v. *Blaisdell,* 290 U.S. 398 (1934); *United States Trust Co.* v. *New Jersey,* 431 U.S. 1 (1977).
7 *Scott* v. *Sandford,* 60 U.S. (19 How.) 393 (1857).
8 *Slaughter-House Cases*, 83 U.S. (16 Wall.) 36 (1873).
9 *Civil Rights Cases,* 109 U.S. 3 (1883). Compare the limited interpretation of the due process clause by the Supreme Court and its 'bad guess' about the equal protection clause: 'We doubt very much whether any action of a State not directed by way of discrimination against the negroes as a class, or on account of their race, will ever be held to come within the purview of this provision.' *Slaughter-House Cases, supra* note 8, at 81.
10 Compare *Strauder* v. *Virginia,* 100 U.S. 303 (1880) (exclusion of blacks from jury), and *Yick Wo* v. *Hopkins,* 118 U.S. 356 (1886) (denial to Chinese of right to operate laundry), with *Plessy* v. *Ferguson* (racial segregation), note 11 below, and the cases refusing to apply the amendment to discrimination that was held not to involve state action, *e.g., Civil Rights Cases* (discrimination by railroads, inns), note 9 above.
11 *Plessy* v. *Ferguson,* 163 U.S. 537 (1896), *overruled Brown* v. *Board of Education,* 347 U.S. 483 (1954), note 32 below.
12 *Bradwell* v. *State,* 83 U.S. (16 Wall.) 130 (1873).
13 *Lochner* v. *New York,* 198 U.S. 45 (1905); *Hammer* v. *Dagenhart,* 247 U.S. 251 (1918); *Adkins* v. *Children's Hospital,* 261 U.S. 525 (1923).
14 *Schenck* v. *United States,* 249 U.S. 47 (1919); *Debs* v. *United States,* 249 U.S. 211 (1919); *Abrams* v. *United States,* 250 U.S. 616 (1919); *Gitlow* v. *New York,* 268 U.S. 652 (1926).
15 In what follows I draw on my book. *The Rights of Man Today,* 1978, ch. 2.
16 See *Duncan* v. *Louisiana,* 391 U.S. 145, 147-9 (1968), and the cases collected there.

17 *Apodaca* v. *Oregon*, 406 U.S. 404 (1972); *Williams* v. *Florida*, 399 U.S. 78 (1970).

18 *South Carolina* v. *Katzenbach*, 383 U.S. 301 (1966); *Katzenbach* v. *Morgan*, 384 U.S. 641 (1966). See the various United States civil rights acts, now in 18 U.S. Code §§241-2; 42 U.S. Code §§1981-85, as interpreted; also the statutes cited in note 45.

19 *Brandenburg* v. *Ohio*, 395 U.S. 444 (1969) (Constitution protects even advocacy of violence, as distinguished from 'incitement to imminent lawless action'); *Collin* v. *Smith*, 578 F.2d 1197 (7th Cir.), *cert. denied*, 439 U.S. 916 (1978) (Nazi demonstrations); compare *Beauharnais* v. *Illinois*, 343 U.S. 250 (1952), a case upholding group libel laws, its authority now questioned; *Thornhill* v. *Alabama*, 310 U.S. 88 (1940) (labour picketing); *Virginia State Board of Pharmacy* v. *Virginia Citizens Consumer Council, Inc.*, 425 U.S. 748 (1976) (invalidating prohibition of advertising of prescription drug prices); *Zauderer* v. *Office of Disciplinary Counsel*, 471 U.S. 626 (1985) (professional advertising); *Memoirs* v. *Massachusetts*, 383 U.S. 413 (1966) (requiring prosecution for obscenity to prove materials 'utterly without redeeming social value'); also *Miller* v. *California*, 413 U.S. 15 (1973).

20 *Tinker* v. *Des Moines School District*, 393 U.S. 503 (1969); but compare *United States* v. *O'Brien*, 391 U.S. 367 (1968) (conviction for burning draft-card upheld); *Buckley* v. *Valeo*, 424 U.S. 1 (1976) (invalidating limitations on political contributions).

21 *New York Times* v. *United States*, 403 U.S. 713 (1971).

22 Compare *New York Times* v. *Sullivan*, 376 U.S. 254 (1964); *Curtis Publishing Co.* v. *Butts*, 388 U.S. 130 (1976); *Gertz* v. *Robert Welch, Inc.*, 418 U.S. 323 (1974); *Time, Inc.* v. *Hill*, 385 U.S. 374 (1967).

23 *Hague* v. *CIO*, 307 U.S. 496 (1939) (parks); *Cox* v. *Louisiana*, 379 U.S. 536 (1965) (street demonstrations); *Richmond Newspapers, Inc.* v. *Virginia*, 448 U.S. 555 (1980) (right of press to attend criminal trial); *Houchins* v. *KQED, Inc.*, 438 U.S. 1 (1978) (press access to jails).

24 *Talley* v. *California*, 362 U.S. 60 (1960) (invalidating prohibition of anonymous leaflets); *Sweezy* v. *New Hampshire*, 354 U.S. 234 (1957) (rejecting inquiry into content of professor's lecture); *Miami Herald Pub. Co.* v. *Tornillo*, 418 U.S. 241 (1974) (right not to publish).

25 *NAACP* v. *Alabama*, 357 U.S. 449 (1958); *Shilton* v. *Tucker*, 364 U.S. 479 (1960); *Abood* v. *Detroit Board of Education*, 431 US. 209 (1977) (right not to join trade union or contribute to its ideological programme); *Roberts* v. *United States Jaycees*, 468 U.S. 609 (1984); *Gibson* v. *Florida Legislative Investigation Comm.*, 372 U.S. 539 (1963); *DeGregory* v. *New Hampshire Attorney General*, 383 U.S. 825 (1966) (legislative investigation); *Baird* v. *State Bar of Arizona*, 401 U.S. 1 (1971) (right of association prohibits exclusion from profession on grounds of membership in particular political organisation).

26 *Sherbert* v. *Verner*, 374 U.S. 398 (1963); *Everson* v. *Board of Education*, 330 U.S. 1 (1947); *School District of Abington* v. *Schempp*, 374 U.S. 203 (1963); *Lemon* v. *Kurtzman*, 403 U.S. 602 (1971). Also *Estate of Thornton* v. *Caldor, Inc.*, 472 U.S. 703 (1985); *Edwards* v. *Aguillard*, 482 U.S. 107 S. Ct. 2573 (1987).

27 *Berger* v. *New York*, 388 U.S. 41 (1967); *Katz* v. *United States*, 389 US. 347 (1967); *Camara* v. *Municipal Court*, 387 U.S. 523 (1967); but cf. *Wyman* v. *James*, 400 U.S. 309 (1971) (refusal to allow visit by social worker may support denial of welfare benefits).

28 *Thompson* v. *Louisville*, 362 U.S. 199 (1960) (loitering); *Robinson* v. *California*, 370 U.S. 660 (1962) (addict); *Weems* v. *United States*, 217 U.S. 349 (1910) (excessive

punishment); *Coker* v. *Georgia*, 433 U.S. 584 (1977) (capital punishment for rape); *see also Enmund* v. *Florida*, 458 U.S. 782 (1982).

29 *Weeks* v. *United States*, 232 U.S. 383 (1914); *Mapp* v. *Ohio*, 367 U.S. 643 (1961) (exclusion of unlawfully obtained evidence); *Gideon* v. *Wainwright*, 372 U.S. 335 (1963) (counsel); *Mallory* v. *Hogan*, 378 U.S. 1 (1964); cf. *Griffin* v. *California*, 380 U.S. 609 (1965) (privilege against self-incrimination). *See also Miranda* v. *Arizona*, 384 U.S. 436 (1966) (obligation to inform person in custody of right not to respond to interrogation).

30 *Bolling* v. *Sharpe*, 347 U.S. 497 (1954).

31 *Smith* v. *Texas*, 311 U.S. 128, 132 (1940) (exclusion of blacks from Grand Jury is unconstitutional 'whether such discrimination was accomplished ingeniously or ingenuously'); also *Lane* v. *Wilson*, 307 U.S. 268, 275 (1939) (Constitution prohibits 'sophisticated as well as simple-minded modes of discrimination').

32 *Brown* v. *Board of Education*, 347 U.S. 483 (1954), *overruling Plessy* v. *Ferguson*, *supra* note 11.

33 *Reed* v. *Reed*, 407 U.S. 71 (1971); *Frontiero* v. *Richardson*, 411 U.S. 677 (1973); *Craig* v. *Boren*, 429 U.S. 190 (1976); *Mississippi University for Women* v. *Hogan*, 458 U.S. 718 (1983).

34 *Griffin* v. *Illinois*, 351 U.S. 12 (1956); *Boddie* v. *Connecticut*, 401 U..S. 371 (1971); but cf. *United States* v. *Kras*, 409 U.S. 434 (1973).

35 *Graham* v. *Richardson*, 403 U.S. 365 (1971); *In re Griffith*, 413 U.S. 717 (1973) (practice of law by aliens); *Sugarman* v. *Dougall*, 413 U.S. 634 (1973) (civil service); but cf. *Foley* v. *Connelie*, 435 U.S. 291 (1978); *Ambach* v. *Norwick*, 441 U.S. 68 (1979) (state may exclude aliens from posts in which they would be exercising 'governmental functions'); *Levy* v. *Louisiana*, 391 U.S. 68 (1968); but cf. *Mathews* v. *Lucas* 427 U.S. 495 (1976) (illegitimate children).

36 *Cruz* v. *Beto*, 405 U.S. 319 (1972) (religious rights of prisoners); cf. *Turner* v. *Safley*, 482 U.S. ——, 107 S. Ct. 2254 (1987) (right of prisoner to marry or to communicate with other inmates); cf. *Goldman* v. *Weinberger*, 475 U.S. 503 (limiting religious right of military officer); *O'Connor* v. *Donaldson*, 422 U.S. 563 (1975) (mental patients); *City of Cleburne* v. *Cleburne Living Center*, 473 U.S. 432 (1985) (discrimination against mentally retarded); *Goss* v. *Lopez*, 419 U.S. 565 (1975) (procedural rights of high school students); *Bellotti* v. *Baird*, 443 U.S. 622 (1979) (abortion for minors); cf. Douglas, J., in *Wisconsin* v. *Yoder*, 406 U.S. 205, 241 (1972).

37 *Kent* v. *Dulles*, 357 US. 116 (1958); but cf. *Regan* v. *Wald*, 468 U.S. 222 (1984) (upholding restrictions on travel to Cuba); *Shapiro* v. *Thompson*, 394 U.S. 618 (1969) (invalidating durational residence requirement for eligibility for welfare assistance); *Dunn* v. *Blumstein*, 405 U.S. 330 (1972) (durational residence requirement for voting); *Memorial Hospital* v. *Maricopa County*, 415 U.S. 250 (1974); but cf. *Sosna* v. *Iowa*, 419 U.S. 393 (1975) (residence requirement for divorce action).

38 *Griswold* v. *Connecticut*, 381 U.S. 479 (1965); *Roe* v. *Wade*, 410 U.S. 113 (1973); *Stanley* v. *Georgia*, 394 U.S. 557 (1969).

39 *Pierce* v. *Society of Sisters*, 268 U.S. 510 (1925); cf. *Wisconsin* v. *Yoder*, 406 U.S. 205 (1972) (compulsory high school attendance law violates Amish parents' freedom of religion).

40 *Wesberry* v. *Sanders*, 376 U.S. 1 (1964); *Reynolds* v. *Sims*, 377 U.S. 533 (1964).

41 See, generally, Henkin, *supra* note 3.

42 *Nebbia* v. *New York*, 291 U.S. 502 (1934).

43 *Hirabayashi* v. *United States*, 320 U.S. 81 (1943); *Korematsu* v. *United States*, 323

U.S. 214 (1944).

44 *Heart of Atlanta Motel* v. *United States*, 379 U.S. 241 (1964); *Katzenbach* v. *McClung*, 379 U.S. 294 (1964).

45 See the Civil Rights Act of 1964, 78 Stat. 241, 42 U.S.C. §2000 (a) (1970); Voting Rights Act of 1965, 79 *Stat.* 437, 42 U.S.C. § 1973 (1970). See also note 18.

46 *Jones* v. *Alfred H. Mayer Co.*, 392 U.S. 409 (1968); *Runyon* v. *McCrary*, 427 U.S. 160 (1976).

47 *Lochner* v. *New York, supra* note 13; *Hammer* v. *Dagenhart*, 247 U.S. 251 (1918); *Carter* v. *Carter Coal Co.*, 298 U.S. 238 (1936); *Pollock* v. *Farmers' Loan and Trust Co.*, 157 U.S. 429 (1895).

48 See generally V. Blasi, *The Burger Court: The Counter-Revolution That Wasn't*, New Haven and London, 1983; see *Lynch* v. *Donnelly*, 465 U.S. 668 (1984) (permitting crèche on public grounds); *Bowers* v. *Hardwick,* 478 U.S. 186 (1986) (upholding laws against homosexual activity).

49 In *United States* v. *Salerno*, 481 U.S. 739 (1987), the Supreme Court upheld legislative provisions requiring courts to order detention prior to trial of persons charged with certain serious felonies if the Government demonstrates by 'clear and convincing evidence' that no conditions for release will reasonably assure the safety of the community.

50 See L. Henkin, 'The Constitution and United States sovereignty: a century of *Chinese Exclusion* and its progeny', 100 *Harv. L. Rev.* 853 (1987).

51 See note 22 above.

52 See *Beauharnais* v. *Illinois*, note 19 above.

53 *Regents of University of California* v. *Bakke*, 438 U.S. 265 (1978); *Fullilove* v. *Klutznick*, 448 U.S. 448 (1980); *Local No. 93, International Association of Firefighters* v. *City of Cleveland*, 478 U.S. 501 (1986); cf. *Wygant* v. *Jackson Board of Education,* 476 U.S. 267 (1986).

54 See note 2.

55 See note 9.

56 See note 16.

57 See notes 9-14.

6

The American constitutional model and German constitutional politics

GÜNTER MOLTMANN
University of Hamburg

The curriculum of every West German secondary school includes a lesson on the United States Constitution, its genesis, underlying principles, and effects on constitutional concepts in the Western world. Every German textbook on history or civics has a chapter, or if not, a long paragraph on the American Constitution. All history or civics teachers in West German high schools must be prepared to explain broadly to their students what the Founding Fathers of the United States resolved in Philadelphia in 1787, how the American government developed, and how it is functioning under the conditions of the original document and its subsequent amendments.

These facts in mind, it is safe to state that every young German with a high school diploma has been exposed to this teaching and has learned something about 1787; that many young people in Germany have some idea of the importance of the American Constitution and of its meaning in general – that it brought about liberty, sovereignty of the people, republicanism, federalism, and that it is on the whole an admirable document; that some Germans have more or less thorough understanding of the functioning of the political system of the United States, of the role of the three branches of power and the system of checks and balances; that few people in Germany are able to interpret United States politics in relation to the American Constitution; and that almost none of them knows that there have been certain interrelations between the American constitutional model and the constitutional politics of Germany, both past and present.

This essay is concerned with the fifth aspect. What was the impact of the United States Constitution on German constitution-making? This question can be discussed within the framework of five historical periods: (a) constitution-making in the United States during the late eighteenth century and its repercussions in Germany; (b) the relationship between the American model and early German liberalism before and during the German Revolution of 1848/49; (c) Bismarck's constitutions for the North German Confederation of 1867 and the Wilhelmian Empire of 1871, and the United States model; (d) the United States Constitution and the Weimar Republic, 1919-33; (e) the United States occupation politics in post-Second World War Germany and the *Grundgesetz* (Basic Law) of the Federal Republic of Germany.[1]

The main part of this essay will be devoted to these five periods. Towards the end, in a more systematic approach, some constitutional principles will be discussed which have been of particular importance in the American–German dialogues on this issue. Also the question of transferability of constitutional elements from one national system to another, in this case from the United States to Germany, will be considered.

During the first period, the era of the American Revolution and the founding of the Union, political interactions between Germany and the newly established United States were at a minimum. People in central Europe were interested observers of exciting happenings and dramatic events in North America. They either criticised disobedience, lawlessness, uproar, and revolution, or greeted with enthusiasm the triumph of freedom, independence, and emancipation. An application of American constitutional principles to the political scene of central Europe was hardly imaginable. In contemporary Germany people, particularly of the lower and middle classes, protested against tyranny and longed for more personal freedom and self-determination, but they were still a long way from demanding a constitution based on the principles discussed in America. This can be explained in part by the political immaturity of the people. More influential probably was the fact that governments in the larger states of the north and south, Prussia and Austria, steered a course of 'enlightened absolutism'. Thus political clashes and conflicts were largely avoided, in contrast, for example, to the situation in France where the misrule of Louis XVI led to the Great Revolution of 1789.

Developments in America had two effects on Germany. As the Austrian historian Fritz Valjavec has shown, the struggle of the colonies for independence from British rule stimulated the emergence of political currents and divisions in the 1770s and 1780s. It raised the level of political consciousness and spurred the forming of conservative and liberal movements, though at the time not yet clearly defined ones.[2] Further, while the making of a constitution and the establishment of a constitutional government in America aroused little interest at the time of the Philadelphia Convention, it prompted a lively and never-ending debate among German liberals in the 1790s. Why this delay? It was of course, the French Revolution, with its effects on all of Europe, its convulsions, wars, and the Reign of Terror, that directed German eyes backwards towards the earlier American Revolution which had led to a political system which was so much more constructive and successful.

Why did Americans achieve things where the French failed? This question was hotly debated in Germany in the 1790s, as Horst Dippel has shown in his book *Germany and the American Revolution, 1770-1800*.[3] Scholars and university professors like the historians Günther Karl Friedrich Seidel and Dietrich Hermann Hegewisch, the economists Johann Georg Büsch and Christoph Daniel Ebeling, extensively discussed the American Constitution in various publications. Seidel, for instance, wrote in 1795: 'The inquiry into the Constitution of the United States of North America is an essential part of the history of their Revolution, for the new Constitution is a result of these notable events; without detailed knowledge we cannot decide whether the Americans profited or lost by their independence from Great Britain.'[4] The deep concern which early German 'Americanists' expressed for the United States Constitution reveals that they foresaw a possible application of its principles to a restructuring of constitutional conditions in the future Germany.

The interest in constitution-making in Germany increased with the formation of the German Confederation of 1815. The old German Empire had collapsed; it was replaced by a confederation with a written constitution *(Bundesakte)*, but one causing great dissatisfaction among progressives who had hoped in vain that the War of Liberation against Napoleon would result in a more liberal political system. Within the growing liberal faction composed mainly of students and professors, lawyers, administrators and businessmen, the study of written constitutions abroad, especially of the American constitution and the French Constitution of 1791, intensified. In 1824, the first German compendium of American constitutional law, Robert Mohl's *Bundes-Staatsrecht der Vereinigten Staaten von Nord-Amerika,* was published in Württemberg.[5] Both models, the French and the American, were attractive because they guaranteed human rights, national sovereignty, the separation of powers, and a representative system. The French model was preferred by Germans on the right who favoured a constitutional monarchy and by Germans on the left who thought of a unified and centralised state; the American model was favoured by those who preferred republicanism and a federal system. Some liberals also saw advantages in the British, Swiss, or Belgian constitutional models.

Examining the debates among liberals before the Revolution of 1848/49

and the voluminous proceedings of the National Assembly at Frankfurt, one can clearly state that the reformer favoured the American pattern more than any other. Few, if any wished to copy it entirely,
but an adaptation of various principles, particularly that of a division of
central and regional powers within a federal system, was considered most
appropriate by many liberals. There seemed to be a striking similarity
between developments in the two countries. The federal system of the
United States, designed in 1787, had replaced the Confederacy of 1777,
ratified in 1781, which had proved weak and inadequate to the exigencies
of the Union. In Germany people wanted to replace the Confederation
of 1815, seen as weak and inadequate in the eyes of nationalists and liberals, by a more perfect union. The new Germany was conceived as a
federal state, though somewhat more centralised than the United
States.[6]

Moreover, the principle of judicial review (Verfassungsgerichtsbar-
keit) was adapted from the American political system. It did not, of
course, originate in the United States Constitution, but through John
Marshall's decision in the important case of Marbury v. Madison in 1803.
Germans followed closely the American pattern and conceived the highest court, the Reichsgericht, in conformity with the Supreme Court.[7]
Universal male suffrage was another element influenced by the political
system of the United States, its basis resting, however, on American
state constitutions as read in the 1840s, not on the Federal Constitution. Thus the German Constitution of 1849, which failed to become
effective, but nevertheless helped to shape later constitutional thought,
reflected the American model at important points.

It is interesting to note that in the constitutional debates of 1848/49
there was not only a one-way orientation of Germans looking to the
United States, anxious to learn and adapt. Americans helped by giving
advice and drafting proposals. An American agent, A. Dudley Mann,
who happened to be in Germany on a special commission from President
Polk to negotiate commercial treaties with the individual German states
against the Prussian-dominated Customs Union, eagerly observed the
revolutionary events. As early as 21 March 1848, Mann had drafted a
constitution for a new German federation. His text, entitled 'Constitution for the United States of Germany', followed closely the American
model, but deviated from it where it did not seem adaptable or appropriate. He thought that it was necessary, for example, to prevent the
supremacy of any state within the federal system, most likely that of
Prussia or Austria. In accordance with the United States system he
suggested a senate composed of two delegates from each state. Not in

accord with the American model, however, was the provision that the federal president was to be elected for a period of three years without possibility of re-election. The first president was to be elected from the member–state with the largest population, the second from the next largest, and so forth, until the last one, from the smallest of the thirty-odd states of Germany, before the process began again.[8]

Mann favoured a republic, but despised the German radical movements of 1848 and 1849. When he saw that the first was not to be accomplished without the support of the second he became disillusioned and retreated to France, only to be disillusioned there again when Napoleon III overthrew the French Republic in 1851.

Other Americans, when asked for advice, commented on German constitutional drafts. John C. Calhoun, then United States Senator from South Carolina, was approached by the Prussian minister in Washington, Friedrich von Gerolt, to give his opinion on a draft prepared by a committee of the old German Diet which favoured a strongly centralised union of German states. Calhoun, a proponent of states rights and outspokenly anti-egalitarian, not surprisingly advised against a closer union and drastic reforms. The old, loosely constructed confederation, he said, could be preserved if a few reforms in practical matters were effected.[9]

The third contribution to the German constitutional debates came from Andrew Jackson Donelson who, from 1846, was United States minister in Berlin and (from September 1848 until November 1849) Envoy Extraordinary and Minister Plenipotentiary at the German Central Power in Frankfurt. In his comment on the same German draft he, like Calhoun, warned against a closer union, and favoured the republican principle, like A. Dudley Mann.[10] It is interesting to see that all three contributions came from Southerners. They seem to reflect the lively Southern debates on states rights which appeared applicable to Germany in 1848/49.

At least one Northerner was also interested, no less a person than Daniel Webster. But he was not to have the opportunity to do what he wished. In March 1849, when the Revolution in Germany was about to collapse, Webster mentioned that the post of an American envoy to Berlin was 'the only place he would like to have, if he were not too poor to take any. That he believed he could do much good in Germany in explaining and recommending our system of government'.[11] It would be most interesting to know what lesson the Whig 'god-like experiencer', as he was called by a sarcastic opponent in the Democratic ranks, would have taught the Germans had he been given the post.

How effective the other three Americans were is difficult to establish. Many constitutional proposals and drafts were discussed in Germany in 1848/49, and the recommendations of Mann, Calhoun, and Donelson may have played a minimal role, or none at all. However, they were symptomatic of the great interest both in Germany and the United States in each other's constitutional schemes. If the US Constitution was not really used as a model for the German one, it served at least as an 'arsenal of arguments' for German concepts of reform.[12] The binational dialogue was short-lived, however – enthusiasm was followed by disillusionment about a progressive German future.

When Bismarck prepared the constitution of the North German Confederation of 1867 and the German Empire of 1871 he could not help looking back at the ineffective Constitution of 1849. He adopted certain ideas from it, including some which the revolutionaries had adopted from the American model. He accomplished what the revolutionaries had fought for in vain: the replacement of a loosely organised confederation by a closely united system (what Americans had done in 1787). However, his concept differed esssentially from the 1849 constitution and even more so from that of the United States. The German Empire was a federation but one in which Prussia was the hegemonial, if not the ruling power. Bismarck and his sovereign, the Kaiser, were popular figures; public opinion played an important role, sometimes influencing political decisions, more often being manipulated by the Chancellor for political purposes. But the Constitution of 1871 did not really provide for national sovereignty. The parliament (*Reichstag*) was elected by the people, but the executive was not responsible to the parliament for many of its decisions. In Prussia the odious three-class franchise system continued. Checks and balances, essential ingredients of the American model, did not control the central power of the Empire. In short, one can hardly speak of an American influence on the constitutional system of Germany established in 1871.

Bismarck was a pragmatist and *Realpolitiker,* but not a man of theories and principles. In his *Gedanken und Erinnerungen* he described the Constitution of the North German Confederation as the 'result of possibilities under existing circumstances with some extensions and corrections permitted by the situation'.[13] The same applied to the 1871 Constitution. Bismarck looked at other constitutions only if they served his purposes. This is well illustrated in a conversation which he had near the end of his chancellorship in 1888 with Carl Schurz, the revolutionary of 1848 who had become an American statesman. Bismarck, at that time apprehending the possible irresponsibilities of young and inexperienced successors to the German imperial crown, like Prince Wilhelm who was to become Emperor Wilhelm II, had asked Schurz about the powers of the American presidents. When his visitor tried to explain them, probably referring to the extensive interpretation which Lincoln had given them, Bismarck exclaimed: 'That is a monarchy with a limited term! Or rather, almost a modern monarchy with a limited term; and it has very much in its favour'.[14]

In contrast with the absence of American influence on the Imperial Constitution of 1871, one can clearly discern a transatlantic impact on the founding of the two democratic German states of the twentieth century, the Weimar and the Federal Republics.

The US Constitution was now one and a half centuries old; it was astonishing that the American political system was still functioning within an eighteenth-century framework, only refined by occasional amendments. Democratic and republican governments had been formed in various countries of the Western world. Discussions of the elements of modern constitutionalism were now commonplace. Admiration for the venerable American system was undiminished, but few constitution-makers considered it to be a suitable model for their own designs and drafts. They still used it as an arsenal of ideas, but there were other arsenals besides the American one; and it was difficult, if not useless, to distinguish between national patterns of origin.

The specific influence of the United States on the Weimar as well as on the Federal Republic resulted from the fact that Germany had twice lost a war and was twice more or less subject to the demands and interventions of the victors. These stated that they wished the defeated country to be politically reorganised in a way that would guarantee justice, peace, and stability.

The American impact on the Weimar Constitution preceded the actual drawing-up of the Constitution by the National Assembly in 1919; it even preceded the collapse of the Wilhelmian Empire in the course of the November Revolution of 1918. President Wilson, during the last month of the First World War, in fact, demanded constitutional reforms in Germany as a precondition for the armistice requested by the German government. In his speech of 4 July 1918, he had expressed his determination not to compromise with a regime neglecting the people's right to self-government.[15] In three notes sent to the German government in October 1918, he became more explicit. In the first he wanted to know whether the German Chancellor, Prince Max von Baden, was 'speaking merely for the constituted authorities of the Empire who have so far conducted the war'.[16] Then, in his second note, he denounced an arbitrary power disturbing the peace and declared that it was 'within the choice of the German nation to alter it'.[17] In his third note Wilson acknowledged certain constitutional reforms which, in the meantime, had taken place in Germany, but wrote that it did 'not appear that the principle of a Government responsible to the German people' had yet been 'fully worked out' nor that any guarantees either existed or were being contemplated so 'that the alterations of principle and of practice now partially agreed upon will be permanent'.[18]

Germany reacted positively in three steps. In October 1918, a parliamentary form of government was introduced. A new clause in the Constitution laid down that the Chancellor had to be confirmed in his position by a vote of confidence in the *Reichstag*. Second, also in October, the two houses of the Prussian Diet conceded equal voting rights to all Prussians, i.e., the elimination of the three-class franchise system. Third, on 9 November 1918, a Republic was proclaimed and the Kaiser was forced to leave the country and, finally, to resign. These constitutional changes, demanded by many Germans, but not effected without pressure from the United States, set the stage for the drafting of the Weimar Constitution. In this, however, the American model did not play a major role. The delegates to the National Assembly could refer to German liberal traditions as well as to various constitutional theories and experiments of modern times which offered help in solving difficult questions.

Germans upheld the federal system although many Liberal and Social Democrats favoured a centralised state. The principle of judicial review was introduced in a limited way: the German Supreme Court, the *Reichsgericht,* was given the power to declare legislative acts of the German *Länder* (states) invalid if they were not consonant with the provisions of the Weimar Constitution. If one considers federalism and judicial review 'America's unique contribution to political science',[19] the political system of the Weimar Constitution took advantage of the American pattern in two important ways.

After the rise and fall of the Third Reich a defeated Germany again faced the task of constitution-making. This time the initiative was not left to the Germans themselves, but rested with the occupying powers in both the West and the East. The result was the emergence of two systems of government and two constitutions in a divided country. The United States was very influential in forming a West German state. What was its specific contribution at this time? In many ways the political system of the Federal Republic of 1949 was predetermined by Western occupation policy and military government as shaped by the United States and its allies, Great Britain and France. Local and regional self-government came first and set the stage for an all-West German government. Its nature was to be liberal and democratic, not based on collectivist and communist principles as in East Germany under Soviet rule.

When, in 1948, the Western powers decided to establish a West German state, they authorised the Prime Ministers of the *Länder* to convene a constituent assembly. According to the so-called Frankfort Documents of 1 July 1948, this assembly was to draft 'a democratic constitution which will establish for the participating states a governmental structure of federal type . . . which will protect the rights of the participating states, provide adequate central authority and contain guarantees of individual rights, and freedoms'.[20] The documents contained no details and were rather general in wording. In an *aide-mémoire* of 22 November 1948, the three occupation powers specified conditions. Most important was their instruction to the West German Parliamentary Council, i.e., the constituent assembly convened in Bonn, to provide for a bicameral system, one chamber strongly representing the German *Länder* and safeguarding their individual interests.[21]

The three Western powers were in full agreement on this programme. The federal principle, always cherished and favoured by Americans and adopted by Germans in the nineteenth century, now again appeared appropriate for a German state. Too much central power in Germany could endanger the stability of the international system. The Wilhelmian Empire and, more so, the Third Reich had provided proof of that. Looking at intergovernmental negotiations behind the directive of 1948, one finds, however, that there were differences in opinion as to how far German federalism should be carried. The British government was less interested in it than the French and United States governments. French politicians preferred decentralisation of power as far as possible to prevent future German aggression, while American politicians advocated it in accordance with their own constitutional system.

In March and April 1949, shortly before the Parliamentary Council had completed its work, a controversy arose between the Council delegates and the military government which, in a second phase, induced a controversy among the occupation powers themselves and revealed a specific American position. What happened, briefly summarised, was that the military governors wanted to give more power to the *Länder* *vis-à-vis* the central government, particularly as far as taxation and general legislation were concerned. General Lucius D. Clay, the American military governor (and a southerner in the states rights tradition), felt very strongly about that. In West Germany the Christian Democratic party and the Christian Social Union party would have followed suit, but the Social Democrats favoured a strong central power which, they thought, was a precondition for the socialist reforms planned for Germany in the future. During the ensuing negotiations between the three occupation powers, the British government, in co-ordination with the German Social Democrats, backed out of the common front and consented to a more centralist solution. The French government then advised its military governor in Germany not to insist on a strong *Länder* policy. Finally after the intervention of the US State Department, which preferred flexibility in occupational politics, the Americans also yielded. Thus, American 'hyper-federalism' as Kurt Schumacher, leader of the Social Democrats, called it, was not introduced into the *Grundgesetz* of the Federal Republic of Germany.[22]

In many ways, of course, the West German Constitution, which became effective on 23 May 1949, corresponded with American constitutional theories and practices. It should be mentioned that the principle of judicial review was implemented again and now received more weight than in the Weimar Republic. A special 'constitutional court' *(Bundesverfassungsgericht)* was formed with the power to examine the constitutionality of state and federal legislation *(Normenkontrolle)*. The competence of this court with regard to judicial review is broader than that of the United States Supreme Court and, it may be noted, was not imposed on the German constitution-makers by the occupation powers.[23] Although the *Grundgesetz,* like the Weimar Constitution, does not reflect the clear division of powers characteristic of the American Constitution, the system of checks and balances was improved and strengthened.

Summing up American impact on German constitutional thought and practice over 200 years, it can be said that more than anything else it was the principle of federalism which attracted the Germans. In Germany local and regional sovereignties had a long tradition; since the Middle Ages they had been counterweights against central rule and the resistance to changes was stronger than the idea of national unity. They could not easily be abolished when a new German state was designed. Not only were there still reigning kings, dukes, and princes, clinging to their power, but the people had developed specific regional identities which they were not willing to sacrifice. Americans had demonstrated how regional and national sovereignties could be brought together in harmony within one governmental system. That example seemed to suit Germans well and to solve major problems.

However, did the Germans really understand the complex structure of American federalism? They favoured a federal system out of respect for traditional sovereignties and local interests but did not agree on territorial reorganisation by which, for instance, very small states would be integrated into more powerful units and, therefore, a balance of weight among the *Länder* could be achieved. Prussia's hegemony remained undiminished, and in 1849, the King of Prussia was elected as the new head of the union. In America the larger states had ceded their territorial claims to western lands in the course of the Revolution and by that had reconciled smaller states to a closer union. The Federal Constitution gave each state, small or large, an equal vote in the Senate, while the German *Länder* were represented in the state chamber in proportion to their population (they still are in the *Bundesrat* of the Federal Republic, in which, however, the states are reorganised and more balanced). German federalism was geared to the past. It preserved conventional powers with all their weights and drives for preponderance, while the rational construction of American federalism was part of a well-balanced system in which no state could dominate the union or develop hegemonial power.

Of course, constitutions are conceived, put into effect, and function under given circumstances and in specific political contexts. The American governmental system was accomplished after the old powers had been overthrown in a life and death struggle for independence. In nineteenth-century Germany the old powers had yielded with more flexibility and new constitutions were not made against a background swept more or less clean by revolution. Moreover problems of the transferability of constitutional schemes are numerous and difficult. Perhaps it is impossible straightforwardly to adopt another country's constitutional framework, no matter what influences may operate.[24]

The republican principle was not adopted by Germany before 1918. In this respect the American model did not serve the Germans. The majority of them were content with a constitutional monarchy, adopting some French or British patterns. They felt safe in having a national representation and restricting the power of the head of state to executive duties, knowing that the President of the United States was also vested with considerable power. They did not or could not take into consideration the fact that the presidential term was limited to four years and that the President could be removed by impeachment. German constitutions of the nineteenth century preserved hereditary monarchy and did not provide for impeachment procedures. Had the monarch been a mere figurehead, this would have been of little importance. But a monarch without such restrictions and invested with strong powers, particularly those held by the Kaisers in the Bismarck Empire, was very different from an American president. Germans did not follow American suggestions for the introduction of a republican form of government, probably for two reasons: they underestimated the limits of power of the American executive provided by the United States Constitution, and they were confronted with powerful *Länder* sovereigns whom they could not easily push aside without the risk of civil strife and domestic turmoil.

So, while Germans discussed many aspects of the American model, they had difficulties in fully understanding its complexity and even more difficulties in adapting it to new conditions. The effective system of checks and balances conceived by the Founding Fathers of the United States to prevent extremes in government was not fully transferred to nineteenth-century German constitutions. It was impossible to copy it because there was not enough room for rational changes; there were too many adverse circumstances which could not be overcome. In 1848/49 enthusiasm about a successful drafting of a constitution and its practical implication ran high, but revolutionaries and reformers had soon to realise that there were not enough safeguards to prevent the resurgence of the old political system. The liberal movement collapsed, perhaps before it had a real opportunity to introduce change.

Comparing such American–German interactions in the nineteenth and twentieth centuries, one comes to a paradoxical conclusion. The more Germans discussed the American pattern, the less elements were adapted from it – as in 1848 – and the less they discussed it, the more it was adapted – as in 1919 and perhaps 1949. This can first be explained by the fact that, in the twentieth century, American constitutional principles, as well as the principles of other democratic systems, had become commonplace; they lacked the novelty which they had had for nineteenth-century liberals. Second, while nineteenth-century Germans studied the American Constitution and tried to adapt its elements to their own drafts, twentieth-century Germans were forced to accept imposed constitutional directions from the United States, the victorious power at the end of two wars. However, many Germans felt comfortable with these impositions since they were not strange to them, but corresponded to the progressive traditions of their own country. Whether based on voluntary self-orientation or forceful imposition, the impact of the American model on German constitutional politics was welcomed. The exemplary achievements of the Founding Fathers of 1787, however deficient they may have been, are still admired and appreciated in Germany today.

NOTES

1 The term *Grundgesetz,* and not 'Constitution', was chosen because Germans wanted to emphasise that the Federal Republic of Germany was to be considered a provisional arrangement since it applied to only one part of the German nation–state which they were longing for.

2 F. Valjavec, *Die Entstehung der politischen Strömungen in Deutschland, 1770-1815,* Munich, 1951, pp. 108-9.

3 H. Dippel, *Germany and the American Revolution, 1770-1800: A Sociohistorical Investigation of Late Eighteenth-Century Political Thinking,* Chapel Hill, NY, 1977, pp. 276-78.

4 G. K. F. Seidel, 'Die Staatsverfassung der vereinigten Staaten', in D. Ramsay, *Geschichte der Amerikaniscen Revolution aus den Acten des Congresses der vereinigten Staaten,* pt. 4, Berlin, 1795, p. 1.; compare Dippel, *Germany and the American Revolution,* p. 277, also E. E. Doll, 'American history as interpreted by German historians from 1770 to 1815', *Transactions of the American Philosophical Society,* New Series, XXXVIII, 1949, pp. 421-534.

5 R. Mohl, *Das Bundes-Staatsrecht der Vereinigten Staaten von Nord-Amerika,* pt. I: *Verfassungsrecht,* Stuttgart/Tübingen, 1824. A German translation of Thomas Jeffeson's *Parliamentary Manual* (1801) was published under the title *Handbuch des Parlamentarrechts,* Berlin, 1819, trans. by L. V Henning.

6 For a detailed discussion of the influence of American Federalism on German constitutional debates in 1848/49 see E. Franz, 'Das Amerikabild der deutschen Revolution von 1848/49: Zum Problem der Übertragung gewachsener Verfassungsformen, *Beihefte zum Jahrbuch für Amerikastudien,* II, Heidelberg, 1958.

7 See K. v. Beyme, *Vorbild Amerika? Der Einfluß der amerikanischen Demokratie in der Welt,* Munich 1986, pp. 119-21.

8 See G. Moltmann, *Atlantische Blockpolitik im 19. Jahrhundert: Die Vereinigten Staaten und der deutsche Liberalismus während der Revolution von 1848/49,* Düsseldorf, 1973, pp. 213-24, 371-5; G. Moltmann, 'Amerikanische Beiträge zur deutschen Verfassungsdiskussion', *Jahrbuch für Amerikastudien,* XII, 1967, pp. 206-26 and 253-61 (draft of constitution).

9 M. E. Curti, 'John C. Calhoun and the unification of Germany', *American Historical Review,* XL, 1934/35, pp. 476-8; cf. G. Moltmann, *Atlantische Blockpolitik,* pp. 224-32.

10 G. Moltmann, 'Amerikanische Beiträge', pp. 225-6, text of comment, p. 262. cf. G. Moltmann, *Atlantische Blockpolitik,* pp. 232-3.

11 Unpublished letter from Francis P. Blair to Martin Van Buren, 3 March 1849, Van Buren Papers, Library of Congress, Washington, DC. See G. Moltmann, 'Amerikanische Beiträge', pp. 210-11.

12 E. Angermann, 'Der deutsche Frühkonstitutionalismus and das amerikanische Vorbild', *Historische Zeitschrift,* CCIXX, 1974, pp. 1-32, esp. p. 4.

13 See O. Becker, *Bismarcks Ringen um Deutschlands Gestaltung,* ed. and enlarged by A. Scharff, Heidelberg, 1958, p. 336.

14 See J. Alden Nichols, *The Year of the Three Kaisers: Bismarck and the German Succession, 1887- 88,* Urbana/Chicago, 1987, p. 238.

15 Address at Mount Vernon, *The Papers of Woodrow Wilson,* ed. A. S. Link, 11,

Princeton, 1985, pp. 514-57, esp. p. 516.

16 Lansing to Oederlin, 8 Oct. 1918, *Foreign Relations of the United States: Diplomatic Papers*, 1918, supplement 1 (The World War), I, p. 343.

17 Lansing to Oederlin, 14 Oct. 1918, *Foreign Relations,* pp. 358-9.

18 Lansing to Oederlin 23 Oct. 1918, *Foreign Relations,* pp. 381-3. For a detailed discussion of Wilson's attitude toward Germany at the end of the First World War see K. Schwabe, *Deutsche Revolution und Wilson-Frieden: Die amerikanische und deutsche Friedensstragie zwischen Ideologie und Machtpolitik 1918/19,* Düsseldorf, 1971, pp. 88-226.

19 *Concise Dictionary of American History*, ed. W. Andrews, New York, 1962, pp. 504-5.

20 *Germany 1947-1949: The Story in Documents*, Department of State publication 3556, Washington, DC, 1950, p. 275.

21 *Ibid.*, p. 278. For a detailed discussion of the controversy see H.-J. Grabbe, 'Die deutsch-alliierte Kontroverse um den Grundgesetzentwurf im Frühjahr 1949', *Vierteljahrshefte für Zeitgeschichte*, XXVI, 1978, pp. 393-418, also H.-J. Grabbe, *Unionsparteien, Sozialdemokratie und die Vereinigten Staaten von Amerika 1945-1966,* Düsseldorf, 1983, pp. 168-76.

22 Grabbe, 'Die deutsch-alliierte Kontroverse', p. 415.

23 Cf. Beyme, *Vorbild Amerika?* pp. 125-30.

24 The problem of transferability is well discussed in Franz, *Das Amerikabild*. For a concise and excellent treatment of the same question see the recent article by Angermann, 'Der deutsche Frühkonstitutionalismus'.

7

France and the American experience, 1789–1875

ODILE RUDELLE

Fondation Nationale des Sciences Politiques, Paris

The reciprocal influences between the political system of France and the United States began very early. One of the first acts of the National Assembly was the passage of the Declaration of the Rights of Man and of the Citizen, a document influenced by American examples. At this time the image of the American Revolution was of one which had culminated in a stable constitutional system.

If the first days of the French Revolution did appear to have inaugurated an 'American era', this only lasted until the fall of the monarchy.[1] The American model, nevertheless, was not forgotten; perhaps it thrived in proportion to French disillusionment with their own petrified development, so that it was seen in a context of regret and nostalgia. The Carnot family is a striking exammple of this. Lazare, a member of the Convention, 'L'organisateur de la Victoire', and a regicide, died in exile. Hippolyte, his son, became the propagandist of the American School; Sadi, the grandson, President of the Republic, was assassinated. In 1863 Hippolyte published a biography of his father,[2] in which he portrayed a good man literally haunted by the personality of George Washington, whose example he had several times presented to Napoleon Bonaparte, telling him to choose his place in history as that either of 'a Cromwell or a Washington'.[3] Lazare moved away from Bonaparte when the latter wished to become Napoleon. During the Hundred Days he hoped that the time for a Constitutional Assembly on the American model had finally come. He refused to return to the War Ministry but became Minister of the Interior, using his last days in power to promote a plan of 'mutual education' wholly inspired by American practices. Exiled, he died in Germany in the arms of his son, Hippolyte, to whom he never ceased talking of the Republic.

Hippolyte Carnot returned to France after his father's death, presenting himself as a follower of the 'American School'. But he discovered that 'the idea of the Republic' was hardly ever cultivated except by those nostalgic for the Year II, now grouped in secret societies. Supporters of political liberty put their hopes in the 'monarchy according to charter'. Hippolyte sought a realistic political programme. At first he found it in Saint-Simonism, then in the electoral activities of the society 'Aide-toi, le-ciel-t'aidera' where he met Guizot.[4] The Revolution of 1830 seemed for a moment to provide a new opening for the 'American era'.[5] La Fayette made a triumphant return to the US; in the *Revue Americaine* brilliant journalists explained to the French that in the United States 'republic and liberty' were synonymous even in the matter of religion. This was the time when Guizot meditated on the life of Washington and completed a long preface to the French edition of his correspondence.

However, returning to power at the end of 1840, Guizot failed to apply the lessons of Washington. If he copied the American's prudence in foreign affairs and in his domestic resistance to the popular party, he never understood the danger of a limited suffrage in a constitutional system increasingly dominated by office-holding deputies.[6] Guizot did not wish to listen to Tocqueville and the main lessons of *Democracy in America*, which explained that the apparent disorder of a liberal democracy is in fact its true harmonising element. He moved away from his old friends. The American School reconstituted itself without him, becoming a curious mixture of old legitimists of the dynastic left and of old Republicans hoping to break with the revolutionary cycle of the First Republic.

But we should not misunderstand this American School which would reappear in 1848. It was nothing else than the bold enterprise of certain writers working to reconcile liberty and revolution. But crushed between Catholic legitimism on the one hand and the nationalistic Jacobinism of the Republicans on the other, torn between religious faith on the right and national pride on the left, its proponents found no response from the heart of French society. And while Tocqueville and his liberal friends thought that the practice of local democracy might be a training ground for liberty, the Republicans preferred to put their hope in popular education, so that the voters could become enlightened.

After the Revolution of 1848 Tocqueville became a member of the Constitutional Commission and Hippolyte Carnot a short-lived minister of public education. Carnot had to resign as a result of patronizing the famous Republican educational *Manuel* written by Charles Renouvier,[7] while Tocqueville wondered how to build a republic with fellow constitutional commissioners who had 'seen nothing, studied nothing, understood nothing, save monarchy'. . . . or Republicans who 'had few ideas of any kind that did not come from the newspapers which they read or wrote for. . .'[8]

The failure of the Second Republic was that of Republicans seized with the fear of universal suffrage. Tocqueville died in 1859. The torch of the American School passed to Edouard de Laboulaye, member of the Institut and professor of the College de France. As a member of 'Commission of 30' he proposed a constitutional amendment in January 1875: 'The government of the Republic is formed of a President and two Houses',[9] which is the quintessence of the American School of balanced power. This was rejected. Nevertheless on the next day the French Republic was finally voted. Laboulaye became Chairman of the Commission and was able to play a leading role for the next six months.

Having now looked at this general background I should like to examine more closely the years 1848 and 1875 in order to discuss why the influence of the American School on the laws of 1875 has generally been forgotten while its role in the Revolution of 1848 has generally been exaggerated.

THE AMERICAN INFLUENCE ON THE CONSTITUTION OF 1848:
A MISTAKEN APPEARANCE

In February 1848 the provisional government placed itself immediately in the tradition of the American Revolution. It was unanimous in its wish to break with the memory of the First Republic. Lamartine stated succinctly that while the First Republic had been a 'battleground', the Second Republic was to be 'government'.[10]

All at that time then began to study the institutions of the United States, the model republic. René Rémond has listed the numerous editions and translations of the US Constitution which appeared in 1848 and the visits of Tocqueville and of Michael Chevalier to the American Embassy in order to obtain certain specific information.[11] This public immersion, soon followed by the decision to create a single executive chosen by universal suffrage, has suggested the direct influence of the United States presidential system. This is where misunderstanding begins, for the very reason that the 1848 Constitution cannot be understood as a presidential system in that it expressly refers to a 'ministerial' responsibility towards the Assembly, something later forgotten by a number of scholars.[12]

This confusion was made possible since ministerial responsibility was mentioned only rather obscurely, and since there was a conflict between the Constitutional Commission and the Assembly, not over the principle of responsibility, but over its formalisation. As was so often the case a solution was achieved by referring the difficulty to a later legal definition ('loi ulterieure'). So Article 68: 'The President of the Republic, the ministers, and the agents of government, who are the depositories of public authority are each responsible for what concerns them in all acts of government and administration.' This expressed the classic principle of the Republic in which all authority was supposed to be responsible authority, although to whom and how responsible was not specified. The Constitutional Commission planned a beautiful hierarchy: the criminal responsibility of the President to the High Court, political responsibility of ministers to the Conseil d'Etat and the responsibility of the civil service according to the usual procedures. This was meant to increase the power of the Conseil d'Etat whose members, chosen by the National Assembly and thus made judges of ministerial political responsibility, would have then become exactly the kind of second Chamber which in fact the National Assembly had previously refused to vote for.[13]

Naturally enough the National Assembly rejected this plan and proposed an alternative: 'a law will determine the other cases of responsibility'. This law was never produced, nor did any long and scrupulous constitutional practice have time to establish itself. These ambiguities in fact produced the later misunderstandings about the so-called influence of the American presidential system.

Between the American and the French Constitution of 1848 there are similarities of vocabulary and procedures. But their thoroughly different political and historical backgrounds produced some complete reversals in the meaning of words.

The US Constitution is a federal Constitution set up to create a 'Union of States', each of which wished to safeguard its own identity. The French Constitution of 1848, by contrast, aimed at the organisation of a republic 'une et indivisible', with a strong centralised administration. The French system asked both for the sacralisation and the self-restraint of Republican power since no procedures are provided to resolve any conflicts. The whole edifice is entrusted to the care of the suffrage of the people, which will express itself as a kind of 'conscience' or to the care of the President – who takes an oath 'before God'.

The American wish to organise a 'Union of States' had translated itself into different procedures: federalism and a single Executive with a veto power; and finally a Supreme Court able to rule on the separation of authority between Union and States. A wise equilibrium between the powers creates a balance which makes compromise the general rule of government: divisions of power between nomination and advice and consent in certain important appointments, between the negotiation of treaties and their ratification, between the impeaching and the judging power, and so on. And the whole is reorganised so that no part of the government will be tempted to believe itself the whole of the nation.

The brief description should underscore the main differences from the French Constitution of 1848 where in spite of an article affirming that the separation of powers is the first requisite for a free government, the Constitution is profoundly unitary. We can give three examples: local affairs; unity of legislative power; and the mode of nomination of the executive.

Local affairs The organisation of local affairs was the object of preliminary discussion in the Constitutional Commission as well as in the National Assembly.[14] Democracy in local government was called for as a school of civics and a safeguard of liberty. Neither Lamennais, the Catholic, nor Leroux, the Republican Socialist, were listened to. Lamennais resigned. Tocqueville, who shared his ideas, revealed himself as powerless to change the prevailing opinion.[15]

It was Armand Dufaure who best expressed the dominant opinion in the Commission and in the Assembly. A disciple of both Bonaparte and Guizot, he was convinced that centralisation was a step in the march of Reason and that France owed her unity and European preponderance to centralisation. Therefore at a time when Germany was in its turn dreaming of unity[16] France could not abandon what had made her a power. The Constitution was to create an order based on political liberty. But this great enterprise would be made more difficult if it was linked to the abandonment of the traditional administrative structure. The 'corps délibérants' – municipal and general councils – were to be elected, but not the heads of the local Executive, who were to be nominated by the central political power and would thus enjoy 'la confiance déléguée'.

But at the same time that this immense power was granted to a central bureaucracy, anxiety arose over the use which the Executive might make of it. This explains why finally the Executive was given limited direct political powers in terms of the power of veto, of the right to be re-elected, of the right of dissolving the Assembly, and so on.

The unicameral assembly. The unicameral assembly was another example of French unitarianism. It was adopted in the name of French particularism when bicameralism was common to most other free nations, as was often recalled in the debates.[17] But on this matter the memory of the Convention and of its decree of 25 September 1792 on the 'République une et indivisible' was too much present to be ignored. Sitting in the aftermath of the September massacres and the battle of

Valmy, the Paris Convention had had nothing in common with that of Philadelphia. Indivisibility had been voted following Robespierre's moving speech against the menace of the 'fédérés'. In May and June 1848 riots in the streets of Paris played something of the same menacing role. These allowed the representatives to think of themselves less as delegates than as the nation's body and the nation's voice. As Lamartine said: 'Against the sects which work on the people, what do you have to oppose? Enlightenment and assistance. And afterwards? The dictatorship of the Constituent Assembly, a single and standing force, the dictatorship not of a man but of a legislative body."[8]

A supporter of bicameralism, Tocqueville took part with sorrow in the Constitutional Commission's discussion of this matter, which was, he wrote, the 'only serious discussion' in the Commission and the only occasion of opposition between the two parties, the 'American' and the 'French' school. It was, Tocqueville stated,

> less a question of bicameralism than of the general character necessary for the new government: to continue with the wise and somewhat complicated system of balance and counterbalance and to place at the head of the republic restricted powers which would consequently be cautious and moderate ones? Or to take the contrary path and to adopt a simpler theory, leaving all matters to a single power, homogeneous in all its parts, without restraint, and in consequence impetuous and irresistible in its actions.[9]

The same kind of difference is to be found in the discussion of the means of election for the head of the executive.

The election of the executive authority. A united and homogeneous executive leads towards direct universal suffrage, whereas the American executive, based on the idea of 'limited powers', has retained indirect electoral procedures through the choice of members of an electoral college whose power is exhausted after they have fulfilled their function. The United States Constitution was silent about voting qualifications, which were deliberately left to the legislators of each state to decide. Leaving aside the question of slavery (one reason among many for federal abstention over voting qualifications), we shall insist only on the philosophical distinctions underlying direct and indirect elections.

Tocqueville was aware of the problem and tried to adapt a system suitable to a French context. If an absolute majority (or at least two million votes out of the ten million voters) had not been obtained in the first ballot, the National Assembly would have to choose, as was the case in the United States where Congress might in some circumstances have to choose the President. But even with this similarity of procedures, the basis remained different. In the one case it was the nation which spoke directly (or indirectly if it was the National Assembly) in order to appoint the President. In the other case it was only a method of designation by a body which could not possibly be taken for the entire nation. In the US the nominating power is never confused with the controlling power.

In spite of these precautions Tocqueville still found that American political life was harmed by the President's desire for re-election. To avoid this evil in France he proposed to forbid the President from standing for re-election, a proposal that was accepted – with the well-known consequences of the *coup d'état*. In his *Souvenirs* Tocqueville had the modesty to admit that it was the only one of his votes that he came to regret.

The bad luck of the Constitution of 1848 was – obviously – that it came into conflict with Louis Napoleon, lover of the *coup d'état* long before he was voted President of the Republic. The coup of 2 December devalued for more than a century a procedure to which the French people (but not the political class) were always attracted. But the failure of the Constitution of 1848 cannot be ascribed to one man's ambition, nor even to the sudden irruption of the 'Republic without Republicans' of which Tocqueville spoke. The failure of 1848 was also a failure in the understanding of the American lesson, that is to say the choice of unicameralism joined to administrative centralisation. Fortified by this lesson the next constitution-makers of Republican France will choose another line; they will follow the American lesson of the 'union between balanced forces'.

THE AMERICAN INFLUENCE ON THE CONSTITUTIONAL LAWS OF 1875: A FORGOTTEN REALITY

The obligation to obtain the Parliamentary Monarchists' consent for the establishment of a republic was the opportunity for the American School and Edouard de Laboulaye. In order to engage in constitution-making the Assembly had to reconstitute the alliance of the 'liberal union' at the end of the Second Empire, an alliance which was formed on the model of American liberty: local liberties, religious liberties, liberties of opinion, and of educational instruction. In France in 1875 the necessity of finding a compromise between Monarchists and Republicans played something of the same role as the necessity of finding a compromise between strong and weak Federalists had in 1787 in the United States. The Founding Fathers had invented a tripartite solution (single Executive, bicameral legislature, and Supreme Court). In order to resolve conflicts, the French put in place a system that was not dissimilar. This contained both a single Executive and a bicameral Congress in which a Senate was related to local structures. In addition, the simple procedures for constitutional revision seemed to promise the solution of major conflicts between Monarchists and Republicans. Neither the organisation of justice nor local institutions are mentioned. The French political system stands alongside an administrative organisation established by the Consulate and continued in 1848. This demonstrates of course the limits of the parallels between American Experience and the laws of 1875 – to which we must now turn.

We can look at three points. The right of revision, the Senatorial method of nomination, and the 'attributes' of the President of the Republic, even if, as one knows, the latter were made purely formal by the crisis of 16 May 1877.

The right of revision. Here the difference from the American model was so flagrant that a regret for it was always present. Since the process of revision had to be simple no fixed majority was declared necessary to start it. A motion for revision voted separately by each of the two chambers gave legality to the meeting of a Congress of Revision. In the same way no ratification by popular vote was provided for, whether in plebiscitary form or according to the American formula of a convention chosen to decide on matters discussed beforehand.

This purely parliamentary procedure for constitutional revision was regretted by numerous eminent persons. Of the American school, Laboulaye always remained firm on this point. On the side of those called the 'plebiscitarian republicans' – about eighty members in a 600-member Assembly – we can mention Alfred Nacquet who, ten years later, was a Boulangiste leader whose best argument would be to criticise this parliamentary monopoly.[20] After the First World War the argument was picked up by the Christian Democrats and, of course, after 1945, by Charles de Gaulle.

There is, however, a point of detail relating to the right of revision where one can note American influence. In 1884 Jules Ferry was the master-craftsman of the only revision of the Third Republic. Wishing to make the Republic the definitive government of France, he was inspired by the American example to prohibit any non-Republican amendments to its Constitution. Parliament's monopoly of revision was replaced by words specifying that: 'the republican form of government cannot be the object of any proposal for revision', which recalls, of course, the words of the US Constitution stating that the United States guarantees a republican form of government to each American state. Once again there is a resemblance here, but not an identity, since by incorporating this provision into the relationship between the Union and states, the US Constitution at the same time expressed both the principle and its guarantee. France, in accordance with the tradition of 1848, proceeded to a proclamatory type of affirmation without any precise guarantee of the least possibility of legal appeal.

Bicameralism with the Senate based on local structures. The necessity of obtaining the Monarchists' agreement decided the question of bicameralism. No discussion was possible on this point. The debate involved the method of nominating Senators. Were they to be nominated for their 'capacities'? Were they to be non-removable? Were they to be elected? If so, who was to elect them? Such questions were the occasion of the most interesting debate during which the reference to the American model was completely explicit.

It was Richard Waddington who proposed to adopt the American principle of a second chamber based on local representation by equating the French departments with the different US states. Waddington proposed that, as in the United States, the French senators would be chosen by the chambers of each department, by the meetings of district councillors (conseillers d'arrondissement) and general councillors (conseillers généraux). This was rejected and support shifted to a moderate proposition – a call to the delegates of the municipal councils. This idea came from Lefebvre-Pontalis, Tocqueville's follower, who explained that 'the variety of local interests would be a guarantee against the danger of homogeneous majorities which always threaten to become oppressive'.

The American example figured equally in the choice of the number of Senators: two by department, Waddington proposed. The commission kept to this general idea, while modulating its application. Thanks to the influence of the great republican leader, Léon Gambetta, this new kind of Senate was accepted by the Republican party which decided to call this second House 'the Great Council of the Commons of France'. Conceived of in the spirit of the American school, this Senate was very far from the French tradition of the First and Second Republics, a tradition of 'capacities', nobility, or universal suffrage. It became allied with a conservative rural type of democracy and its American origin was quickly forgotten.

Attributes of the President of the Republic. In the laws of 1875 the President of the French Republic is viewed as head of the Executive, a fact largely forgotten after the crisis of 1877. In the debates of the time the American example is several times quoted on two subjects: the power of veto and the time of election. The President was not given a veto power although his obligation to promulgate the law is accompanied by a reserve power of a right of second deliberation – a feeble echo of the American right of veto.[21] The only American influence which was accepted related to the time of the election of the President, set to take place one month before the expiry of his predecessor's term. In the US, of course, the elections took place several months in advance.

After 1875 the influence of the American model varied with circumstances. When the French Republic developed in the direction of endemic ministerial instability, the US system was evoked in a nostalgic fashion. This nostalgia was no longer, as it had been under the Empire, one for liberty but for Executive stability. Ministerial instability also fed endemic antiparliamentarianism, of which the Boulangist crisis is the most celebrated episode. Boulanger had been chosen by Gambetta to represent France at the centenary celebrations of Yorktown where he became acquainted with the American system. But despite support from Naquet, Boulanger never developed any real constitutional thought. From prudence or from ignorance he saw nothing in the American model, except the image of a stable executive power settled on a popular basis. Contrary to the legend of the failed *coup d'état*, Boulangism was never anything except an unhappy electoral adventure. But after Boulanger's failure (and his rather pitiful suicide on his mistress's grave) Boulangism joined the category of forbidden things, like the Bonapartism and Caesarism which were always present as false temptations within French democracy. Ideological crystallisation after Boulanger made later attempts at analysing institutions or revising the French constitutional equilibrium very difficult. As a result there was a silence, an ignorance, in the first part of the twentieth century about the American model in general and what the laws of 1875 in particular owed to the American school. The radical Republicans as well as the French socialists thought of themselves as part of the mainstream of unitary Republicanism. Only the advent of the Fifth Republic with the growing influence of the 'Conseil Constitutionnel' after the coming to power of the 'Union of the Left' resulted in the rediscovery of American constitutionalism.

In conclusion I think we may say that the American model has been present in French history more as an example of the practice of liberal government than because of American declarations about the rights of man, since the latter are seen as a peculiarly French contribution to world history. Evidence for this practical weight of the American example is given added force by consideration of a letter written on 14 May 1948 to General de Bénouville by Charles de Gaulle, ten years before his return to power. It is a synthesis of de Gaulle's politics since the Liberation and includes a description of his method of 'drowning' the Communist Party in the democratic system:

> At the time that you are leaving for the United States, I think it is useful to be more precise about a few ideas that can help you in our discussions.
>
> To make our American friends comprehend the fundamental reasons for our action, you should always remind them about the situation in France at the moment of the Liberation. The IIId Republic in 1940 had been engulfed in disaster. The shock produced by the Vichy government risked plunging France into anarchy. The Communists were organised in such a way that they could seize power if they found the occasion or the means.
>
> My first task was both to finish the war and to stop the increasing power of the Communists. I did it not without blows or opposition but without bloody conflict. In particular I dissolved the armed groups that the Communists had organised for their own purposes and incorporated into the regular army all the healthy elements of the Resistance which were indeed of a very high quality and I reinstated normal administration and regular justice.
>
> That achieved I reestablished democracy by calling for free elections at first of municipal councils, then of general councils, finally of a constituent national assembly. Thus the Communists found themselves drowned in democracy. At the same time the political parties renewed themselves – unhappily in a manner more divided and exclusivist than ever before. In the regime that the parties instituted for their own purposes, without any regard for the national interest, my action and even my presence became impossible without at least a coup d'état – which I rejected entirely even as an idea. That is why I retired from power.
>
> However the country recognised by this experience that because of the problems surrounding it, the exclusive regime of parties could not continue and that the separation of powers is a necessity to restore at the same time and separately, both the government and the parliament. As for me, I have proposed, as is known, an organisation of powers which would largely take into account the example furnished by the United States Constitution and one in which the fundamental liberties of the individual will be guaranteed by a state sufficiently solidly organised to do so.[22]

One hundred and fifty years after Carnot, one century after Tocqueville, the American school had made a new convert. Renouncing any imperial or Cromwellian ambitions, General de Gaulle accepted a place in the school of George Washington.[23]

NOTES

1 From Georges de La Fayette *(Oeuvres,* Vol II, p. 251) quoted by Bernard Gilson *L'invention de la présidence,* Paris, 1968, p. 304.

2 Hippolyte Carnot, *Mémoires sur Carnot par son fils,* Charavay, Mantoux, Martin, éditeurs, Paris, 1893 (new edition).

3 *Ibid,* p. 213.

4 On the first years of the republican party and the return to France of Hippolyte Carnot see Georges Weill, *Histoire du Parti républicain; 1814-1870,* Paris, 1900.

5 René Rémond, *Les Etats-Unis et l'opinion publique française,* Paris, 1962, 2 vols.

6 See Pierre Rosanallon, *Le moment Guizot,* Paris, 1986.

7 Charles Renouvier, *Manuel républicain de l'Homme et du Citoyen,* 1848, new edition by Maurice Agulhon, Paris, 1981.

8 Alexis de Tocqueville, *De la démocratie en Amérique, Souvenirs, L'Ancien Régime et la Révolution,* Paris, 1986, p. 826.

9 *Journal Officiel de la République Française,* partie officielle, Débats parlementaires, 30 January 1875, p. 769.

10 *Le Moniteur de la République Français,* Débats parlementaires, 13 June 1848, (intervention of Lamartine).

11 Rémond, *Etats-Unis,* pp. 838ff.

12 Gilson, *Invention,* p. 322.

13 See Odile Rudelle, 'L'élaboration de la Constitution de 1848', in Christian Bidegaray and Paul Isoart, *Des Républiques en France, Economica,* Paris, 1988.

14 *Journal Officiel de la République Française,* Débats parlementaires, Pierre Leroux, 4 June 1848.

15 Tocqueville, *Souvenirs,* p. 828.

16 *Le Moniteur de la République Française,* Débats parlementaires, intervention of Armand Dufaure, September 1848, p. 2903.

17 Armand Marrast, 'The reason quoted from London or Washington is bad because it comes from there.' Quoted in Gilson, *Invention,* p. 321.

18 *Le Moniteur de la République Française,* 1848, p. 2841.

19 Tocqueville, *Souvenirs,* p. 829.

20 On Boulangism as an electoral revolt against Parliament's selfishness see Odile Rudelle, *La République absolve,* Paris, 1986.

21 See *Journal Officiel de la République Française,* Débats parlementaires de l'Assemblé Nationale, 17 June 1875, p. 5444. Lefévre-Pontalis: 'The Constitutional Committee has refused (and I think it was wrong) to give the French president of the Republic the veto right that has belonged to the American president for nearly a century. The Committee has merely given the president the right to ask for a second reading).'

22 Charles de Gaulle, *Lettres, Notes et Carnets, Mai 1945-Juin 1951,* Paris, 1948, p. 249.

23 On de Gaulle and Washington see Odile Rudelle, *Mai 1958: de Gaulle et la République,* Plon, Paris, 1988.

8

Some British views of the United States Constitution

J. W. BURROW
University of Sussex

To attempt in a single essay to review British responses to and judgements of the American Constitution may seem an impossibly ambitious task. Not only is there a variety of sometimes contradictory opinions to be considered, precluding any possibility, of course, of speaking of *the* British view, but the variables by which those opinions were shaped have been many and diverse: the individual characters and stances of the commentators, themselves sometimes changing with advancing years; the constantly shifting features of both British and American public life and political culture, with each mutation altering respectively either the object or the perspective from which it was seen; and, not least, the volume of influential commentary produced by American jurists, scholars, and publicists, which in turn has naturally helped to shape British perceptions. Lord Acton, for example, copiously quoted from Southern spokesmen, notably Calhoun, sometimes at more than a page's length.[1] James Bryce naturally made use of 'native informants', and relied extensively in *The American Commonwealth* on the authority to whom he submitted his manuscript, Judge Thomas M. Cooley.[2] From the 1860s, personal friendships between British and American scholars have become common, as, in this century, have been protracted academic visits. All this suggests that we should approach with a certain caution not merely the notion of *the* British view of the American Constitution which is clearly absurd, but even that of *British* – in the sense of distinctively British – views of the American Constitution. Not infrequently the particular British view will represent at most a preference for one American view over another.

It is worth reminding ourselves at the outset, too, that even on the British side alone we are not speaking simply of a collection of disparate opinions, but to some extent at least of a connected tissue of political culture bound together by personal contact and intellectual influence.

The commentators I shall speak of in this essay formed members of a closely-knit political and academic culture. Bryce and A. V. Dicey travelled to America for the first time together,[3] and the latter was one of the dedicatees of *The American Commonwealth*, while Bryce had fallen, as an undergraduate at Trinity College, Oxford, under the influence of Edward Freeman.[4] Henry Maine, whose views were criticised by Bryce,[5] was his and Dicey's colleague at Oxford. Acton and Bryce were of course known to each other and the former wrote perhaps the most famous early review of *The American Commonwealth*. In the ensuing generations, Harold Laski knew Bryce, though he did not think very highly of him,[6] and was taught at New College by Bryce's biographer H. A. L. Fisher, while Laski wrote the foreword to Denis Brogan's 1933 book *The American Political System*. It was a narrow world.

That we can see it in this way is partly the consequence of the benign limitation of our concern here specifically to views of the Constitution rather than simply views of American politics. To speak of British opinions of the latter, or, as it would probably have been called in the earlier period, of 'American democracy', would call for a much wider net and finer mesh. But in speaking of views of the Constitution as such we are justified in trawling only for the bigger fish, for views of some elaboration, argumentative weight, and, given our period, academic analysis. The mention of period also suggests two other limitations. One is a voluntary restriction; the other is, I suggest, inherent. The former is simply that in this historical survey, I shall not venture beyond the first half of our own century. and shall not deal, except very briefly in conclusion, with the frequently eager interest shown at the moment by British jurists, historians, political scientists, and journalists in the working of the American Constitution; they can speak for themselves. The other limitation, I think, is less arbitrary, in that I shall have little to say of the period before the American Civil War. One reason for this is the existence of the admirable book by David P. Crook, *American Democracy in English Politics, 1815-1850*, on which I shall extensively rely for that period. The other is that until the beginning of the second half of the last century, and the American Civil War, the prevailing interest of British writers seems to have been not so much in the peculiarities of the US Constitution as in the specific feature in which it differed so radically, but also, some hoped and many feared, prophetically, from the British Constitution before 1867. In other words interest was focused primarily on the United States as a democracy, a term which, particularly following Tocqueville, could be interpreted socially as much as politically. Essentially, it seems, and particularly before the stabilisation of English politics by the Reform Act of 1832,[7] the American polity was seen, in large terms, as 'democracy' rather than as the complex mechanism it actually was.

Radicals naturally exalted its lacunae, which stood for all possible merits: no king, hereditary aristocracy, church establishment; Tories deplored the same things. Radicals often ignored the Whiggish character of the Constitution, its elaborate checks and balances. Jeremy Bentham, who denounced the cherished Whig notion of 'balance' in an English constitutional context as a confidence trick, managed to reconcile his contempt for it with his favourable view of the American polity largely, it seems, by ignoring the elaborations of the latter, while he specifically rejected bicameralism,[8] though, on the other hand, in what looks like a tribute to the American precedent, in his own proposed Constitutional Code the Prime Minister was not to sit in Parliament.[9] Whigs on the other hand adumbrated, in the years before and after 1832, many of the themes we encounter later in English judgements of the United States Constitution. Thus the Constitution might suit Americans, but it was not for export.[10] This was in conformity both with the pervasive Burke-anism of English Whig and also much Tory political argument and also with the increasingly sociological perspective of nineteenth-century political theory, which insisted that political arrangements must be matched to the national character and circumstances, and normally would in fact be moulded by them.[11] American circumstances were often declared to be special, even unique. No general inferences could be made for the workings of democracy from a country in which class-conflict was checked by the ready availability of land and the absence of here-ditary aristocracy.[12] The 'success' of the American polity was also some-times seen even in the middle of the last century, when racial language was less common than it became later, in terms of 'Anglo-Saxon' heritage, racial as well as institutional.[13]

The argument of special circumstances could be run both ways, of course; if American conditions were more often seen as exceptionally favourable, they could also be interpreted in terms of handicaps, particu-larly by those who, in Britain in the 1860s, wished to argue for a further extension of the franchise and to discount conservative references to the deplorable character of the American example. Thus, colonial manners were rough and uncultivated; Americans were commercially minded and little interested in careers in public life; the influence of Irish and Ger-man immigrants distorted the politics of the great cities.[14] These argu-ments, though hardly gratifying to American pride, were democratic, not conservative, though they derived in part from decades of well-established, almost commonplace snobberies, fastidiousness, and condescension in English, particularly but by no means exclusively conservative English, attitudes to the United States. The supposed relation between American society and the American polity could be, and was, in the years before Britain's own constitutional 'leap in the dark' in 1867, interpreted in a number of different ways, each with its own kind of contemporary political purchase. Thus the United States was the pure type of democracy, representing an ideal, or possibly less than ideal but inevitable, future for Europe; this was the naive radical and also the sophisticated Tocquevillean view. Or, *as* a pure democracy, in Tory eyes wearing the classical spectacles, Aristotelian and Polybian, through which educated nineteenth-century Englishmen saw so much of their political world, it was in its nature licentious and doomed to inevitable anarchy and equally inevitable despotism, with Andrew Jackson as the most obvious candidate for Caesar or Bonaparte.[15]

Against these 'pure type' notions was the doctrine of special circumstances, run either way: American democracy only worked because of highly favourable circumstances or the defects of American politics afforded no argument against democracy because of the handicaps imposed on it by American conditions. Finally, and most sophisticated perhaps, there was the perception – a perception which seems in England to have been a distinctively Whiggish one, though it also appears among intelligent Tories – that the American Constitution was arguably, because of its elaborate construction, not even particularly democratic, and had been designed by its makers to check rather than to express the popular will. Generally speaking, during the Jacksonian period and up until the Civil War, English views of this character, while approving the intention to restrain democracy, often despaired of the outcome, or at least viewed it with anxiety.[16] It was not altogether an unsympathetic stance, but it was one which precluded any desire to take the American Constitution as a model for Britain; that was to come later. This stance was the one taken by the most celebrated English analysts of the American scene of the 1860s, Acton and Bagehot.

Both saw the crisis of the Union as a demonstration of the failure of the Founding Fathers to devise effective long-term constraints on popular sovereignty, though the remedies they would themselves have prescribed were different, and in fact opposed: Acton's centrifugal, Bagehot's centripetal. Acton, following for the most part Calhoun, was for the further sanctification of states' rights, including the right of secession. Bagehot, following the model he was to establish for his contemporaries as the English Constitution, was for the fusion of executive and legislature and a restricted franchise. These were responses to crisis and obviously this was an unlikely time for admiration of the American Constitution even by the most sympathetic. Bagehot was complaining that the Constitution was too rigid, Acton that it was not rigid enough. Acton's criticism was an understandable one at the time, even if it was arrived at through preoccupations which had little to do with America and everything to do with Europe. But there is no doubt that Bagehot's has been the more common English criticism, though the circumstances of the 1860s gave it a special persuasiveness. Bagehot's and Acton's comments reflect acute anxieties, not so much for the American Union, which is merely their reflector, but for the future of English and European liberalism in an age of advancing democracy which Tocqueville as well as historical events had taught English liberals to regard as their probable fate and against which they often sought anxiously to build dykes and barriers. Later, in the 1880s, when the United States after Reconstruction seemed again a success, liberals of this stamp, notably Dicey and Henry Maine, were to see in the American constitutional example precisely the safeguards they sought in vain in the British parliamentary tradition. But in the early sixties, understandably, the United States seemed not a model but a dire warning and dreadful failure.

Acton, in particular, saw the Civil War in universal and apocalyptic terms, as a global event comparable to the Declaration of Independence. The latter, was, as he wrote towards the end of his life, of such significance because it was 'the system of an international, extra-territorial universal Whig, far transcending the English model by its simplicity and rigour'.[17] Acton was not one of those Englishmen who sneered at the concept of a revolution based on principle; on the contrary, it was this for him that gave the American revolution its universal significance. But Acton's liberalism was complex, because it was both theoretical and highly principled *and* Whiggish so while he responded to the Declaration he also admired the Constitution. He lauded the political wisdom of the Convention and asserted the English origins of the constitution: 'Far from being the product of a democratic revolution and of an opposition to English institutions,' he said, 'the constitution of the United States was the result of a powerful reaction against democracy, and in favour of the traditions of the mother country.'[18] It was the very merits of the constitution and of the intentions of its founders that made its failure – an inevitable failure, Acton at that point, in 1861, was prepared to argue – a tragic one. Acton largely discounted all the checks and balances of the Constitution except the federal one; it was in federation above all that he saw 'the true natural check on absolute democracy' while 'states rights are at the same time the consummation and the guard of democracy."[19]

The agent of the Civil War and of the break-up of the Union Acton saw as a strong federal authority which had become an instrument of a theory of the omnipotence of the popular will, recognising no restraints. The federal constitution had been corrupted by Jacksonian democracy, a phenomenon which Acton saw in European, which for him meant universal, terms; it was the American equivalent of 'the spurious democracy of the French Revolution', which now had 'destroyed the Union, by disintegrating the remnants of English traditions and institutions.'[20] If the attempt to combine the English Whig heritage of liberty with democracy was to survive, its future must be with the Confederacy. The popular will would be forced, by the very character of the Confederacy's origin, to recognise some untransgressible limits, some boundaries set to political will by established rights. The Confederacy's existence was 'a distinct repudiation of the doctrine that the minority can enforce no rights, and the majority can commit no wrong. It is like passing from the dominion of an able despot into a constitutional kingdom.'[21] As Acton wrote to Lee after the war, 'secession filled me with hope, not as the destruction but as the redemption of Democracy'.[22]

The clue to Acton's attitude to secession was apparent from the beginning; his concerns were not primarily American but European, even, primarily, continental. As he wrote in 1861, secession 'is chiefly important in a political light as a protest and reaction against revolutionary doctrines, and as a move in the opposite direction to that which prevails in Europe'.[23] Acton tended to see the conflicts of nineteenth-century Europe, the secular republican, democratic and nationalist movements which threatened the existence of multinational states like Austria and the independence of the Catholic Church, in terms of a struggle for the political future of Europe between the English Whig principles of corporate rights and the rule of law, democratised and as it were universalised in America, and a French, Robespierrean and, as later generations might say, totalitarian version of democracy.[24] In those terms, the Confederacy stood for the English tradition of liberal constitutionalism, while an overmighty federal authority, corrupted by Jackson, stood for the French.

Some of Acton's views, particularly their continental and Catholic dimensions, were peculiar to himself; others, of course, given the common upper-class English bias towards the Confederacy, were less so. Of all English writers at the time of the Civil War the one who gave closest attention to the strictly constitutional aspects of the crisis was, as one

might expect, Walter Bagehot, and the similarities between him and
Acton are close enough to make the differences instructive. With
Bagehot, indeed, though his articles on America are not his most pre-
scient, we reach a new level of detail in British analysis of the American
Constitution. Bagehot approached the crisis of that constitution as a man
with two overriding preoccupations: cabinet government and the education of public opinion. The former he sometimes seems to speak of
almost with the proprietary rights of a discoverer; the latter he saw not
only as a large part of the function of Parliament and public men but as
his own role in life, the role of mediator between the insider's and the
spectator's view of public affairs, in a world in which the spectator was
also the vital electorate, the ultimate court of appeal of the nation.[25] In
both respects, the smoothness of executive government achieved by the
cabinet as a committee of the legislature, and the representative assembly
as the educator of public opinion, the great forum of the nation, he found
the American Constitution defective, even apart from the special conditions of the early 1860s, though he held that the specific defects of the
Constitution played a major part in creating those conditions. Unlike
Acton he had no admiration for federation as such,[26] and it was Presidential compared with cabinet government that drew his closest attention.
He agreed with Acton that the Union had been destroyed by the growth
of an uncontrolled democracy, but more explicitly and emphatically than
Acton he held up the details of the English model as the preferable alternative. 'The American constitution was, in its very essence, formed upon
an erroneous principle. Its wise founders wished to guard against the
characteristic evils of democracy; but they relied for this purpose upon
ingenious devices and superficial subtleties. They left the sovereign
people, sovereign still'. The ingenuities of the founders had been
counterproductive, and 'they have neither refined the polity, nor
restrained the people'.[27] Bagehot made a number of detailed criticisms.
The delay in the handing over of the presidental office had allowed the
crisis to worsen; the legalistic habit of mind fostered by the Constitution
disabled the Americans from taking a large view.[28] Later Bagehot was to
argue that it hampered the federal government in the task of reconstruction; he thought that the South should have been governed for a while
like a British crown colony.[29] The system of indirect presidential election
produced election by caucus and more or less ensured mediocrity in the
successful candidate;[30] Bagehot at that point shared the usual English
view of Lincoln as an uneducated mediocrity, though he recanted it
later. But the crux, for Bagehot, was the separation of Executive and
Legislature, which had both hindered the political education of the

nation and helped to precipitate the crisis. Because Congress and the President sit for fixed terms, the Constitution makes the government unresponsive to shifts in opinion and fails to educate that opinion by the spectacle of a vivid parliamentary life. The English 'have a daily critical, eager opinion on parliamentary issues, because those issues are decisive'.[31] In America, because of the separation of powers, 'Those who act cannot speak and those who speak cannot act . . . An English debate is conducted by our principal politicians towards a proximate result'.[32] Because of the fixed terms, and the hiatus between election and assumption of office, 'The Americans may be governed by the opinions of the supreme people, but it is by yesterday's opinion'.[33] And because of the fixed term, in a fluctuating situation a presidential election stakes all on a single irrevocable decision:

> the choice of a president being a much less remediable transaction than the choice of an English prime minister, it has more tendency to induce acts of popular resistance such as we have recently seen. [The Southern States might not have acted so violently] if a congressional defeat could at any moment have relieved them, as a parliamentary defeat does in England, of their unwelcome master.[34]

The defect of the Founding Fathers had been, of course, that they shared in the mistaken belief of their age that the essence of the English Constitution was a separation of powers and did not understand the nature of cabinet government. Their political understanding was indeed English and Whig, but it was eighteenth-century English Whig and, being rigid, the constitution they created had been unable to evolve as the English one had done.

> The constitution-makers of North America were not unnaturally misled by the political philosophy of their day . . . at that time no speculative politician perfectly commprehended that the essence of the English Constitution resided in the English Cabinet . . . [and] By keeping the two careers of legislation and of administration different they rendered the life of a high politician, of a great statesmen, aspiring to improve the laws and to regulate the policy of a great country, with them an impossibility. They have divided the greatest department of practical life into two halves, and neither of them is worth a man's having.[35]

Bagehot's claim may have been anachronistic in seeming to speak of the English Constitution in the eighteenth century as identical with its functioning in the mid-nineteenth but his fundamental argument was of wider application: a written constitution necessarily fastened a particular view of the Constitution upon posterity and perpetuated its errors.

Both Bagehot and Acton were able to see the survival of the Union, which they had declared impossible. Their later words were naturally more sober, without really amounting to retraction. Bagehot came to see American 'legalism' as having virtues as well as vices,[36] but on the Constitution itself his final judgement was one which has frequently been echoed by British authors since, including James Bryce and Denis Brogan: not an endorsement, certainly, but a kind of wondering admiration at the ability of the Americans to make their cumbersome institutions work so relatively well. 'They are so full of loyalty to their Constitution, so ingenious in resource, so sober-minded in danger, so active in repairing a mistake, that they may make almost any blunder they please, and yet not suffer for it as any other nation would suffer for a less blunder.'[37]

By the time Bagehot wrote that he could even have experienced a twinge of envy, for the obstacle to democratic misdemeanours which he had relied on in Britain had been thrown down by the second Reform Act in 1867. In the early 1860s he had been able to read lessons to the Americans, and probably to his own more democratically inclined countrymen, on the real means for restraining democratic excesses: not constitutional ingenuities, but simply a restricted franchise: '*Our* security against tyranny is the reasonableness, the respectable cultivation, the business-like moderation of the governing class itself' (my emphasis).[38] But after 1867 (and still more after the further extension of the franchise in 1884 which Bagehot dreaded, though he did not live to see it) no conservative liberal of Bagehot's type would be able to talk with that particular kind of confidence again. From the 1870s to the 1890s English constitutional self-congratulation was often replaced by acute anxiety. The period saw not only the third Reform Act but what liberal intellectuals saw as Gladstonian populism; they denounced as pandering to Irish peasant insurrection the tampering with the rights of property in Ireland, and reacted to the threat of the disintegration of the United Kingdom posed by Irish Home Rule. In the House of Commons itself the gentlemanly conventions by which it had been able to conduct its business were exploited to the point of anarchy in the procedural onslaught of the Irish members led by Parnell. All this made British constitutional confidence harder to sustain than at any time since the 1820s, or up until very recently. The 1880s and 1890s are pre-eminently the decades in which respected British authorities have expressed envy, as distinct from merely respect, for at least some specific aspects of the American Constitution, most notably judicial review, the powers and composition of the Upper House, and Federalism.

The most extreme of these advocates was the jurist and former Indian administrator, Sir Henry Maine, in his attack on democracy published in the mid-eighties under the title *Popular Government*. A substantial part of the book was given over to an encomium on the American Constitution compared with the British. The apparent lesson of the 1860s seemed reversed. It was the American Constitution wich seemed the success, while the 'flexibility' of the British had permitted its subversion by democracy, while preserving the old forms, with a minimum of hindrance. Maine agreed with Acton and Bagehot on the essentially British origins of the American Constitution, just as he agreed with Acton in contrasting the American and French republics to the advantage of the former, but the message of Bagehot's parable was reversed. Maine is, indeed, more detailed and specific than Bagehot or Acton on the connection between the American constitution and that of Britain in the eighteenth century. The former 'is in reality a version of the British constitution, as it must have presented itself to an observer in the second half of the last century'.[39] Maine explicitly sets that view of the constitution against Bagehot's: 'Mr Bagehot insisted that the great neglected fact in the English political system was the government of England by a Committee of the legislature, calling themselves the Cabinet. This is exactly the method of government to which George III refused to submit.'[40] The Founders of the American Constitution have taken George III's view, not that of the English Whigs. The only difference is that the presidency is elective and for a fixed term. Bicameralism, too, is part of the English heritage, and no constitution but the British could have suggested money bills arising only in the lower house.[41] The Supreme Court's mode of action – this was of course, to become a cliché – 'is entirely English. No general proposition is laid down by the English tribunal, unless it arises on the facts of the actual dispute submitted to it',[42] and it is largely to this that the success of the Supreme Court is due.

It was wise for Maine to establish the essentially English character of the United States Constitution in presenting it as an object of admiration, and possible imitation. More daring is his effective reversal of Bagehot's argument; the fact that the United States Constitution reflects an eighteenth-century English view is not its demerit but its virtue. The Americans took their stand at the right point; English constitutional evolution had in recent years become a corruption to which English 'flexibility' gave its opportunity. The Americans confronted early the problem, democracy, which the English have now to meet, and the Americans left their successors rich in expedients for controlling it and rendering it relatively harmless, while the British stand naked before it.

Maine contrasts the obstacles, procedural and substantive, to a bill before Congress, to those offered by the British system. America has a fundamental law – the sanctity of contracts – which would have rendered the Irish Land Act invalid; 'it is the bulwark of American individualism against democratic impatience and socialist fantasy'.[43] Moreover the fusion of executive and legislature in Britain , the fact, of which Bagehot so approved, that there the fate of the government is staked on the fate of a bill, militates against proper and cautious deliberation by the legislature. The crux of Maine's argument is that what are in effect constitutional amendments, like the Reform Act of 1884, can be passed with no more procedural obstacle than any other legislation and with the full weight of the Executive behind it. Maine also incidentally offers perhaps the earliest expression of what appears to have been, until recently, a rare English view, a preference for the slow grinding of Congressional investigation as compared with the brisk and often flippant British parliamentary question as a means of wringing information from the Executive.[44] But above all what was needed was to remove constitutional amendment from the ordinary process of legislation.

Maine and Bagehot represent extremes of the adulatory and the hostile in English views of the American Constitution. Since their political sympathies were not fundamentally dissimilar, the difference has to be accounted for almost entirely in terms of the sea-change undergone by British political life in the two decades between Bagehot's writings on the Civil War and Maine's *Popular Government*. One wonders what the radical admirers of the United States of the early nineteenth century would have said to find its constitution being held up for admiration and envy by a bitter critic of democracy. But Maine was extreme even in the 1880s. His fellow-jurist and Oxford colleague, A. V. Dicey, was on the whole more temperate, though he shared all Maine's gnawing anxieties and aversions. Dicey's tone in his *Introduction to the Law of the Constitution,* published in the same year as Maine's polemic, and furnished with an important new introduction in 1915 towards the end of his life, was, as befitted a textbook, judicial, even at times equivocal. Like others we have looked at he is anxious to trace English origins for the United States constitution: the relation of the Privy Council to the colonial legislatures, for example as the precedent for the Supreme Court.[45] As for almost every Victorian liberal intellectual, France was the awful warning, though Dicey's most obvious aversion was expressed as hostility to *droit administratif* rather than primarily to the Rousseauist doctrine of natural rights which Maine so detested; it was the common-law heritage which ranged Britain and the United States together against the political model represented by France. Like Maine, Dicey clearly hankers for some additional restraint on legislation which could be called 'constitutional', and unlike Maine he is tempted by the referendum, which he sees as essentially conservative, since it can only respond to the question put to it.[46] Like Maine and unlike Bagehot he approved the idea of detaching the fate of a particular bill from the fate of the ministry, and like Maine he envies the United States' constitutional sanctification of contracts.[47] But he sees the drawbacks as well as the attractions of judicial decisions on disputed political questions: respect for the impartiality of the judiciary may be compromised.[48] Above all Dicey was circumspect about the American example because he, as an ardent opponent of Irish Home Rule, was resistant to the notion widely canvassed in Britain at the turn of the century, of federal solutions to the problems both of preserving the United Kingdom in the face of Irish discontent and also of preserving the unity of an empire of self-governing dominions and providing for imperial defence.[49] Dicey makes the obvious points in rebuttal: the greater diversity of the Empire compared with the thirteen states, the danger of the creation of divided allegiances where none exist, and the fact that federalism was 'foreign to the historical and, so to speak, instinctive policy of English constitutionalists'. If some form of imperial federation was to come about it must grow rather than be developed 'by arduous feats of legislation'.[50]

Compared with Maine's implied call to constitutionalists to save the nation from itself by precisely such feats, Dicey preserved a more Burkean and gradualist stance. So, even more obviously did the third of this triumvirate of English lawyers of the 1880s, the leading British authority on the American Constitution, James Bryce, whose *American Commonwealth* was first published three years after Dicey's in 1888. Bryce's book in fact belongs as much to the cultural history of the United States, or even more so, as to that of Britain. We are told that over 200,000 copies of Bryce's book were bought in the United States in the fifty years after its publication.[51] Moreover, if we remember that Bryce said that five-sixths of his book came from conversations with Americans and one-sixth from books,[52] it is no criticism of its author if we feel that in many respects in reading him, America was only taking back in transmuted form what it had given. Not the whole of America, it has been pointed out, but, rather, an educated, Protestant and Yankee America.[53] All the same, if Bryce's attempted overview of the public life of the United States was inevitably taken from a particular perspective, his efforts to contain those multitudes were as much as could reasonably be expected of any one man. Bryce's tone, genial, tolerant, on the whole indulgent, certainly not infrequently condescending, can easily now seem smug, epitomising his historically conditioned limitations; Acton in his review spoke of Bryce's 'cheery indulgence for folly and error'.[54] One of the American celebrants of the half century of the *American Commonwealth*, which produced a commemorative and corrective volume in 1939, appeared to complain of a contrast when he said that 'Noted as a defender of liberal causes in his own country Bryce accepted the views and espoused the principles of the conservative, aristocratic and anti-democratic groups in American life',[55] a remark which betrayed no great understanding of mid-nineteenth-century English liberalism. This was to do Bryce less than justice. Moreover the equability and judiciousness of tone that he achieved was not given him automatically by his time, country and milieu of educated and academic liberalism. We have Maine as witness to that. The decade in which Bryce's book was written was in Britain a deeply troubled one, if in the United States it seemed one of expansiveness and success. It is relevant that Bryce, like Edward Freeman, who achieved a comparable geniality without envy towards the constitution of the United States, which to both of them was a mutation of the English adapted to new conditions,[56] was a Gladstonean Liberal and by English standards at the time a democrat as well as a Whig. Bryce neither envied nor on the whole gratuitously sneered. His complacency was a kind of achievement, and it gave him a clearer eye than the others we have considered. If his judgements on the American Constitution seem now often rather dully judicious and obvious and piecemeal compared with the fireworks of Maine or Bagehot, if it seems a matter of ticks and crosses of graduated sizes, a tick for the Senate and the Supreme Court, more criticism for the presidency and the House, this piecemeal approach was surely sane and reasonable. His commendation of a 'rigid' constitution as a substitute for more social and organic sources of conservatism was frank without being hysterical, and he recognised that the constitution was not in fact wholly rigid.[57] Above all, pervading Bryce's particular favourable and adverse verdicts there was a Burkean sense that the endurance of the Constitution, and the reverence in which Americans hold it, is something before which detailed criticism is humbled. The American Constitution, a century after its creation, seemed to Bryce no less a revered work of time than the English constitution itself,[58] and it was, accordingly, not for imitation. If there is a polemical sub-text in *The American Commonwealth* it is a polemic against Maine: 'Direct inferences from the success or failure of a particular constitutional arrangement or political usage in another country are rarely sound'[59] – this dictum at the opening of Bryce's book was no doubt a platitude, but it was not an empty one.

It was often noted of *The American Commonwealth*, by way of paying tribute to its stature, that it appeared fifty years after the work of Tocqueville.[60] When Harold Laski introduced the work of the young Denis Brogan to the British public in 1933, he appeared to lay claim to the same demi-centennial succession for it, rather sacrificing arithmetical pedantry to the requirements of symbolic numerology.[61] Arithmetic apart, it was not an absurd comparison. Brogan's book stands out in its period as Bryce's did in his, though its character was very different. Brogan's work and the work of Laski himself offer the opportunity for a comparison between the character of British interest in the American Constitution in the middle and later Victorian period and in the first half of the present century. There is, it seems, a slacking of urgency, at least in interest in the purely constitutional comparisons provided by America. To some extent Bryce may be responsible. The Survey provided by *The American Commonwealth* was so comprehensive that it must for a long time have discouraged imitation or anything but relatively specific emendation. In that sense *The American Commonwealth* is the climax of a whole period of commentary. But there are surely more deep-seated reasons. First the American Civil War and then a series of constitutional innovations in Britain, culminating in the Parliament Act of 1911, and the development of the self-governing Dominions within the Empire,[62] gave the American Constitution, from the 1860s until the early years of this century, a particular fascination. Democracy was, of course, the central issue, and the Americans were there first, with their constitutional survival-pack, in that unknown and probably hostile territory. The years between the First World War and the middle of this century provided no similar source of acute constitutional interest in America. In so far as British views of the working of American institutions were anxious, the anxiety attached not so much to the notion of the United States as a constitutional model or warning as to the effect of those institutions on America's capacity to sustain its new role as leader of the democratic and/or capitalist world. British views were, it seems, shaped for the first time less by events peculiar to Britain than by those in Europe and in America itself; the rejection of the League of Nations, the rise of Nazism and Communism, the Depression, the New Deal, Franklin Roosevelt's conflict with the Supreme Court, the anti-Bolshevik and anti-communist crusades which followed the two world wars. And in being so shaped they appear less distinctly British perhaps, though it may be that it needs an American eye to see just how much an outsider's views they nevertheless remain.

This in some ways more 'American' perspective did not entail, however, any greater generosity towards American constitutional idiosyncracies. With greater intimacy went the insider's prerogative of criticism, and the fellow-feeling was for the more critical spirits in America itself. It also, more surprisingly perhaps, but intelligibly given the intellectual climate of the time, went with a pressure to fit American tendencies, as Acton had done from a very different perspective, into a European (rather than distinctively British) pattern, and into a general view of the character and future of industrial society. Brogan's 1933 book *The American Political System* is a striking case of this. Bryce's tolerance was, for the moment at least, in abeyance. The criticism is as harsh as Bagehot's and occasionally similar.[63] It is plainly a young man's book: impatient, prodigal of advice, and, the author clearly felt, perhaps impertinent,[64] with a short way with constitutional pieties.

It is a mark of the times that Brogan's book actually began with the Supreme Court and mixed some praise with a good deal of criticism. Again, drawing clearly on the views of American scholars, epitomised by Charles A. Beard's 1913 book *An Economic Interpretation of the Constitution,* Brogan proclaims in blunt language the class origin of the Constitution, relatively neglecting the problems of local autonomy that federalism was designed to solve. The Constitution 'has shown its temper in the comparative ease with which it has been adapted to the needs of the rich and the astonishing difficulty with which it has been twisted into an instrument of the needs or wants of the poor'.[65] American legalism has been divisive and liberty in America has been no more secure than in other countries.[66] Judicial review makes legislation irresponsible and uncertain and judges are likely to be inherently conservative. Weakening the Supreme Court is made a high priority.[67] The presidency must be strengthened to meet the needs of the times.[68] Brogan's constitutional judgements are not all adverse, but 'the problems now facing the Americans are of the European type, and they are problems which the American government is much less fitted to deal with than are most European governments'.[69] For 'when all allowances are made, the spectacle of the American people living its political life according to canons laid down in the late eighteenth century to serve the political ideals and the economic rights of the American bourgeoisie almost beggars description'.[70]

Harold Laski, in his admiring Foreword, pressed equally hard the theme that it was Europe that showed the future to America – a kind of ironic inversion of Tocqueville. American politics too will become class-dominated and it is America, not Europe, which is under-equipped to meet them; 'the sources in which our own security is to be found are largely to seek in America', Laski goes on to instance the supremacy of the legislature over the judiciary, the neutrality of the civil service, local government largely free of business corruption, a method of discovering leaders better than a lottery, and a party organisation reflecting 'the total economic interest of the country'.[71] Bagehot would have agreed with all that except the last, and Laski had indeed, a decade earlier, confessed to Justice Holmes his agreement with Bagehot's view of the American Constitution,[72] Laski, who in his youth had been a pluralist and supporter of states' rights, became as time passed more and more hostile to the United States constitution as a barrier to 'the positive state'.[73] His 1940 book on the Presidency (dedicated 'To F.D.R. with affection and respect'[74]) called for large increases in presidential powers, and his 1949 book *The American Democracy* did little more than rehash the themes of the 1930s and announce more stridently than ever the imminent advent of class politics and the necessity for an American Labour Party on the British model.[75]

Brogan's trajectory took the opposite course. In an ironic Preface to a new edition of *The American Political System*, written in wartime in 1943, he confessed to something like a *volte face*:

> Eleven years ago one could be more finicky than is wise today. A reluctance to lay rash hands on 'that great work of time' the working constitution of the United States seems, today, more reasonable than it did in 1932. And that not only because the dangers of such a rash course seem more evident, but because the existing political system has proved capable of far more adaptation . . . than seemed likely . . .'[76]

In other words, in the Europe of the 1940s there seemed worse things than having a constitution made by eighteenth-century gentlemen, and Roosevelt and the New Deal had done their work. The constitutional frame had not been changed but the nation's political life had revived within its boundaries. In 1933 he had pictured America as a sort of Prometheus, weighed down by its constitutional chains. In 1943 the image seemed more that of a Houdini, chains unbroken, offering to perform the trick again wherever required. And by the time we come to Brogan's 1954 book *An Introduction to American Politics*[77] the tone is unabashedly celebratory. Those who think of the constitution as a bourgeois confidence trick are rebuked;[78] the emphasis is on union, charisma, solidarity; whatever its failings, the Constitution has proved itself by the national success it has permitted and the reverence it attracts. America was not another but somehow politically retarded Europe; it was its own place, with its own lights and pieties, its resiliences almost inexplicable to the outsider.[79] We seem to have come full circle back to Bryce: 'a constitution can survive in a form that makes it less and less adequate for the needs of the society it purports to serve . . . This has not happened in the United States. The constitution is still at the centre of American government and politics'.[80] The verdict could hardly be more emphatic.

This survey has been a brief and selective one, but even so it has made it clear that it does not readily yield a neat summary; divergences of opinion within Britain at any one time and the shifting variables of American and British politics preclude that. Some elements of approval and disparagement have, it is true, been fairly constant, though not, of course, necessarily only in British views. That the United States Constitution had been derived from the British precedent in various ways, rather than created *a priori*, has been, after the very early years, common ground among British commentators of many shades of political opinion. Its origins were seen, indeed, by the Victorians in terms of a distinctly conservative version of English Whiggism, by largely ignoring the question of Lockean or Radical Whig and *philosophe* inspiration. Acton was perhaps something of an exception here, though he drew, of course, the obvious distinction between the Declaration of Independence and the Constitution, and he fully shared in what seems to have been the general Victorian, intellectual liberal adulation of Hamilton and denigration of Jefferson.[81] But his catholic feeling for natural law made him more receptive than other English Whigs and liberals to that aspect of the thought of the eighteenth century, and he saw the American Revolution as a very much a real one even if the Constitution had to be seen as an attempt to curb it. Bryce, he thought, had neglected the power of the revolutionary element: 'ideas rooted in the future, reason cutting clean as Atropos'.[82]

The Constitution then, in British eyes, has consistently been seen as an adaptation, more or less successful and at least in some degree necessary, of British Whig constitutional notions and established English and colonial practice to a kingless independence and a society without an hereditary aristocracy but with strong traditions of local autonomy. The separation of legislature and Executive, however, has been often criticised and seldom envied, though Freeman allowed that the American model was probably not only the best for the Americans themselves but more suitable for British self-governing colonies, where the Westminster system had not been a success.[83] The Supreme Court, on the other hand, has drawn considerable respect and intermittent envy, with reservations about legalism and the mixing of political and judicial questions. The Senate, too, has been generally approved, while the most that has usually been found to say for the House of Representatives is that it does no particular harm. Verdicts on federation have naturally fluctuated depending on circumstances, deprecation of an *imperium in imperio* being matched by liberal endorsement of the value of variety [84] and conservative envy of the obstructions offered by a pluralistic polity to ill-considered innovation.[85] Bryce's view of the state legislatures as political laboratories was, as it were, the political scientist's gloss on conservative–liberal predilections.

Some elements of the American political system have almost always seemed alien and reprehensible in British eyes: not only, obviously, the electoral college, but the election of some judges, the locality qualification for representatives (which Bryce saw as an undesirable feature of democratic egalitarianism, differences in political capacity and experience being taken too lightly),[86] and the spoils system. Yet there has been a sigificant shift of emphasis generally in attitudes to the American Constitution in Britain in recent years, with more favourable views being taken, sometimes, on both right and left of the political spectrum. Calls for a bill of rights and judicial review are one symptom, and, we have seen, they are not unprecedented. Admiration for the 'openness' of American government epitomised in congressional investigating committees, on the other hand, seems of very recent, post-Watergate growth, and tends, of course, to come from a different point on the political spectrum, though the earlier example of Maine reminds us that this is not a constant[87] and may vary with political circumstances. To speak from memory for a moment, the inquisitorial powers of Senate committees, shining light into dark places, were not an object of liberal enthusiasm in Britain thirty years ago, when probably the only member of the Upper House the average Briton could have named was Joseph McCarthy.

The other main British preoccupation with the working of the American Constitution, this time a critical one, continues a long-standing adverse judgement of its effects on the formation of a consistent and coherent foreign policy. What has changed, of course, is the feelings which lie behind this criticism, Victorian irritation being replaced by twentieth-century anxiety. Admittedly, in the last century the blame was often attributed to 'democracy' rather than to the separation of powers, but the main lines of criticism are still familiar. America, as Tocqueville had said, was poorly equipped to conduct a foreign policy, but she hardly needed one. It has often seemed to anxious British observers that only the latter part of the judgement needs revision.

NOTES

1 E.g., 'Political causes of the American Revolution', in the *Rambler,* n.s., 3rd ser., V, May 1861, pp. 17-61, reprinted in *Selected Writings of Lord Acton,* ed. Rufus J. Fears, 3 vols. Indianapolis, 1985, I, pp. 240-43.

2 According to Edmund Ions, 'Historically Bryce's standpoint was largely that of a highly educated Protestant American living in the 1880s.' Edmund Ions, *James Bryce and American Democracy, 1870-1922,* London, 1968, p. 141. Bryce's use of Cooley was adversely commented on by Charles G. Haines in *Bryce's American Commowealth. Fiftieth Anniversary ,* ed. Robert C. Brooks, New York, 1939, p. 8.

3 H. A. L. Fisher, *James Bryce,* 2 vols., London, 1927, I, p. 135.

4 Ions, *James Bryce,* p. 29. See also H. A. Tulloch, 'Changing British attitudes towards the United States in the 1880s', *Historical Journal,* XX 4, 1977, pp. 825-40. Tulloch rather exaggerates, I think, the importance of Freeman's influence.

5 Stefan Collini has pointed to the manuscript evidence for Bryce's irritation with Maine when composing *The American Commonwealth.* Stefan Collini, Donald Winch, and John Burrow, *That Noble Science of Politics. A Study in Nineteenth-Century Intellectual History,* Cambridge, 1983, p. 241.

6 E.g., Laski to Justice Holmes, 18 October, 1921, *The Holmes–Laski Letters. The Correspondence of Mr Justice Holmes & Harold J. Laski, 1916-1935,* ed. Mark de Wolfe Howe, 2 vols., London, 1953, I, p. 375.

7 Crook sees 1832 as something of a turning-point in British attitudes to American democracy, ushering in a period of more informed and moderate comment. David P. Crook, *American Democracy in Engish Politics, 1815-1850,* Oxford, 1965, pp. 201-2.

8 *Ibid,* p. 21.

9 M. J. C. Vile, *Constitutionalism and the Separation of Powers,* Oxford, 1967, p. 115.

10 E.g., Francis Jeffrey quoted in Crook, *American Democracy,* p. 79, n. 2.

11 For the influence of this on nineteenth-century political ideas, see Collini *et al., That Noble Science,* pp. 19-20, 239-46, and especially chs. iv, v, and vi.

12 Crook, *American Democracy,* pp. 23-4, 81-90.

13 W. R. Greg was referring to the American's 'Anglo-Saxon race' in the *Edinburgh Review* in 1852. Cited Crook, *American Democracy,* p. 90. Cf. *Ibid.,* p. 83.

14 This argument formed part of the response to Robert Lowe's citation of the defects of American democracy in the public debate surrounding the 1867 Reform Act. See, e.g., Leslie Stephen, 'On the choice of representatives by popular constituencies', in *Essays on Reform,* London, 1867, pp. 99-100. Cf. A. O. Rutson, in the same volume, pp. 284-5.

15 Crook, *American Democracy* pp. 112, 120, 150.

16 *Ibid.,* pp. 143-7.

17 'Lectures on the French Revolution', in *Selected Writings of Lord Acton,* ed. Rufus J. Fears, I, p. 198.

18 'Political causes of the American Revolution', in Fears, *Selected Writings,* I, p. 219.

19 'Lectures on the French Revolution', in Fears, *Selected Writings,* I, p. 211.

20 'Political causes', in Fears, *Selected Writings,* I, p. 261.

21 'The Civil War in America' (1866), in Fears, *Selected Writings,* I. p. 277.

22 Acton to Robert E. Lee, 4 November 1866, in Fears, *Selected Writings,* I, p. 363.

23 'Political causes', in Fears, *Selected Writings,* I, p. 262.

24 See particularly his review of Erskine May's *Democracy in Europe* in Fears, *Selected Writings,* I, pp. 54-85.
25 On this see Collini, *et al., That Noble Science,* pp. 166-7, 178-81.
26 Bagehot argued at this point (1861) that federation was a fair-weather constitution and intrinsically brittle. 'The American Constitution at the present crisis', *The Collected Works of Walter Bagehot,* ed. Norman St John Stevas, 9 vols. London, 1965-78, IV, p. 291.
27 *Ibid.,* p. 313.
28 *Ibid.,* p. 283.
29 'The American difficulty' (1876), *Collected Works,* VIII, p. 369. Bagehot added: 'they have constitutionalism on the brain'.
30 'The American Constitution at the present crisis' (1861), *Collected Works,* IV, pp. 305-6.
31 'The federal government responsible for federal apathy' (1863), *Collected Works,* VI
32 *Ibid.,* pp. 170-1.
33 *Ibid.,* p. 169.
34 *Collected Works,* IV, p. 238.
35 'The American Constitution at the present crisis', *Collected Works,* IV, pp. 309-10.
36 Essentially this amounted to the Constitution's having been able to generate its own kind of deference. 'It is the prepossession, the prejudice, in favour of the Constitution . . . which has given that Constitution its great success. Political institutions cannot work without a great deal of blind belief in them.' 'The American difficulty', *Collected Works,* VIII, p. 369.
37 *Ibid.,* p. 368.
38 'The American Constitution and the present crisis', *Collected Works,* IV, p. 301.
39 Sir Henry Maine, *Popular Government,* London, 1885, pp. 207-8.
40 *Ibid.,* p. 213.
41 *Ibid.,* p. 230.
42 *Ibid.,* p. 223.
43 *Ibid.,* p. 248.
44 *Ibid.,* pp. 236-9.
45 A. V. Dicey, *Introduction to the Law of the Constitution,* 8th ed., London, 1915, p. 160.
46 *Ibid.,*pp. xcvii-xcviii.
47 *Ibid.,* p. xcix. Dicey also makes the point (p. 170) that in the United States the Irish Land Act would have been declared unconstitutional and void. W. E. H. Lecky, who was an Irish Protestant, made the same point about the constitutional protection for the sanctity of contract in his generally admiring view of the American Constitution (as distinct from his considerably less favourable view of current American politics) in his *Democracy and Liberty,* new ed., London, 1899, 2 vols. I, p. viii.
48 Dicey, *Introduction,* p. lxxviii.
49 E.g., *Imperial Federation and Colonization from 1880-1894. Papers and Addresses by Lord Brasser,* ed. Arthur H. Loring and K. J. Beadon, London, 1895, pp. 126, 133. On this issue see James Bryce, 'Flexible and rigid constitutions', in his *Studies in History and Jurisprudence,* 2 vols., Oxford, 1901, I, pp. 245-9, and Dicey, *Introduction,* pp. lxxii-lxc.
50 Dicey, *Introduction,* p. lxxvi.
51 Brooks, *Bryce's American Commonwealth,* p. 76.
52 Ions, *James Bryce,*

53 *Ibid.,* pp. 138, 141.

54 Fears, *Selected Writings,* I, p. 397.

55 Charles G. Haines in Brooks, *Bryce's American Commonwealth,* p. 4.

56 James Bryce, *The American Commonwealth,* London, 1910, 2 vols., I, pp. 34, 408. Cf. E. A. Freeman, *Some Impressions of the United States,* New York, 1883, pp. 116-17, 122, 135, 138.

57 A 'rigid' constitution 'tends to render the inevitable process of modification gradual and tentative'. Bryce, *The American Commnwealth,* I, p. 407.

58 *Ibid.,* p. 305n.

59 *Ibid.,* p. 8.

60 E.g. Brooks, *Bryce's American Commonwealth,* p. 16.

61 D.W. Brogan, *The American Political System,* London 1943 (1st. ed. 1933). Foreword to first edition by Harold J. Laski, p. xxxi.

62 Dicey pointed out that the British North America Act (1867) spoke in its preamble of the analogy between the constitution of Canada and the United Kingdom, where 'Kingdom' was a 'diplomatic inaccuracy' for 'United States'; 'no one can study the provisions of the British North America Act, 1867, without seeing that its authors had the American Constitution constantly before their eyes'. Dicey, *Introduction* p. 162. In a footnote in later editions he acknowledged that Canada had a ministerial, not a presidential, system and stressed that he was speaking essentially of Federation.

63 E.g., 'The Spirit of the America Constitution is the spirit of the lawyer.' Brogan, *American Political System,*

64 *Ibid.,* Preface to 1st edition.

65 *Ibid.,* p. 17.

66 *Ibid.,* p. 33.

67 *Ibid.,* p. 23, 33, 381.

68 *Ibid.,* p. 381-2.

69 *Ibid.,* p. 380.

70 *Ibid.,* p. 35.

71 *Ibid.,* p. xxxii.

72 Letter to Holmes, 13 April 1923. *The Holmes–Laski Letters,* 1, 494. Earlier Laski had described the constitution to Holmes as 'the worst instrument of government the mind of man has conceived'. *Ibid.,* p. 475.

73 See, e.g., Harold J. Laski, *Studies in the Problem of Sovereignty,* Oxford, 1917. At that point Laski doubted 'whether, fundamentally, there is truth in the judgement that federalism is conservative' (p. 275).

74 Harold J. Laski, *The American Presidency. An Interpretation,* London, 1940.

75 These adverse judgements are confirmed in Herbert A. Deane, *The Political Ideas of Harold J. Laski,* New York, 1955, pp. 304-7.

76 Brogan, *American Political System,* p. vi.

77 Published in the US as *Politics in America.*

78 D.W. Brogan, *An Introduction to American Politics,* London, 1954, p. 8.

79 *Ibid.,* p. 10.

80 *Ibid.,* p. 2.

81 Hamilton's chosen means might be regarded as mistaken, but his intentions were generally applauded.

82 Fears, *Selected Writings,* I, p. 404.

83 E. A. Freeman, 'Presidential government' (1864), in *Historical Essays,* 1st ser., 3rd. ed., London 1875, pp. 396-7, 405-6. Cf. Freeman, *Some Impressions of the United*

States, pp. 121-2.

84 Bryce spoke the liberal slang of his generation when he referred to its mitigation of 'the terrible monotony of life', *The America Commonwealth* I, 345.

85 This was a long-established conservative view, put by the Tory spokesman John Wilson Croker in the 1830s. See Crook, *American Democracy,* p. 144.

86 Bryce, *The American Commonwealth,* I, p. 197.

87 See above, n.44.

9

The Supreme Court and the Constitution after one century

A. E. CAMPBELL
University of Birmingham

Constitutional law [wrote a commentator in 1900], although based upon a fixed form of words, seems to be a barometer peculiarly susceptible to changes in that strange atmosphere termed, for want of a better word, public opinion. . . . Although not so sensitive as a mere statute, a constitution sometimes appears more like a legislative act than a rule of law; for its interpretation varies – rightly or wrongly – as varies the legislative mind of the people.[1]

As we celebrate the two-hundredth anniversary of the Constitution of the United States, the air is loud with debate about how and how far a fundamental law so old can be brought into line with the felt needs of a modern society greatly different from anything the Founding Fathers could have envisaged. Some argue that the time has come for a thorough-going revision, something not to be undertaken lightly but surely not inappropriate every couple of centuries or so. On a slightly lower level the debate rages between those who argue that judges must try to discover the 'original intent' of the framers – the school of which Judge Robert H. Bork was pushed to the forefront by his ill-fated nomination to the Supreme Court – and those who contend that such an enterprise is impossible (at least in any full sense) and that the effort to undertake it leads to confusion and to the invention of the past.

Centenaries concentrate the mind, and this is the second centenary of the Constitution, not the first. A hundred years ago or so, men also were conscious of the great differences between their society and that of the Founding Fathers, and of the need to adapt the Constitution to their time. If the high point of the debate came rather after the centenary, as it did – in the Progressive period rather than in 1887 itself – it may be that the explanation lies in the shadow of the Civil War. The North–South division had dominated national life for a generation before 1861, and constitutional discussion with everything else. After the war the desire to get back to normal, the need to rebuild the Union and to cut back the powers of the federal government, and perhaps the need to digest three Reconstruction amendments, may well have delayed formal consideration of the Constitution. The victors in what had been a highly conservative Civil War had some reluctance to question the instrument under which – perhaps even for which – the war had been fought. Nevertheless changing times and changing needs had their imperatives at the end of the nineteenth century as at the end of the twentieth. Today, however, we can look back not only on the Constitution but also on its critics of a century ago with the eyes of historians. Some similarities and differences may throw light on our own problems.

As it is approached by philosophers of law, the problem of how a text of one era can be reinterpreted in another is always the same problem, however much answers may differ. To historians, however, the problem is always specific to time and place and thus always different. So with this one. In one sense, a written constitution is an obvious thing for a state to have. The world is full of them. Britain is something of an anomaly in lacking one. Every state embodies certain principles and practices. Why not set them down, as clearly as possible, so that the nation and the world may know what they are? But more importantly, every constitution is an attempt to guard against certain dangers, and that, of course, is particularly true of such parts of it as may come to be called a bill of rights. The historian, then, may properly ask from what quarter danger is thought likely to come. If that changes over time, so too must the interpretation of the Constitution – if it is not amended.

* It is surely clear that the tyranny of government was still a lively fear when the Constitution was written. The Founding Fathers quietly took precautions against the tyranny of the mob, but they were forced to concede more explicit restrictions on the power of the federal government than they had wanted. The contrast enshrined in the Constitution is that between the people and a government distinct from them – and all too distant from them – with interests and temptations not theirs. By implication 'the people' on the one side and 'the government' on the other are both in some sense unitary, almost possessed of personality. They are not equal, of course, for one is the creature of the other, yet the fear was that the creature might take on a life of its own, might, so to say, rebel against its master.

If that had remained the perceived danger, there would probably have been little discussion of the Constitution, from its ratification to our own day. The Constitution does not engage the affections of Americans. The celebration of independence was quickly and enthusiastically made the very centre of American political ritual; the Constitution was never so · worshipped. So obvious is the point that it is hard not to feel that if the Constitution is being celebrated in 1987 it is in much the same spirit as that in which the Constitutional Union party was formed in 1860. The coming of the Civil War, of course, is evidence that a very different kind of danger overtook the first. Two groups within the country, at odds with each other, were each trying to ensure that the federal government acted to protect what each claimed as its rights. No government could have satisfied both; and – for a variety of incidental reasons not here germane – the war came. By the victory of one side, and by constitutional amendment, the issues of the Civil War were settled. They could not have been settled by compromise, and the problem was not one the Founding Fathers had foreseen or addressed.

It would be absurd to pretend that the United States today is in any danger of falling apart. Nevertheless there are important similarities between claims made today and those made in ante-bellum days. One element in President Reagan's political rhetoric is a distraction. The contention that the federal government has become too large, too powerful, too burdensome, is not the fear of 1787 realised. Rather President Reagan, like Mrs Thatcher in this country, has chosen to speak for one constituency, those who pay taxes, as against another, those who benefit from tax expenditures. That is an old debate – who gets what?, who pays what? – but it has never proved impossible to reconcile in democratic societies, though stubborn presidents or prime ministers may make it harder. Nor, more importantly, is the Constitution drawn essentially into the argument, for a federal income tax is now part of it.

What is happening today, surely, is that once again different groups within society, whose interests and principles are opposed and ultimately irreconcilable, are demanding the protection of the federal government for their rights – real or alleged – and are insisting that the Constitution guarantees those rights. Consider the arguments that spun like a tornado round the confirmation of Judge Bork. The right-to-life lobby against the right-to-abortion lobby. The advocates of 'creation science' against opponents who plead the separation of Church and State. Those for creative discrimination in favour of minorities against those opposed to it. In none of these debates is 'the government' set against a united citizenry. In all of them each of two opposed groups claims that the Constitution – properly interpreted – supports its position. As one polemicist recently put the point, 'Americans of left and right no longer share the same religion, the same values, the same codes of morality; we only inhabit the same piece of land.' And he went on to develop a contention that John Brown or William Lloyd Garrison might well have applauded, that strength of conviction on a moral issue justifies extra-constitutional activity. The words are those of an immoderate man, and journalism has its own rules, but the cleavage described is not one to be bridged by constitutional interpretation or even amendment.[2]

The years around and following the first centenary of the Constitution saw a quite different danger, and one with quite different consequences for constitutional debate. To recapitulate, the need seen after the Civil War was that the power of the federal government, enlarged by war, should be diminished. As the century neared its end, however, the perceived danger was that the power of governments, and especially of the federal government, was too little, not that it was too great. When the Constitution was criticised it was because it unnecessarily limited the power of the federal government to take necessary action on behalf of the people. In a word, the people were again made unitary, almost possessed of personality, and so was the federal government; but they were now not opposed. They were on the same side. Who, or what, then, were on the other side? Against what was the Constitution being invoked? Where was the danger? Most importantly, it was now from men of excessive power, whose use of that power denied democratic equality and liberty. The hue and cry in the late nineteenth century was against what Tudor England knew as the over-mighty subject.

The typical over-mighty subject of earlier historical eras had been of a particular sort. He had been a creature of the government – a creature of the king – whose powers had waxed until he forgot their origin and turned them against their grantor. The charge against him was summed up in Queen Elizabeth I's famous injunction to an arrogant bishop to 'remember what you were before I made you what you are'. The favoured subject had benefited from government grants, and public hostility against privileges so granted was endemic in European history while they survived. The American example is Andrew Jackson's struggle against the Second Bank of the United States, for it was a large part of the charge against Nicholas Biddle that his bank had been given a privileged position which it was now using against the public welfare. In the late nineteenth century, however, no such charge could be made. A Rockefeller, a Carnegie, a Morgan, owed no part of his dominance to governmental favour. If monopoly had been created, it was by means initially open to all. That was a larger challenge. Hostility to privilege had been built into the American system from the start; but the whole thrust of nineteenth-century jurisprudence had been to encourage private enterprise, to allow and reward the release of creative energy.[3] If that policy were now to be reversed or modified in any degree, fundamental changes in American attitudes would be needed, and, moreover, they would have to be introduced into the law. Nothing in the tradition of American thought made that easy or obvious. Americans lacked an intellectual framework to accommodate such change. It is not surprising that they groped their way towards new rules, as towards new attitudes, in a hesitant, piecemeal and often contradictory fashion. The search for order, to borrow Robert Wiebe's well-known phrase, was a sort of national hunt-the-thimble – the country sometimes warmer, sometimes cooler – rather than planned progress.[4]

Paradoxically, some such process was implicit in American constitutionalism. Then as now the people had the constitutional right to be wrong, and the constitutional right to change their minds. What was needed was a change of practice that did not imply a rejection of the past. In such a process legislation, both state and national, of course played a large part; but it is hard to deny that the courts, and especially the Supreme Court, were extraordinarily important in mediating change, bringing in small shifts in this case or that, while usually insisting on some point of difference from earlier rulings to justify the change. In a democracy it is not unprincipled, it is necessary, for courts to see to it that the law does not stray too far from the main thrust of public opinion. If that is 'following the election returns', so be it. But that can only be done when there *is* a main thrust of public opinion, a basic consensus. Then there was, just as in some highly important matters there is no such consensus today. One reason forming that consensus was the sheer speed of change. A line of argument that looked new and dangerous one day – at least to conservatives – was shown to be excessively timid and inadequate the next. American society was not splitting, it was adapting. Even when the political battle raged most fiercely – and perhaps its climax was the presidential election of 1896 – it did not move outside an arena formed by shared American middle-class values.

The best evidence for that is to be found in the relationship among the three co-ordinate branches of the federal government. The reaction against the Civil War had seen thirty years of congressional leadership, with the presidential role downgraded. Presidents exercised such leadership as they did exercise by quiet and unobtrusive means. They were not without influence, but it was greatest when least noticed. To that rule Theodore Roosevelt, undeniably a noisy president, was the first and greatest exception; but while he found the White House a 'bully pulpit', exhortation is what a pulpit allows. He made no claim – hardly even in foreign affairs – to escape from the control of Congress or to set up the presidency as an independent power centre, and his requests for legislation were always controlled by a nice sense of what Congress, and public opinion behind it, could be persuaded to stand. Roosevelt was a man who, like President Reagan, took his right of nomination to the Supreme Court seriously, and sought justices who broadly shared his view of what the national interest required. Yet his three appointments were not seriously challenged by an organised opposition objecting to the nominees' constitutional views; nor, for that matter, had been the appointments of his predecessors. Provided that his legal credentials were respectable, what a president then needed was the approval of the Senators of the nominee's state.[5]

It is not easy to derive evidence of clear purpose from the cases tackled by the Court in the last decade of the nineteenth century, and the first years of the twentieth. The Court was busy, and even then it had some right to select those cases it would hear. The Court was a varied one. Most of its members were fairly recent appointments, but they had been appointed by several presidents, of both parties, and by presidents of generally conservative disposition until Theodore Roosevelt's succession. It was not, on the whole, a distinguished Court. Field had been eminent, but he continued to serve distinctly too long and was now at the end of his career. Harlan was eminent, but he was increasingly old-fashioned and increasingly to be found in dissent. Holmes, arriving in 1902, became eminent, but again his most notable contributions were made in dissent. The rest of the Court were grey men. Even a surprising number of the important decisions were by narrow majorities, and a surprising number of the opinions had omissions or logical weaknesses that later scholars have not failed to point out. Probably, too, the legal style of the time was more discursive than modern practice approves.

Nevertheless there was a sort of drift to the decisions, especially in the economic matters with which many of them dealt. The essence of it was a growing recognition that economic life was not merely composed of the clash of private interests, which the state must in some way try to mediate, but that there might be a public interest, or even a sufficient collectivity of private interests, which the state must act more positively to protect or advance. In another aspect, the change was away from the old idea of liberty as freedom from government interference, and towards the larger idea of liberty as the ability of the individual to fulfil his purposes, an idea that was to dominate at least the first six decades of the twentieth century. As one standard text puts it, 'In the late nineteenth century the dominance of the corporation, based to a very great extent on laissez-faire law and policy, served to discredit the idea of negative liberty.⁶ What is remarkable, in historical perspective, is the ease, if not the speed or elegance, with which so large a philosophical change was accomplished.

Because of the revolution in transport and communications, with the consequent development of a national market and of national corporations, some matters could be regulated only by the federal government if at all. Historians who have seen the Court as an obstacle to reform may well have given too much attention to one or two dramatic cases, chief among them *Pollock* v *Farmers' Loan and Trust Co.*⁷ (essentially 1895, though it was heard twice), which struck down the federal income tax and surprised many competent observers by doing so, and *United States* v *E. C. Knight Co.*⁸ (1895), which seemed to restrict unduly the power of Congress to regulate commerce. Yet the Pollock case (long nullified, of course, by the Sixteenth Amendment) took very narrow ground and was one of the five to four decisions of those years; and the Knight decision provided little in the way of precedent. As Fuller, C.J., pointed out, hardly anything did not affect interstate commerce in some degree. If any effect, however indirect or slight, were to allow federal interference, the Constitution's careful enumeration of federal powers would be nullified.⁹ Yet a total ban would also have that effect. No restriction imposed by the Court could be other than arbitrary. What mattered was that the Court was aware of the difficulty, and of the new problem that the nation was facing. *Knowlton* v. *Moore*¹⁰ (1900) and *McCray* v. *United States*¹¹ (1904) show the Court moving in the other direction in taxation matters, while *Champion* v. *Ames*¹² (1903) as well as the Northern Securities Co.¹³ case in 1904 show it doing so in the control of interstate commerce. These counter-examples are certainly late, and have sometimes been cited as evidence of the Court's disposition to follow the election returns. It takes time for a case to reach the Court,¹⁴ but the important argument is not that the Court was steadily moving towards the regulation of business. (The Northern Securities Co. decision was by five to four with Oliver Wendell Holmes, Roosevelt's first nominee, leading the dissenters.) What is more important is that the Court was quietly allowing the extension of Congressional activity, if in a haphazard and sometimes inconsistent way. Though the first Roosevelt was a combative man who did not take kindly to opposition, there developed no serious sense that the Court was acting to frustrate necessary, government-led reform.

If the Court was broadly ready to defer to the right of Congress to determine matters of policy, it was ready also to see presidential power enlarged. The case of *Field* v. *Clark*¹⁵ in 1892 allowed the delegation of power to the president to determine when to invoke the terms of a tariff

law and *Buttfield* v. *Stranahan*[16] in 1904 allowed him the same power
with respect to an act governing the import of tea. In each case – the first
decided by a seven-to-two majority and the second unanimously though
by a Court of seven only – the question at issue was whether there had
been an improper delegation to the executive of power confined by the
Constitution to the legislative. Perhaps neither case was particularly
important in itself, and the rulings were in accord with common sense,
but the separation of powers had been weakened and was to be further
weakened later.

An example of a different sort but pointing in the same direction was
the famous case of *In re Debs*[17] of 1895. There the Court upheld the
issuing of an injunction, by a lower federal court, against the strikers in
the great Pullman strike of 1894. The injunction had been issued at the
request of the President, but against the protest of Governor Altgeld of
the State concerned, Illinois. This is one of the cases often cited as evidence of a pro-business, anti-labour bias in the Court. It cannot, however, be cited as evidence of any distrust of an enlarged executive. That
the governor, had he so wished, could have asked for an injunction is not
in dispute. But did the President have any right to ask for it? He could
not have grounded that right in common law, and no reference was made
to any federal law authorising him to act. The distinction between legislative and executive branches, and the careful restriction of federal
powers, were both being whittled away. The Court was begining to
speak and think as if the identity of interest between Congress and president, and between federal government and country could generally be
assumed.

If the general effect of the Court's work was to enlarge the powers of
the federal government, it was not at the expense of state governments.
Governmental power still had to be divided, but increasingly there was
more of it to divide. Where the states were concerned, the effect was
chiefly made by weakening the clause of the Constitution (Article I,
section 10, 1) prohibiting a state from passing a 'law impairing the obligation of contracts'. The point was finally spelt out in *Manigault* v.
Springs in 1905, which laid down that no law of contract could 'prevent
the State from exercising such powers as are vested in it for the promotion of the common weal, or are necessary for the general good of the
public, though contracts previously entered into between individuals
may thereby be affected'.[18] Long before that date, however, it is safe to
say that the contract clause had not proved useful in efforts to strike
down state laws.

Yet the charge most commonly made is that the Fourteenth Amendment was used to inhibit state action, by extending the idea of due process from the procedural to the substantive. It can, of course, be contended that the Fourteenth Amendment had had the effect of bringing state and federal governments more into line. The federal government had long been prohibited – by the Fifth Amendment – from depriving any 'person' of 'life, liberty, or property, without due process of law'; and the passive form of that article, which did not identify any government, might well have been taken to cover state governments also. Nevertheless, it was thought necessary to extend the ban specifically to state governments in the Fourteenth Amendment, section 1. By implication the federal government, once the more restricted, had been put on an equal footing, a significant shift if one little noticed at the time of the Amendment. Yet whatever the shift in the relations of the two American governments, was not the more significant development the enlargement of the concept of due process? That contention weakens on enquiry, and it does so largely because of the uncertainty of the Court's rulings. The strongest evidence is from a late case – *Lochner* v. *New York*[19] in 1905 – but that was a five-to-four decision, the dissenters already foreshadowed some of the arguments that Louis Brandeis was later to use to such effect, and the Court had already taken a somewhat different tack in earlier cases. Again, in the cases concerning railroad rates, the Court took narrow ground. The way remained open for different rulings in different cases – and every case is, by definition, different. The conception of substantive due process might indeed be used to limit state action. In practice it was usually not so used and, more particularly, it was not used in a manner to preclude later reconsideration. The Court in these years was not notable either for slavish adherence to precedent or for precise and unambiguous reasoning. These may be legal weaknesses; they are sometimes political virtues.[20]

One other area of Court activity deserves special attention – that of race relations in the broadest sense. Perhaps the best-known case of the whole period is *Plessy* v. *Ferguson*[21] of 1896, the case which allowed the provision of 'separate but equal' accommodation for blacks and whites on railroads, and set the precedent which lasted until it was overturned by *Brown* v. *Board of Education* sixty years later. Yet that was only one case to make clear the significant streak of racism in American society at the time. The danger from racial minorities loomed as large as that from ideological minorities. Again the thrust of the Court's decisions was towards enlarging governmental power. The *Chinese Exclusion* Case[22] of 1889 allowed the exclusion of a Chinese who had already been granted a re-entry permit to the country, and *Fong Yue Ting* v. *United States*[23] four years later declined to interfere with a deportation order made in conformity with an act not passed when Fong had entered the country. Still more important were the so-called 'insular cases' just after the turn of the century, in which the Court groped its way towards an entirely new doctrine controlling the nation's new possessions, the doctrine that only after these had been 'incorporated' into the United States – a matter completely in the discretion of Congress – did the full protection of the Constitution extend to their peoples. Until then they were entitled to fundamental rights, but not to those 'procedural, remedial, or formal', nor, of course, to citizenship. Here was a grant of power to Congress which cannot be derived from the Constitution. It is hardly too much to say that some such doctrine was needed and so it was invented.

What do such developments, taken together, allow us to say about the Constitution at that time, and about American society as viewed through the constitutional lens? They do not allow us to identify any deliberate or clearly formulated shift in jurisprudence. The decisions are too diffuse and inconsistent for that. Nor do they show any consistent economic bias, either in favour of business or against it, either in favour of organised labour or against it. They do show a general concern that governments should not be denied necessary powers, and a sense that those 'necessary' powers were now greater than they had been a century before. Given that belief, lines of demarcation between state and federal authority could not be drawn with logical clarity but they could be drawn without much difficulty. A comment of 1956 could have been written sixty years earlier:

> Once it was thought that the test of what states may do is what the nation may not do, or that the test of what the states may not do is what the nation may do, but the criteria are no longer so clear cut as that. The involutions of state power must be considered with greater particularity than can be compressed into a formula.[24]

Given that belief, too, the Constitution was adapted surprisingly easily. With the possible exception of Harlan, all the Justices recognized the need for change. None prefigured the arguments of present-day legal conservatives. For all their differences they would not have thought the immediate intentions of the Founding Fathers an adequate guide.

If the ease of the adaptation is surprising, it is because of its scope. What was happening was a change greater than any under discussion today, nothing less than the change from the concept that governments are to be distrusted and checked to the concept that they are the natural agents of the people in carrying out national purposes. That implies that there are such purposes, and therefore that the people has a large degree of unity. Such public unity is, of course, never quite complete. For all the intensity of the debate over the making and ratification of the Constitution, sufficient unity existed in 1787. So one hundred years later, but it was of a different kind. The first unity had been the shared commitment of self-reliant men to freedom from unnecessary government interference. The second was a communal unity which made the United States more nearly a nation–state like other nation–states, a power among the powers, than it has been before or since. The United States was more fully the embodiment of an ethnic culture than before or since. American racism at the time was not something incidental; it was an essential aspect of American unity as then felt.

Where the necessary degree of social cohesion exists, it appears that a constitution can be modified, or indeed wrenched to purposes quite unforeseen by its framers, with little difficulty; where it is lacking, the Constitution, like everything else, is drawn into a controversy whose origins are elsewhere. This must suggest that those historians who have seen the Populist movement, for example, as a serious and fundamental criticism of American values, or who have identified a 'psychic crisis' in the country at the end of the nineteenth century, are at least exaggerating.[25] The 'legislative mind of the people', as interpreted by the Supreme Court, was not divided against itself.

NOTES

1 John Gorham Palfrey, 'The growth of the idea of annexation, and its bearing upon constitutional law', *Harvard Law Review* XIII, 1900, pp. 371-99, at p. 371.

2 Patrick Buchanan, 'Congress in the dock', *The Times*, 21 July 1987, p. 10 (reprinted from *The Washington Post*). Patrick Buchanan was a member of the staffs of both President Nixon and President Reagan.

3 On this point see James Willard Hurst, *Law and the Conditions of Freedom in the Nineteenth-Century United States*, Madison, Wis., 1956, especially ch. I.

4 Robert H. Wiebe, *The Search for Order, 1877-1920*, Chicago, 1968.

5 There was a good deal of opposition to McKinley's nomination of Joseph McKenna, his Attorney-General, on the grounds that McKenna had demonstrated incapacity as a lower court judge. Before Cleveland succeeded in appointing Rufus W. Peckham in 1895, he had failed with more than one entirely respectable nomination, including that of Peckham's older brother, for no other reason than political rivalry with the Senators from New York. Cleveland, of course, like all his nominees for that seat, was a New Yorker. See the entries for McKenna and Peckham in the *Dictionary of American Biography* and in *The Justices of the United States Supreme Court 1789-1969. Their Lives and Major Opinions*, ed. Leon Friedman and Fred L. Israel, New York, 1969, Vol. III; and, for McKenna, Willard L. King, *Melville Weston Fuller. Chief Justice of the United States 1888-1910*, New York, 1950, pp. 228-30.

6 Alfred H. Kelly, Winfred A. Harbison, and Herman Belz, *The American Constitution. Its Origins and Development*, 6th ed. New York, 1983, p. 731.

7 *United States Reports* (hereafter U.S. with, as usual in legal citations, the volume number preceding), vol. 158, pp. 601-715.

8 156 U.S. 1-46.

9 156 U.S. 16.

10 178 U.S. 41-111.

11 195 U.S. 27-64.

12 188 U.S. 321-75.

13 193 U.S. 197-411.

14 *Champion* v. *Ames*, for example, was testing an act of 1895.

15 143 U.S. 649-700.

16 192 U.S. 470-98.

17 158 U.S. 564-600.

18 199 U.S. 473-87, at 480. Brown, J. here spoke for an unanimous Court.

19 198 U.S. 45-76. The dissenters' arguments from fact are at pp. 70-2.

20 David P. Currie, 'The Constitution in the Supreme Court: the protection of economic interests, 1889-1910', *University of Chicago Law Review*, LII, 1985, pp. 324-88, especially pp. 387-8.

21 163 U.S. 537-64.

22 130 U.S. 581-611.

23 149 U.S. 698-764.

24 Thomas Reed Powell, *Vagaries and Varieties in Constitutional Interpretation*, New York, 1956, p. 85.

25 See Lawrence Goodwyn, *Democratic Promise: The Populist Movement in America*, New York, 1976; Richard Hofstadter, *The Age of Reform*, New York, 1955.

10

Political power and the modern Supreme Court

RICHARD HODDER-WILLIAMS
University of Bristol

I

The recent nomination of Judge Robert Bork to the Supreme Court was indeed a reminder of what is now generally acknowledged: the Supreme Court is a very political institution exercising political power. Ronald Dworkin, for one, noted recently that 'Reagan made no effort to disguise the political character of Bork's appointment" and throughout the summer of 1987 supporters and opponents of this nomination continued to lobby actively.[2] From the British perspective, this was a peculiar, indeed unseemly, performance. But it was not new; even on occasions where the political consequences of a new appointment have not seemed as obviously significant as in Bork's case, there has always been intense lobbying.[3]

It was peculiarly appropriate to consider the political power of the modern Supreme Court in 1987, not only because the Constitution which established it celebrated its bicentennial but also because precisely fifty years before the Court was again in the thick of political controversy; and on that occasion a single change of personnel (Hugo Black for Willis van Devanter) ushered in the modern era of the Court's jurisprudence. Since the Court has been so often embroiled in political disputes (and the modern period is not special in this respect), debates on the political role of the Court have been myriad. It is, indeed, a field well ploughed, even to the condition of a dust bowl. But there is some virtue, I think, in looking more closely than is usually done at what is *meant* by the political power of the modern Court.

The central problem, as I see it, is that the concept of political power is loosely employed. It has both technical meanings (that is, a variety of characteristics noted by political scientists) and popular connotations. Very often, those who argue talk past each other because they are not actually examining the same things even if they might be using the same words.

II

Let me start substantively, then, with one of the technical senses in which the Supreme Court may be said to be exercising political power. One of the most common definitions of 'the political system' is that provided in the early 1950s by David Easton; he distinguished those activities which produced 'the authoritative allocation of values' in a society.[4] In this conception, any action – whether performed by the legislative, executive *or* judicial branch – is definitionally political to the extent that it makes decisions binding upon members of a society. In this sense, therefore, all courts of last resort *must* be political. Since the disputes which they are called upon to resolve rarely, if ever, lack argument on both sides, judges must exercise their 'sovereign prerogative of choice' and prefer their values to others'.[5] Unlike a piece of string whose length can be objectively determined, the legal disputes which reach courts of last resort (for all the certainty of the participants and their backers) are characterised by indeterminacy. The divided votes in both the Supreme Court and the Judicial Committee of the House of Lords testify to the non-mechanical nature of the process of judging.

But the observation that the Supreme Court *must* be political and exercise political power is only the start of the inquiry. For there is, at first sight, a qualitative difference in the freedom to allocate values authoritatively between, on the one hand, the Court and, on the other, legislatures. A Court is by nature 'a substantially passive instrument, to be moved only by the initiative of litigants'.[6] The extent to which courts are involved in issues which are normally considered to be the domain of the more obviously political branches depends primarily on the readiness of political actors to litigate. Americans are a litigious people and make every use of the constitutional provisions open to them to protect, or advance, their interests.[7] There is little doubt, in my view, that interest groups of every kind now litigate in the United States as a normal tactic in their overall political strategies.

Interest group litigation is not entirely new. The railroad interests, the anti-Saloon League and many progressive causes, for example, were involved in litigation a century ago.[8] But the practice has become much more common; test cases are sought; public interest law firms seek out litigation to sponsor and support; the Washington offices of interest groups watch out for cases in which *amicus curiae* briefs may be submitted; in short, many cases which now reach the Supreme Court are less like classic idealised lawsuits between two individual parties than the

interest group pluralism associated with the American legislative process.[9] Administrations, too, for some time have consciously used litigation to advance their political agendas, especially in the social field.[10] Of
no administration is this more true than the Reagan Administration,
which has invested much time and energy in attempts, not entirely successful, to prosecute its social agenda through the courts.[11] In short, the
courts in the United States (and that means ultimately the Supreme
Court) are drawn into the political business of allocating values by the
American people themselves; and this is compounded by congressional
legislation which invites parties to go to the courts to establish and
defend what they consider to be their rights.

The Congress has not only encouraged parties to bring suits with a
high public policy profile to the courts; it has also acknowledged in its
own legislation that the Supreme Court is indeed the ultimate authoritative allocator of constitutional values. In the Gramm–Rudman–Hollings
amendment, intended to create a balanced budget, the legislation provided a quick route for testing its constitutionality and a fall-back position should one crucial section be found unconstitutional, as indeed it
was.[12] And the Executive, too, has emphasised this role of the Court in
its haste, for example, to test the 1965 Voting Rights Act.[13] It was also
deeply involved in the litigation which legitimised the 1964 Civil Rights
Act.[14] The point is that the Supreme Court's political role (in the sense
which I am now discussing) has been enhanced not primarily by its own
volition but by the demands and pressures of a litigious people, the
actions of the national legislature and the encouragement of the Executive branch.

In stressing this point (and reconfirming the wisdom of Alexis de Tocqueville), I do not want to absolve the Court itself from all responsibility
for these developments. The modern Court has shown itself readier than
its predecesors to grant disputants access to the courts; it has made class
actions easier to bring;[15] it has narrowed the exclusions protected by the
marvellously flexible concept of the 'political question';[16] it has encouraged groups who lose out in the legislatures of the several states to litigate
by giving its support to some very visible and unpopular minorities. The
two developments have gone side by side, each encouraging the other;
and this should be a cause of no surprise. The personnel of the Court,
nominated by an elected President and confirmed by an elected Senate,
roughly reflect the dominant forces in Washington over time and hence
provide a mirror to major changes in national ideology.[17]

If the growth in the visibility of the Supreme Court's system-deter-
mined political role is *essentially* quantitative, there is also one distinctly

qualitative change. On constitutional issues, the Court has traditionally been a yea or a nay sayer; in other words, it has either authorised or forbidden a particular practice. Its allocation of values operated negatively by excluding certain practices; it did not act positively and creatively, as legislatures and executives do, to fashion policy. Herein lay one of the fundamental differences in the *nature* of the power exercised by each branch. But this has changed. Sometimes the creativity is very clear; in *Gideon* v. *Wainwright*, for instance, the obligation to provide legal assistance to those accused in state courts, with all its financial consequences, was imposed upon the states.[18] Sometimes it is less clear and, like Popperian social science 'proof', creativity is the logical consequence of a series of negatives which leave only one course of action available; the Fourteenth Amendment's application to the dual school systems or to district electoral boundaries come to mind.

Sometimes, of course, the Court's involvement in matters which are not, on first inspection, litigation at all is manifest. Bostonians will be well aware of the judges Garratty (one state, one federal) in effect establishing the prison system and the public school system respectively; all over the nation, judges have been creating school systems, legislative districts, affirmative action programmes, and penitentiary systems. This, as some would have it, is the authoritative allocation of values out of control, an impermissible usurpation of legislative and executive business. And, of course, in a sense it is. But what the criticism fails to address is the underlying cause of such overt judicial policy-making. It does not follow, in my view, from judges egotistically seeking such power so much as from the failings of legislatures to perform *their* duties under the Constitution. One has only to examine the tenacious way in which many legislatures have consciously and determinedly attempted to circumvent the clear intentions of the Court's generalisations to feel some sympathy for the politico-judges who catch the headlines. People like James Thayer and Felix Frankfurter hoped, perhaps even believed against all the lessons of history, that justice could be learned through the democratic process;[19] but it was Tom Clark's frontal attack on Frankfurter's warnings against entering the political thicket and mathematical quagmire which showed more political understanding: 'the majority of the people of Tennessee', he wrote in his *Baker* concurrence, 'have no practical opportunities for exercising their political weight at the polls'.[20] Sometimes the only remedy by which claimed rights can actually be exercised may be through consent decrees or court-ordered redistricting plans.

The function of the court of last resort under a written constitution with an entrenched bill of rights is in part necessarily political. It may be that more issues of an avowedly political nature are now brought to the Court. The growth of the administrative state, the outcome of new interest group strategies, and the consequence of an ideological shift in the United States, as elsewhere, towards a greater concern for individual rights could be important causes. Using one conception of politics, I would argue that the Court is not doing anything intrinsically new; it is merely doing more of what earlier courts did and the responsibility for this lies largely (although not exclusively) outside its ambit.

III

A more common context in which the concept of power may be used is a situation where one actor makes another do what he or she would not otherwise have done.[21] I have no wish on this occasion to dig deeply into the political science fraternity's complex analysis of the concept 'power', but would rather accept for the time being this usage which is common to most studies of political systems. The study of politics is often defined as the study of the exercise of power; in the Supreme Court's case, the question becomes this: to what extent does the Court *make* people do what they would not otherwise do?

We immediately face a difficulty. In one important sense, the Court does not possess the requisite coercive power to *make* people obey its judgements. Its police have no remit outside the confines of the Marble Palace. So it is entirely possible for its judgements to be disobeyed; indeed, the instruction in *Brown II* to desegregate the public schools with all deliberate speed remains the classic example of non-compliance.[22] But it does not stand alone. Judgements designed to prevent public authorities denying blacks the vote did not enfranchise blacks;[23] judgements outlawing the saying of prayers or reading of the Bible at the beginning of the school day did not at once put an end to these practices in the South;[24] the outlawing of the legislative veto has had a surprisingly small impact on legislative–executive relations.[25] Even in matters of life and death, the Court's will has been thwarted. When it handed down its opinion in *Williams* v. *Georgia* (1955), it explicitly 'rejected the assumption that the courts of Georgia would allow [Aubrey Lee Williams] to go to his death as a result of a conviction secured from a jury which the State admits was unconstitutionally impanelled'.[26] The Georgian Supreme Court, however, read the Justices a lecture on the Tenth Amendment and reaffirmed the death penalty; on 30 March 1956 Aubrey Williams died in the electric chair. There was nobody in the

Supreme Court who could take the Georgian judges to court for murder.

I have, of course, quite carefully chosen the best classes of cases to illustrate the simple point that the Supreme Court needs the voluntary assistance of others if its judgements are to be effective. These others are of two discernible kinds. In the first place, elected legislators and executive offices can act, as Eisenhower did to enforce desegregation in Little Rock, and as the Congress acted in the 1960s. It was the Civil Rights Act of 1964 and the Voting Rights Act of 1965 which provided the bases for the integration of schools and the enfranchisement of blacks; it was the action of the Departments of Health, Education and Welfare and of Justice which brought federal law and federal prosecutors to bear on these problems. Indeed, it was the Health, Education and Welfare Department guidelines which were employed, first by Appeals Court judges and then by the Supreme Court, to provide the framework for deciding upon the constitutionality of desegregation programmes in the public schools.[27] Without the commitment of legislature and executive, it is doubtful whether the changes sought by the Supreme Court would have been achieved in the 1960s at all.

In the second place, the American people grant the Court authority because they believe it is a legitimate source of the 'authoritative allocation of values'. One may attribute this to the reverence granted to the Constitution and vicariously to the Justices who are its guardians. No doubt there is some truth in this idealisation; but there is too much attitudinal evidence for us to accept this vision as it stands.[28] Of course, the Constitution is seen by many Americans, perhaps most Americans, as encapsulating their political ideals; however it can only play this part over time ('totem and fetish', as Lerner described it fifty years ago[29]) if its performance broadly consolidates this attitude. The readiness to obey would be dramatically reduced if the Court's judgements ran counter to popular opinion for any length of time.

Where emotions are intense (as with desegregation or abortion rights) either the willingness to obey by *some* people is withdrawn or the Court's legitimacy is openly challenged. What is interesting to me is the fact that the Court's decisions on many highly salient issues over the last three decades have been so much in line with the public opinion of the day or the direction of a shifting public opinion.[30] Of the major salient issues only in matters of Church and State and bussing is there a large discrepancy between its landmark decisions and national trends. In other words, the Court has tended either to reflect or anticipate public opinion.

FIGURE I

PUBLIC OPINION ON FIVE ISSUES

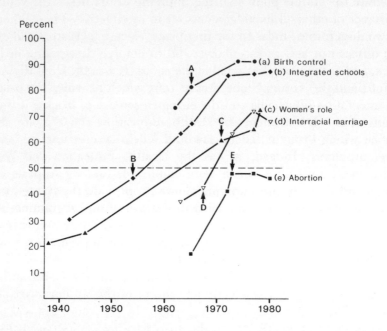

Sources Smith, *A Compendium of Trends on General Social Survey–Questions* (Chicago: NORC, 1980); *General Social Surveys, 1972-1980: Cumulative Codebook* (Chicago: NORC, 1980) *SRC-CPR American National Election Studies* (Ann Arbor: ICPSR, 1960-80).

Percent answering 'Yes' to: 'Do you think birth control information should be available to anyone who wants it, or not?' (NORC).

Percent answering 'Same schools' to: 'Do you think white students and Negro students should go to the same schools or separate schools?' (NORC).

Percent answering 'Approve' to: 'Do you approve or disapprove of a married woman earning money in business or industry if she has a husband capable of supporting her?' (NORC).

Percent answering 'No' to: 'Do you think there should be laws against marriages between Negroes and whites?' (NORC).

Percent answering 'Yes' to: 'Please tell me whether. . . you think it should be possible for a pregnant woman to obtain a legal abortion if she is not married and does not want to marry the man?'(NORC).

Note: Cases are: (A) Griswold v. Connecticut, 381 U.S. 479 (1965); (B) Brown v. Board of Education, 347 U.S. 483 (1954); (C) Reed v. Reed, 404 U.S. 71 (1971); (D) Loving v. Virginia, 388 U.S. 1 (1967); (E) Roe v. Wade, 410 U.S. 113 (1973).

Source: David Barnum, 'The Supreme Court and public opinion: judicial decision making in the post-New Deal Period', *Journal of Politics*, XLVII, 1985, p. 656. Used by permission.

One crude measure of Supreme Court power would involve quantifying those cases decided 'for' the government and those 'against' the government. I calculated some figures for the decade from 1975 to 1986. Three things were striking: 'pro'-government figures fluctuated between 59.1 and 79.7 per cent, averaging out at 66.4 per cent, high figures when it is remembered that the vast majority of instances where government prevailed in the lower courts are not reviewed; the Supreme Court is a great legitimiser. Second, apart from the 1977 Term, there was a marked disparity between civil and criminal cases; in the 1981 and 1983 Terms, indeed, the Court was on the government's side over 90 per cent of the time on *criminal* and habeas corpus cases; the evidence does suggest that a majority of the Court sees its primary role as protecting individual *civil* rights. Third, and most significantly, there is a marked disparity in the treatment of cases originating in the federal system from those originating in the state courts, where deference to government is much lower[31] (why is *certiorari* granted if there is not a predisposition to reverse a state Supreme Court's judgement?). The impression of Court power is, I suggest, largely generated from those cases which strike down state regulations.

TABLE 1

CASES DECIDED 'PRO-GOVERNMENT' 1976-86 (%)

Term	(a) In favour of government in all civil actions from inferior federal courts	(b) In favour of federal government in civil actions from inferior federal courts	(c) In favour of government in federal criminal and habeas corpus cases	(d) In favour of state governments in all cases granted certiorari from state courts
1976	67.1	(56.7)	66.7	40.0
1977	64.9	75.0	(50.0)	50.0
1978	69.7	(67.6)	86.7	61.1
1979	59.1	55.3	72.0	33.3
1980	72.6	75.6	83.3	50.0
1981	64.9	79.4	91.3	36.4
1982	60.0	61.8	83.3	68.0
1983	79.7	88.9	93.7	40.7
1984	62.3	77.8	77.8	54.5
1985	63.9	71.1	76.7	60.0
1986	70.3	74.3	55.0	61.5

Source: Harvard Law Review: annual statistics published in November issues, vol. XC (1976) – vol. CI (1987). Reprinted by permission.

Some observers of the American scene have noticed the Supreme Court's intervention in state death penalty law, state abortion law, state schooling and prison practices, and state regulation of pornography and have concluded that the Court is the most powerful of the three branches of the federal government. This is surely an illusion. It ignores the congruence between *national* opinion and judgements of the Supreme Court of the United States; it underplays the Court's need for voluntary acquiescence, which itself is effective only if the Court does not in fact confound the people's will; and it lacks, I suggest, a sense of relative power. Just as the stress on the centralisation of the federal system underplays the simultaneous and massive expansion of state government, so the stress on the Court's important role in establishing aspects of American social policy should not forget the far greater, and far more directly initiated, contributions of the federal legislature and executive. The Great Society, the Vietnam War, the barrage of legislation and executive orders issuing forth each year from either end of Pennsylvania Avenue, these are the dominant Washington forces affecting life – and death – among American people. It is only when the perspective is state-centred and rights-centred that the Court looms really large; and, even here, that perception differs from place to place. This irregularity of impact plays a very central part in what I referred to earlier as the popular connotations of the Court's power and to which I shall shortly return.

IV

In many ways, the concept of political power which I have been looking at is a very crude one. It seems to assume that power is only exercised in direct, observable situations where command and response can both be documented and measured. But there is also a 'second face of power'[32] where the range of choices *realistically* open to citizens is circumscribed by means other than the command–response model. The role of education in internalising values (very much an American concern) or of the media in establishing models and judgements on politicians and their policies come immediately to mind. The power to set the public agenda or form popular prejudice is also very real and, in a contemporary democracy, can be of decisive importance.[33]

It is here, I think, that the primary significance of the Supreme Court may be found. It does help to set an agenda; and it does highlight values. I observed earlier that the desegregation called for in *Brown* would probably not have taken place when it did had there not been congressional action; but I would also argue that the congressional action would not have been so high on the political agenda if the *Brown* decision had not lent legitimacy to black civil rights demands and placed the issue of race discrimination unequivocally, if embarrassingly, on the public agenda. Similarly, the simple, (perhaps over-simple) moral underpinning to *Miranda* or *Reynolds* made the subsequent actions of public officials both necessary and broadly acceptable.[34] Because the Court has such a high profile and because its legitimacy does normally result in its judgements being honoured, its major decisions translate what in reality is often a squalid set of facts into a principle of national significance. Ernesto Miranda was hardly the stuff of which heroes are made; and Norma McCorvey, the Roe in the abortion case of *Roe* v. *Wade*, was a ticket seller for a freak-animal sideshow in a travelling circus when she was raped in Georgia and immediately made off to friends and support in Texas.[35] To argue that the Court, independently and self-motivatedly, thrust suspect rights or abortion on to the national agenda is too simple; and it is too simple for a reason beyond the necessary fact that it was only because Ernesto Miranda's lawyer appealed through the Arizona courts and Norma McCorvey's lawyer through the federal courts that the issues ever reached the Supreme Court.

Americans may speak loosely of appealing their cases right to the Supreme Court. But even when they do, only a tiny percentage of appeals in fact get heard. Here, then, is a different form of agenda-setting. The process of selection, of granting *certiorari*, is clearly an exercise of power;[36] some applications are successful; most are not. Many of the latter are certainly not worthy of review; a very large number are understandable attempts by prisoners in state gaols to escape their punishment; some are quite ridiculous, such as the claim that prohibition against left-hand turns denied a motorist his right to travel.[37] At the margin, however, the choice is close and debatable. It is interesting to note that there are some scholars who hold that substantial matters are being omitted and others who believe the opposite, that too many unnecessary cases are being granted *certiorari*.[38] It is unlikely that both can be correct.

Striking the balance is not easy. But three observations are pertinent. The study of past justices' papers makes it abundantly clear that a majority of the Court does come to feel that a particular issue, previously ignored, requires attention. This conclusion, however, arises less from personal predilection than from the empirical observation that a disturbing amount of litigation is going through the lower courts on the issue and often being disposed of in different ways in the various Courts of Appeal; the failure of states to redistrict is a case in point.[39] Second, it is also clear that, once an issue has been identified, there is often a deliberate search for the 'right' case to use to address that issue; *Gideon* and *Coker* are cases in point.[40] Third, some of the winnowing out is, in fact, done by the executive branch in the person of the Solicitor-General; he has authority to decide the cases which the United States will appeal and he uses this authority to select those which he wants the Court to hear, either because they are the most suitable from his professional point of view or because they raise questions to which the executive branch wants answers.[41] The Supreme Court has traditionally accorded the Solicitor-General's choice special respect. In the 1983 Term, for example, 79 per cent of the Solicitor-General's appeals were granted against an average of 2 per cent while 78 per cent of the cases brought by others but on which the Solicitor-General had filed a supportive position were granted.[42] Clearly to a very important extent the Court is abnegating some aspect of its agenda-setting power to the judgement of an agent of the executive branch.

The agenda-setting function of the Court stems from the 1925 Judges Act and from more recent amendments to it which have, effectively, permitted it to control its own docket. But that control is tempered by a proper respect for the Solicitor-General's judgement and an empirical assessment of the issues that demand a place on the agenda. In both cases, the initiative lies outside the Court. Once placed upon the public agenda, however, the very fact of Supreme Court consideration confers a saliency to the issue; when the Court pronounces upon the new issue, the pronouncement puts down a moral marker, expresses for the time being an authoritative, perhaps *the* authoritative, statement on the matter which becomes the starting point for the ensuing public debate. Segregated schools are unconstitutional; women have a right to an abortion in certain circumstances; suspects must be treated in a certain way. These statements *are* a 'second face of power', putting their opponents on the defensive and challenging them to justify their positions with arguments broader than self-interest.

V

For the many people for whom the political power of the Supreme Court is exemplified by the readiness of the Justices to do what they consider to be the politician's business and to use judicial power to advance their own policy agendas, I have not yet even begun to examine the *real* issues. One scholar has recently argued that the Justices use the Constitution 'as a kind of letter of marque authorising them to set sail at will among laws, striking down any they find displeasing'.[43] I call this the popular sense in which the phrase 'political power' is used, even by scholars and attorneys-general. Its constituent parts are the assumption that justices have a complete freedom in their judging (especially in areas where they are supposed to have no right to stray) and the belief that this freedom is exercised entirely in line with their own predilections. Even if the extreme version is diluted to exclude such obviously excessive words like 'entirely', 'complete' and 'any', the indictment is a severe one. It is also a pragmatic, instrumental one; the niceties of political science categories are made redundant by the concentration on what in fact happens, what results.

Schools *have* been desegrated; children *are* being bussed; affirmative action plans *have* been approved; Bible-reading at the start of the school day *has* been outlawed; limitations on abortions *have* been set aside; electoral districts *have* been equalised. It is plain for all to see. It would, of course, be absurd to deny this. But it would also be misleading, as I have already argued, to imagine that these fundamental changes were achieved by the Supreme Court and the lower federal courts alone. And there is a hidden aspect of the popular view of the judiciary's political power which needs teasing out; underneath much of the criticism is the implicit assumption that the Court's views are improper because they undemocratically predominate over those of the elected authorities and their agents. They are, in short, illegitimately counter-majoritarian.

This is not the place to get too deeply embroiled in the continuous debate over the philosophical justification for judicial power of the kind exercised by the Supreme Court. But there are two very obvious points which do need repeating. The United States Constitition was never majoritarian, if this implies a belief in the ultimate legitimacy of elected majorities. The whole constitutional edifice was designed in part precisely to prevent a single majority enjoying sovereign power; Federalism, the separation of powers, a bicameral legislature and, above all, the so-called Bill of Rights testify to this. There is necessarily going to be a conflict between limited government and crude democratic assumptions. This is one of the unresolved contradictions bequeathed by the Founding Fathers and one which, as we celebrate the Constitution's bicentennial, is still unresolved and is, I believe, irresolvable.

My second point also draws attention to another constitutional contradiction. Within a federal system of government, there is now a national bill of rights. The effective incorporation of virtually all the rights set out in the first nine amendments to the Constitution into the Fourteenth Amendment (and hence applicable to the individual states) has created a major source of tension in which the contemporary Court is now forced to participate. It is little wonder that localised hostility to the Court's actions is incurred; the federal system, for all the homogenising and centralising developments of the modern period, reflects major differences in the priorities, values and ambitions of the several states. Inevitably, therefore, a national institution espousing national values will tread on parochial toes; attempts to permit local variations (in, for example, what counts as pornographic) have been tried but have only recently been dropped as unworkable.[44]

The dispute at a generalised level is about the extent to which judicial power should be exercised; but positions tend to follow from specific complaints. Some legal scholars, naturally, can live with both a personal approval of the morality of the Court's decision and also criticism of that decision; Ely's position on the abortion cases is probably a case in point.[45] Politicians in particular, however, find this Janus-like dichotomy too uncomfortable to live with. Ideological conservatives praised the Court's activism in the 1930s but attacked it in the 1950s; ideological liberals attacked the Court's activism in the 1930s but defended it in the 1950s. Thus public criticism of the Court's philosophy of judicial action normally hides opposition to its substantive action. The public approves of judicial power but disaffected constituencies disapprove of particular exercises of that power.

Disapproval often brings with it a distinctly jaundiced view of the Justices, who are thought to do no more than translate their particular political preferences into judicial form. Judging is often idealised as a comparatively simply process of 'discovering' the law; if the 'discovery' runs against the observer's preferences, therefore, clearly the fault must lie in the perverted practice of the errant Justices. There is something implausible about this view. And yet it contains within it a rather more sophisticated truth. Conceptions of the judicial role differ and these different conceptions naturally produce different outputs.[46] Those who stress the importance of limited government and the Judiciary's fundamental purpose as protecting individuals and unpopular minorities against government will inevitably be activist in the sense of constraining some actions of elected governments. Whether a commitment to liberal values in the 1980s leads to such a judicial philosophy or such a philosophy leads to liberal outputs is a moot point. But what is clear is that there are competing views about what a Court *ought* to do within the American constitutional system. There is no simple relationship between activism and a goal-oriented jurisprudence. Activist justices can be principled in a way that for the most part excludes personal judgements; Hugo Black, by and large, was activist in terms of outcome (until the middle 1960s) but self-restrained in terms of process; John Harlan, by contrast, was less activist in terms of outcome but much more so in terms of process. He, like his mentor Felix Frankfurter, would agonise on a case-by-case basis before deciding whether a state's action did, or did not, infringe on the principles of ordered liberty or sear the conscience.[47]

Popular judgements of the Court often misconceive the process of judging. While the votes of most justices on most issues can be safely predicted, it is certainly not the case that votes are always easily cast. One thing *The Brethren* has shown is that justices are often plagued by indecision and doubt;[48] the private papers of justices indicate that they sometimes change their minds;[49] many a drafted opinion never saw the light of day because it was challenged and intellectually subverted;[50] the variety in the make-up of majorities suggest that the translation of personal beliefs into votes on the merits is mediated by a range of factors; nor should we forget that in the 1981 to 1985 Terms, for example, 35.3 per cent of the cases with full opinion were unanimous, William Brennan agreeing with William Rehnquist. In the end, the Court's opinion will often and necessarily so, be a compromise between different lines of argument; Harlan Fiske Stone, professor turned justice, wrote to an old academic colleague to defend his writing on just these grounds.[51] Political scientists are not surprised. But this necessary realism does provide academic lawyers with a field day, as they point out the internal contradictions of a majority opinion whose author often knows it is internally contradictory.

The popular connotations of judicial political power – that it is exercised 'at will' and strikes down 'any' law a justice finds displeasing – are very real and in the political arena have a motive force of their own which cannot be ignored. But they are, I believe, based essentially on misperception and misunderstanding. Most (but not, I hasten to add, all) justices develop their jurisprudence over time as the kaleidoscope of litigated facts passes before their eyes and their judicial philosophy becomes more settled. Unpopular outcomes provoke protest, as though the *only* explanation for such outcomes was to be found in a moral fault in the Justices. That is hardly fair. But losers are tempted to cry 'foul'; Carl Lewis, well beaten by Ben Johnson over 100 metres in Rome, claimed briefly that his victor had shot the gun;[52] in the United States, the defeated are also tempted to deny to a current Supreme Court majority the dignity of an honest jurisprudence.

VI

The Supreme Court has been openly attacked by members of the Reagan Administration in an almost unprecedented manner; not since 1937 has the challenge been so open. Politicians are joined by scholars, too. And there is plenty of *prima facie* evidence to suggest that the Court has been exercising its judicial muscles with relish and widespread effect. There is always likely to be an undercurrent of concern about the Supreme Court's exercise of judicial power with policy consequences. Whether this is the ideal method of resolving many American problems remains debatable. However, I would contend that it is by far and away the best *practical* method of constitutional amendment actually available to the American people. Indeed, the celebrations of the Constitution's bicentennial can only take place, in my view, *because* the Court has, in effect, rewritten parts of it.

What I hope to have done in this essay is to make four comparatively simple points. First, I take it as axiomatic that the Court must exercise political power because it 'authoritatively allocates values' but it is the American political process (interest groups, legislators in Washington and Administration officials alike) which forces issues on to the agenda. Second, I suggest that its *direct* impact on society is perhaps not as great as is often made out;[53] its nationalising tendency certainly treads on delicate state corns (and loud is the outcry), but its fiat runs only so far as the American people and their elected officials permit. Third, I state that its *indirect* impact is, however, considerable; enjoying the beneficient penumbral aura of the Constitution, the Court's judgements establish the moral benchmark in many areas. Finally, I point out that the Court is, after all, the third branch of the federal government system, which means two things: it *is* part of the governmental structure (and will necessarily decide issues in ways that some parties dislike), but it is also less potent than either legislature or executive.

NOTES

1 Ronald Dworkin, 'The Bork nomination', *New York Review of Books*, 13 August 1987, p. 3.
2 See *Time* (European edition), 24 August 1967, p. 16.
3 See e.g., the classic study of Pierce Butler's appointment by David Danelski, *A Supreme Court Justice is Appointed*, New York, 1964, and the account of Harrold J. Carswell's failure to be confirmed in Richard Harris, *Decision*, New York, 1971.
4 The most accessible presentation of his general framework is 'An approach to the

analysis of political systems', *World Politics*, IX, 1956-57, pp. 383-400.

5 The phrase, of course, is Oliver Wendell Holmes's.

6 Robert Jackson, *The Supreme Court in the American System of Government*, Cambridge, Mass., 1955, p. 12.

7 Jethro K. Liberman, *The Litigious Society*, New York, 1981.

8 Clement Vose, *Constitutional Change: amendment politics and Supreme Court Litigation since 1900*, Lexington, Mass., 1972.

9 The National Association for the Advancement of Colored People (NAACP) is the standard example of such an interest group. But conservative groups, too, are now litigating in great numbers and with greater seriousness. See Lee Epstein, *Conservatives in Court*, Knoxville, 1985.

10 For the Eisenhower years, see R. Huston (ed.), *Roles of the Attorney-General of the United States*, Washington DC, 1968; for the Kennedy years, see Victor Navasky, *Kennedy Justice*, New York, 1971.

11 Lincoln Caplan, 'Annals of law', *New Yorker*, 10 August 1987, pp. 29-58, 17 August 1987, pp. 30-62.

12 *Bowsher* v. *Synar*, 106 S.Ct.3181 (1986).

13 *South Carolina* v. *Katzenbach*, 383 U.S. 761 (1966).

14 *Heart of Atlanta Motel* v. *US*, 379 U.S.241 (1964); *Katzenbach* v. *McClung*, 379 U.S. 294 (1964).

15 *Flast* v. *Cohen*, 392 U.S.83 (1968); but see *Worth* v. *Seldin*, 422 U.S.490 (1975) and Gregory J. Rathjen and Harold J. Spaeth, 'Access to the federal courts: an analysis of Burger Court policy-making', *American Journal of Political Science*, XXIII, 1979, pp. 360-82.

16 *Baker* v. *Carr*, 369 U.S. 186 (1962), *Powell* v. *McCormack*, 395 U.S. 486 (1969). See generally Phillippa Strum, *The Supreme Court and 'Political Questions': a study in judicial evasion*, Birmingham Ala., 1974.

17 The classic exposition of this view is R. A. Dahl, 'Decision-making in a democracy: the Supreme Court as a national policy-maker', *Journal of Public Law*, VI, 1957, pp. 279-95. Although some of his arguments have been challenged, this generalisation still seems sound. But see David Adamany and Joel B. Grossman, 'Support for the Supreme Court as a national policymaker', *Law and Policy Quarterly*, V, 1983, pp. 405-37.

18 *Gideon* v. *Wainwright*, 372 U.S. 335 (1963)

19 Thayer's views are cited in David F. Forte (ed.), *The Supreme Court in American Politics*, Lexington, Mass., 1972, p. 85; Frankfurter's appear regularly in his opinions.

20 *Baker* v. *Carr*, 369 U.S. 186 (1962), at 258-9.

21 Robert A. Dahl, 'The concept of power', *Behavioural Science*, II, 1957, pp. 201-5.

22 *Brown* v. *Board of Education of Topeka, Kansas*, 349 U.S. 294 (1955). For some picture of what happened thereafter, see, for example, J. W. Peltason, *58 Lonely Men: southern federal judges and school desegregation*, Urbana, 1961, and J. Harvie Wilkinson III, *From Brown to Bakke*, New York, 1979.

23 Richard Claude, *The Supreme Court and the Electoral Process*, Baltimore, Md., 1970.

24 H. Frank Way, 'Survey research on judicial decisions: the prayer and Bible reading cases', *Western Political Quarterly*, XXI, 1968, pp. 189-205.

25 Louis Fisher, 'The administrative world of *Chadha* and *Bowsher*', *Public Administration Review*, XLVII, pp. 213-19.

26 *Williams* v. *Georgia*, 349 U.S. 375, (1955), at 391.

27 *U.S.* v. *Jefferson County Board of Education*, 380 F2d 385 (5th Circuit, 1967).
28 For a recent review, see Gregory A. Caldeira, 'Neither the purse nor the sword: dynamics of public confidence in the Supreme Court', *American Political Science Review*, LXXX, 1986, pp. 1209-26.
29 Max Lerner, 'Constitution and Court as symbol', *Yale Law Journal*, XLVI, 1945-46, p. 1294.
30 David G. Barnum, 'The Supreme Court and public opinion: judicial decision-making in the post-New Deal period', *Journal of Politics*, XLVII, 1985, pp. 652-66.
31 Philip Kurland, *Politics, the Constitution, and the Warren Court*, Chicago, 1970.
32 Peter Bachrach and Morton S. Baratz, *Power and Poverty: theory and practice*, New York, 1970. For a shorter discussion, see Steven Lukes, *Power: a radical view*, London, 1974.
33 See, in the Supreme Court context, Gregory A. Caldeira, 'The United States Supreme Court and criminal cases, 1935-1976: alternative models of agenda building', *British Journal of Political Science*, XI, 1981, pp. 449-70.
34 *Miranda* v. *Arizona*, 384 U.S. 436 (1966): *Reynolds* v. *Sims*, 377 U.S. 533 (1964).
35 Fred W. Friendly and Martha J. H. Elliott, *The Constitution: that delicate balance*, New York, 1984, p. 202.
36 See David O'Brien, *Storm Center: the Supreme Court in American Politics*, New York, 1986, pp. 157-212.
37 As reported in William J. Brennan, 'The National Court of Appeals: another dissent', *University of Chicago Law Review*, XL, 1973.
38 Henry M. Hart, 'The time chart of the Justices', *Harvard Law Revew*, LXXII, 1959-60, pp. 84-125; Samuel Estreicher and John E. Sexton, 'A managerial theory of the Supreme Court's responsibilities: an empirical study', *New York University Law Review*, LIX, 1984, pp. 681-822.
39 *Baker* v. *Carr*, 369 U.S. 186 (1962). The Court's discretionary power is well exemplified when it chooses not to consider some issues where the Courts of Appeal differ.
40 *Gideon* v. *Wainwright*, 372 U.S. 335 (1963); *Coker* v. *Georgia*, 433 U.S. 584 (1977).
41 Robert Scigliano, *The Supreme Court and the Presidency*, Glencoe, 1971, pp. 161-96.
42 Caplan, 'Annals of Law', 10 August 1987, p. 35, Caplan argues that this traditional deference, especially when *amicus* briefs are filed, is weakening. In the 1985 Term, for example, the Court granted review to only 57 per cent of cases where an *amicus* brief was filed. 'Annals of Law', 17 August 1987, p. 55.
43 Walter Berns, 'The least dangerous branch, but only if . . .' in Leonard J. Theberge (ed.), *The Judiciary in a Democratic Society*, Lexington, Mass., 1979, p. 15.
44 *Pope*, v. *Illinois* 107 S.Ct. 1918 (1987).
45 John Hart Ely, *Democracy and Distrust: a theory of judicial review*, Cambridge, Mass., 1980.
46 For a useful example of examining Supreme Court behaviour through the 'role theory' lens, see Mark Silverstein, *Constitutional Faiths*, Ithaca, NY, 1984.
47 This perspective is delightfully set out in Norman Reddich, 'A Black–Harlan dialogue on due process and equal protection: heard in Heaven and dedicated to Robert B. McKay', *New York University Law Review*, L, 1975, pp. 20-46.
48 Bob Woodward and Scott Armstrong, *The Brethren*, New York, 1979.
49 J. Woodford Howard, 'On the fluidity of judicial choice', *American Political Science Review*, LXII, 1968, pp. 43-56. For a somewhat contradictory view, see Saul

Brenner, 'Fluidity on the United States Supreme Court: a re-examination'; *American Journal of Political Science*, XXIV, 1980, pp. 527-35.
50 See Bernard Schwartz, *Unpublished Opinions of the Warren Court*, New York, 1985.
51 Thomas Alpheus Mason, *Harlan Fiske Stone: pillar of the law*, New York, 1956.
52 *The Times* (London), 31 August 1987. Perhaps he should have mentioned drugs.
53 Charles A. Johnson and Bradley C. Canon, *Judicial Policies: implementation and impact*, Washington DC, 1984.

11

Is the US Constitution adequate for the twenty-first century?

JAMES L. SUNDQUIST
Brookings Institution

It is appropriate, at this point in our bicentennial colloquium, to return to that part of the Constitution that is in fact 200 years old this year – the part establishing the structure of the United States government, which was the actual product of the Philadelphia convention – as distinct from the Bill of Rights, which is only 196 years old and will have its own bicentennial in due course. In discussing the adequacy of our constitutional structure for our third century of national life, one can use almost any day's headlines as the starting-point. For the news in America is normally dominated by conflict between the executive and legislative branches – the President and Congress – and this is the outcome, indeed the *intended* outcome of the constitutional structure bequeathed to the twentieth and twenty-first centuries by the wisdom of the eighteenth.

So let us start with the subject that has dominated the news for most of the spring and summer of 1987, and has absorbed public attention for 250 hours of often dramatic televised public hearings – what we call the Iran–contra affair.

In his own summation of the Iran–contra events, in an address to the nation, President Reagan spoke of the 'failure' of his policy, of a 'policy that went astray', of the 'damage that's been done'. Then he went on to say that the 'lies, leaks, divisions, and mistakes' grew out of mistrust between the Executive and legislative branches. And he proposed the usual remedies: The 'executive and legislative branches of government need to regain trust in each other' and 'need to find a way to co-operate while realizing foreign policy can't be run by committee'.

Well, nobody is for mistrust and against trust. But how do we get there from here? How do we get trust and co-operation in the U.S. system of government? Just by replacing people – the ones who lied to Congress and made the mistakes and ran a secret foreign policy out of the White House that the Secretaries of State and Defence were opposed to and part of which they, and the President himself, did not even know about? The President agreed with the view that 'the failure lay more in people than in process' and took pride in having appointed a new national security adviser, a new CIA director, and a new Chief of Staff in the White House – all of whom he said he had explicitly instructed to please let him into the policy-making process. And, of course, Admiral Poindexter and Lt.-Col. North had long since been reassigned. But is that enough to restore trust and bring about co-operation?

If Iran–contra were an isolated episode – or, rather, two isolated episodes – one could perhaps say yes. But these events are far from isolated.

What we have been seeing almost continuously for more than twenty years is a *pattern* of mistrust between Congress and the Executive branch, a pattern of deceit, of conflict in which each branch attempts to vitiate, and often succeeds in vitiating, the policies of the other. The pattern appeared most spectacularly in the case of Vietnam, but it was evident also in the quarrels over Angola and Cyprus, trade negotiations with the Soviet Union, the Carter *Salt* II agreement, arms sales to Arab countries, and most recently aid to the Nicaraguan contras. If Congress had known about what the administration was up to in Iran, there would have been conflict over that as well.

When what we might consider to be exceptional conduct becomes not the exception but the rule, in a wide range of circumstances with many different individuals involved, we have to look for *systemic* causes. And that such causes do exist is beyond question. Since the bicentennial year of celebration, we are constantly reminded of the wisdom of the Founding Fathers in bestowing upon our country its unique system of separation of powers, of checks and balances. What we see in the Iran–contra scandal is checks and balances at work.

On the plus side, we have seen the way in which checks and balances facilitate exposure when mistakes are made. The scandal has been separately, and intensively, investigated by all three branches. The President had the Attorney-General inquire into the case, then appointed the Tower Commission, which did a thorough – and thoroughly independent – job. Meanwhile, Congress plunged in, with separate House and Senate committees that combined for joint hearings. And an independent counsel (formerly called the special prosecutor) selected by a panel of judges went to work on the criminal aspects of the matter. If the President himself was not on trial, certainly the presidency has been. The way in which the separation of powers serves to hold our highest officials to account is the envy of people in other countries. At the time of Watergate, I was in Europe and repeatedly heard people say, 'If something like that had happened here, the difference is that nobody would ever have found out about it.'

But exposing mistakes, and even putting people in jail, are remedies only after the fact – after the damage has been done. The more important question is how the failures and mistakes could have been prevented in the first place. And here is where we come to the minus side of checks and balances. Referring again to the current cases, were they not simply the errors, or misbehaviour of the Executive branch alone? Then why did the President blame what happened on mistrust and lack of co-operation *between the branches?*

In the Iran case – the trading of arms for hostages – the President admits that he was 'stubborn' in insisting on pursuing a mistaken policy. 'Presumably he did not inform Congress – in defiance of the law – because he was afraid the legislators would prevent his carrying out the policy. He has already overridden the misgivings of his Secretaries of State and Defence; having to override congressional objections too would have made his course far more difficult, and there was always the danger that the legislators would take the issue to the public by leaking secret information. (The information eventually reached the public, of couse, as it was bound to do, but by way of leaks at the Iranian end of the transaction, not the U.S. end.) What the President was saying, in effect, was that trust and co-operation between the branches would have saved him from himself. Congress would have checked him.

This is clearly, then, a systemic problem not a people problem. Every president is bound to believe in his policies, more or less stubbornly. If Congress is likely to inhibit his chosen course, he and his subordinates are motivated to conceal, to deceive, to lie, and cover up – as has been our experience for twenty years, and in many instances before then as well. They are going to find loopholes in any law requiring the sharing of information and co-operation between the branches. Just changing national security advisers, or even presidents, is not going to solve the problem. It is systemic.

That systemic problem can be defined as the absence in the U.S. constitutional system of the restraints, and safeguards – truly effective checks and balances, if you will – that flow from collective responsibility. In parliamentary countries, the doctrine is that a prime minister does not embark on foreign and military adventures without consultation with the cabinet, and its concurrence. Some at least of the cabinet members are important political figures in their own right with independent bases of support. If the foreign minister and defence minister both opposed a prime minister's proposal, it would be hardly likely to be carried out. Yet in the United States major foreign policy decisions are presidential, not cabinet matters, individual, not collective. A president is never obliged to consult with his cabinet on any matter, much less get its approval. Besides, his cabinet is made up of his own appointees. The president gives them their status and power, they are wholly dependent on him, they rarely have political bases of their own. So a cabinet member is not likely to carry objections to presidential policy very far, and is even less likely to resign in protest. And when one occasionally does, the country does not pay much attention.

The only officials with enough independent political strength to serve as a genuine check and restraint on the president are the leaders of Congress. But as we have seen over and over again, laws requiring that they be consulted can be easily evaded. Congress can be kept completely in the dark, and the presidency can become then a one-man show, the 'imperial presidency', the 'runaway presidency', as it was called back in the Vietnam days. Congress thought it had laid the imperial presidency to rest, when it finally took matters in hand and forced President Nixon to resign, but the dealings with Iran showed it to be alive and as well as ever.

Our constitutional system of checks and balances creates one kind of problem, then, when it is evaded and we are left with no real restraint on the presidency at all. It creates another when it works. The other part of the Iran–contra affair – the contra part – illustrates that as well as any case in history.

In brief, what happened is that President Reagan, upon assuming office, set out to topple the Sandinista regime in Nicaragua by supporting the contra forces. For a time Congress authorised limited assistance to the contras. But eventually it revolted, restricting its aid to the contras to humanitarian purposes, and through the Boland amendment prohibited any military assistance. Congress wrote a foreign policy by law – or thought it did. Then the President's men set out to evade that law, protecting him, giving him deniability, as the phrase goes, by not telling him. They sent some of the profits from the Iranian arms sales to the contras in disregard of the law.

Now, just what good does it do in circumstances like this for the President to plead for trust and co-operation between the branches? The problem here is a fundamental policy difference between them. Can either branch be expected to co-operate in carrying out a policy of the other branch which it strenuously opposes? The President is right in saying that they have to, for any policy to succeed, yet the systemic prob-

lem is that much of the time they do not and, because of their deep-
seated disagreeements, cannot realistically be expected to.

Consequently, under such circumstances, the United States cannot
have a foreign policy that works. The President's Nicaragua policy, if
Congress supported it, might be decisive and strong enough to be effective. Congress's policy, if it had presidential backing, might work too.
Both those postulates are conjectural, but what we can be *sure* of is that
with the two branches going in opposite directions, the weak compromises they eventually work out stand little prospect of success.
Maybe the Central American countries will work something out now,
but in our years of acting alone we have been meddling just enough to
gain for the Sandinista government a lot of sympathy and support both
at home and abroad, but not enough to give them any real trouble. There
is a good analogy here with Vietnam, when the country could never
adopt either of two decisive policies – either to go in with enough force
to win the war, or pull out early and gracefully. As it was, we just
suffered all those casualties for nothing.

Let's move to the domestic area for a moment. Here the central problem is our budget deficit, which has been running close to $200 billion a
year since the great tax cut of 1981 took effect. The national debt stands
at $2 trillion, and has doubled in the last six years. The United States
has suffered the shock of becoming the world's leading debtor nation,
living by borrowing from abroad. Our trade deficit, our shortfall in
investment, high interest rates, are all blamed on the inability of the
government to bring its budget deficit under control. For all these
economic reasons – as well as for sound moral reasons – the country has
had for some time now a political consensus that this has got to stop.
The President calls the deficits an outrage and a disgrace, and wants a
constitutional amendment to prohibit them – after he leaves office, of
course. The Democrats who lead Congress denounce them with equal
fervour, as do all the current fourteen presidential candidates in both
parties. But, as in the case of Central America, the country has no policy
and no programme. The President has his plan to reduce the deficit, but
Congress will not accept it. The Democratic majorities in Congress have
hammered out their programme, but the President promises to veto it if
they send it to him. There is always the hope that, this year, the two
sides will finally gather at a summit meeting and negotiate a compromise.
But they have not been able to get together in other years, and at this
point this year, after wrangling since January and with the new fiscal
year shortly to begin, they are still arguing about the shape of the conference table.

These are the checks and balances in operation. Intense conflict, interminable delay, deadlock, ineffective and watered-down compromises – these are the characteristics of the American system, in foreign and domestic policy alike. And they are what call into question the adequacy of the consitutional system for the third century of the American republic.

My description of how our system works is not a partisan one. Conservatives and Liberals in the United States, Republicans and Democrats, will generally agree that the checks and balances do what they were intended to do, when they are allowed to operate; the branches do check one another, constantly. What Americans have disagreed on is whether those consequences are, on balance, good or bad.

Traditionally, Conservatives have thought the sludginess of our governmental processes to be good. The separation of powers slows things down, compels a high degree of consensus for any new departure, prevents mistakes – mistakes of commission at least – and provides many points at which powerful minority groups like people of wealth and property or southern segregationists can interpose a veto to prevent the majority from acting. 'That government is best which governs least' has been the slogan of conservatives for our whole two centuries.

Liberals, on the other hand, have tended to deplore the obstruction and delay and they have wanted government to be capable of action. And, in so far as the constitutional structure has been criticised (notably during the Great Depression) it has been from that quarter. *Now*, however, we have a new breed of conservatives – vigorous and activist – who are not satisfied just to stop the advance of the welfare state but want to dismantle it. Now some of them are beginning to bemoan the constitutional system that prevents *them* from carrying out *their* programme. That thwarts Ronald Reagan from repealing the New Deal and wiping out the Sandinistas, and outlawing abortion, and all the rest.

So some Conservatives and some Liberals, of both parties, including an impressive roster of former high officials and elder statesmen, have now come together over the past half-dozen years to undertake the most serious and responsible – and best organised – re-examination of our basic constitutional structure that has been attempted at any time since its adoption. Early this year, the Committee issued its report and recommendations, which I commend to you.

Those who question the constitutional structure are asked, in effect, who do you think you are to reject, and overturn, the wisdom of the Founding Fathers? The best answer to that is that the Founders themselves, almost as soon as they began to run their new government,

rejected the basic principle of the model that they had written into the
Constitution and that we are living with today. They overturned their
own wisdom.

Those of you who have read the proceedings of the 1787 Convention,
as recorded by Madison and others, and the *Federalist* papers, know
that the framers' model was a government *without* political parties – what
we may call the Madisonian model. Only the most rudimentary forms of
today's parties then existed in the States, or anywhere else, but in so far
as the framers referred to these groupings at all, they condemned them.
They rarely termed them parties, but factions or cabals, and they were
blamed for the 'corruption' and 'intrigue' that the delegates saw in the
legislatures of the new states as well as in legislative bodies elsewhere.

It was to prevent the control of the entire government by any one
individual or group – and for group, read faction or cabal or party – that
the separation of powers doctrine was embraced in the Madisonian
model and the checks and balances devised. A house of representatives
might be seized by a transient popular majority but the Senate would be
a stable body of distinguished elders with long overlapping terms who
would rise above factionalism, and the President – with his veto – would
be the very embodiment of the non-partisan ideal. That is why the
framers rejected popular election of the President, or even his election
by Congress, and conceived the electoral college as a non-partisan
apparatus – like the search committee which a corporation or university
or city council sets up to select a new chief executive – but made up of
men who did not know one another, would not be in communication
with one another, and hence, as Madison put it at the Convention, 'there
would be little opportunity for cabal, or corruption'.

No more powerful diatribe against political parties has ever been
penned than the *Federalist*, particularly Madison's No. 10. He speaks of
the 'violence of faction', of the instability, unsteadiness, confusion,
oppression and 'schemes of injustice' that flow from 'that dangerous
vice', those 'sinister combinations' – factions and factionalism.

But before George Washington's first term was up, what became the
Federalist and Republican parties were taking form, and they developed
so quickly that in his celebrated Farewell Address, Washington felt constrained to warn his countrymen 'in the most solemn manner against the
baneful effects of the spirit of party generally' – what he called the 'worst
enemy' of democratic governments everywhere, leading to 'riots and
insurrections', 'corruption', and all the rest. Ironically, each year since –
including this year – a senator and representative arise in their respective
chambers on Washington's birthday to solemnly intone those words to

their colleagues, who have *all* been elected on *party* tickets, have organised their respective chambers through *party* caucuses and *party*-line votes, and have entrusted the conduct of legislative business to *party* organisations and leaders.

By 1800, two national parties were in full-fledged operation, with candidates for president and vice-president. The electoral college had been converted from a search committee with the gravest of responsibilities to a rubber stamp, its members pledged to the parties' nominees. 'The election of a President of the United States is no longer that process which the Constitution contemplated', one of the framers, Rufus King, remarked in an 1816 Senate debate. Parties, James Madison acknowledged in his retirement years, are 'a natural offspring of Freedom'. By that time, of course, Madison had been elected and re-elected President as a party nominee.

Why, then, are parties natural? (And they must be, because they have appeared in every democratic country of the world, without exception.) They are natural because people who share a common background or philosophy or approach to government, or all of these, want control of government in order to enact their policies and their programmes, and the means to that end has to be a political organisation. When the organisation, or party, wins an election, it does what it promised – or tries to, anyway – and then takes responsibility, at the next election, for the results. We can call this the responsible party model.

The responsible party model does what, in America, the Constitution, built on the Madisonian model, was explicitly designed to prevent. Adoption of the responsible party model, this violation of the spirit and philosophy of the Constitution, began with the framers themselves, except only Washington, who was consistent to the end. And it has continued ever since. No party ever said, 'We only want the presidency', or the Senate, or the House. They say, give us *total* responsibility. In the 1984 election, Ronald Reagan's Republicans said, give us control of the House and Senate, as well as the presidency, so we can enact our programme. And so did Walter Mondale's Democrats.

In other words, our country's political leadership, of every party, for two centuries, has organised and utilised political parties not to support the constitutional system – but to overcome it. And the discipline of political science has been overwhelmingly in favour of their doing exactly that. In fact, the organised discipline went more or less officially on record to that effect in 1950, with the famous report of its Committee on Political Parties. Political science textbooks call parties the tie that binds, the glue that cements, the web or the bridge that unites the disparate organs of the government to make the constitutional structure work.

And there is every evidence that the people have accepted the responsible party model, too. Rarely, until thirty years ago, did they fail to elect each four years a president and congress of the same party. In the nineteenth century, that was largely an artefact of the election process. Parties printed the ballots and the voter selected the ballot of his choice, which was a party slate. But even after the secret ballot was invented and ticket-splitting was made not only possible but easy, the overwhelming majority of voters continued to vote a party ticket, and one part or the other, at each presidential election, was given control of both elective branches of the government. In this century, the Republicans had complete control in the 1900s and 1920s, and the Democrats, with one two-year hiatus, during the two decades from 1933 to 1953.

In 1956, however, the country passed through a momentous transition, the historic importance of which has simply not been understood in America, a transition from a system of single-party government nearly all the time to one of divided government most of the time. In that year, for the first time in more than seven decades, the people denied to an elected or re-elected President, Dwight Eisenhower, a Congress controlled by his own party, and they repeated that decision in four of the next seven presidential elections. As in 1956, in 1968 and 1972 with Nixon and 1980 and 1984 with Reagan, they placed Republican presidents in the White House but sent Democratic majorities to the House of Representatives, and in the first three of those elections to the Senate as well. Neither party was given full responsibility, with corresponding accountability.

Does this mean, then, that the people, beginning at mid-century, came to reject the concept of responsible party government that, until then, they appeared to have accepted? By no means.

I won't go through the mathematics here, but it is demonstrable by both polls and election returns that most people still vote straight tickets for President, Senate, and House. It is the minority (never more than 20 per cent and in most elections many fewer than that) whose ticket-splitting between a Republican for President and Democrats for Congress gives us our divided governments. A very small minority is getting what it wants, and denying responsible party government to the country.

When two parties split the control of government, as has been the case two-thirds of the time since 1954, deadlocks are inevitable. If the President sends up a proposal, the opposition party in control of a legislative body *has* to reject it. Otherwise, it is saying, the President is a wise and prudent leader, and it is building him and his party up for the next election. And if the opposition majority in Congress initiates a measure, the President has to veto it – or he is saying, in effect, my opponents are right and statesmanlike, and he is building *them* up. Eventually, something emerges after a stream of recriminations and vetoes, but it is apt not to reflect the views of either party, and be a pale and ineffective compromise. Neither party takes responsibility, neither can be held accountable, each can point the finger at the other if things go wrong.

In countries with parliamentary systems, coalition governments that try to combine the major right-wing and left-wing parties are adopted rarely, either accidentally, as in Israel today, or in response to the deepest crisis, for it is the business of the major parties to discredit and defeat each other, and they can, and should, lay aside their normal partisanship only under extraordinary circumstances and for short periods. Yet in the United States, such coalition governments, governments divided between left and right, are now routine. And they have been marked, as one would expect, by the confusion and conflict in foreign policy and ineffectiveness in grappling with the deficit and other domestic problems that I described earlier.

How might we change our Constitution, then, or our political practices, to make divided government less likely? The answer unfortunately is, as a practical matter, we can do nothing.

Two approaches are theoretically possible. Since divided government is the result of ticket-splitting, the simplest remedy would be to prohibit it – go back, in effect, to the nineteenth century when the ballots were designed in such a way that people were compelled to vote the straight ticket of one or another party, and divided government was therefore a rarity. Voters could be required to choose between party slates, or 'team tickets', consisting of a party's candidates for national office (presidency, vice-presidency, Senate, and House). That would virtually assure the President's party control of the House, and usually of the Senate also. A second approach would be to award the party that won the presidency enough bonus seats in Congress to assure a majority of both houses.

These two proposals, however, illustrate the practical problems that constitutional reformers face. Because the amendment process requires extraordinary majorities – two- thirds of the House and Senate and three-fourths of the states it demands, in effect, bipartisan agreement. Therefore, both parties would have to see benefit in the change. But since redistribution of power always creates both winners and losers, one party is bound to lose. In the current case, it would be the Democrats, for had either of the reforms been in effect it would have given the Republicans control of Congress during much or all of the time that they have held the presidency. The Democrats in Congress would never take a second look at any team ticket scheme that would make them stand or fall with a George McGovern or a Walter Mondale – that would convert their majorities into minorities every time their candidate for president was beaten. And even the Republicans wouldn't buy it. They'd remember how many seats they would have lost with Barry Goldwater back in 1964.

So those of us who believe that divided government is the gravest of all the weaknesses in our constitutional system reach the discomfiting conclusion that nothing can be done about it. There is no remedy that would be both effective and plausibly acceptable. We simply have to hope that historical events will occur that somehow will solve the problem for us, by restoring party loyalty, and consequent straight-ticket voting for national offices, to the level we were accustomed to a generation or two ago. I have written elsewhere about what those events might be.

What are some of the other problems of the constitutional structure as we look ahead to the twenty-first century? Next on my list is the extremely short time-horizon the Constitution imposes on our elected leaders. Put simply, the difficulty is that our mid-term congressional elections are too frequent. No other major democracy in the world gives its elected legislature only a two-year term. The result, for us, is that House members are constantly campaigning, unless they happen to come from absolutely safe seats, and at any given time one-third of the senators – except the few who have announced their retirement – are also running frantically for re-election.

The current House was elected in November 1986, sworn in in January 1987, and by February its members were already making the rounds of the Political Action Committees, starting to raise money for next year's campaign and making the inevitable promises that these Committees demand in return for their cash. Members who expect tough challenges dashed home almost every weekend throughout 1987, and in 1988 *every* weekend. The senators up for re-election in 1988 will have been heavily engaged in money-raising for a year or two beforehand. Senators, with their six-year terms, have a saying that in the first two years you can be a statesman, in the second two you're a politician, and in the last two you're a demagogue. By that token, House members are demagogues all the time.

It is now accepted as a fact of American political life that whatever an administration hopes to accomplish in its term, it all has to be done in the first year. That's called the one-year 'window of opportunity'. In the second year, everybody – Congress and the Administration both – are distracted by the mid-term election. And that election almost invariably sets the President back. The opposition party is strengthened, and becomes more aggressive. A deadlock is created, or if it already exists is intensified. The presidential campaign gets under way immediately, and then everyone waits for that election, which will presumably resolve matters. A four-year term would open that 'window of opportunity' somewhat wider.

Defenders of the two-year term say that a short tenure keeps representatives close to the people, and that is a fundamental principle of democracy. It is, of course. But how close is close enough, and how close is *too* close? In autumn 1986, members of the House went through an intensive period of closeness, listening to constituents constantly for two solid months, expounding their views, and asking for a mandate. Should not the winners, who received their mandate, have a breathing spell to do what they promised to do before they must again be back in the intimacy with their constituents of the campaign period? It is not as though they are ever completely out of touch – with the telephone, the post, the media, and the public opinion polls. But if they had more time before they had to face the voters, House members would have a chance, like senators, to be statesmen for a while, and do the difficult, unpopular things that sometimes have to be done – as, in our current situation, to raise taxes, which a majority of the members of both the House and the Senate will admit privately is absolutely necessary to reduce the dreadful budgetary deficit.

Longer terms for House members is one constitutional reform issue that has been seriously considered a number of times. The last time was at the end of Lyndon Johnson's presidency, when he sent up a special message urging that an amendment be adopted for four-year terms, all members to be elected simultaneously with the President. Just before his message went up, one senior congressman had taken a poll asking the members' preference, and as might be expected they were overwhelmingly in favour of the longer term. So when President Johnson's message arrived, you would expect the members would approve it by a big majority – right? Wrong. The reaction of the members was to ask, when that wheeler-dealer from Texas proposed this nice gift for members of Congress, what was his *real* motive? And then his attorney-general, testifying for the proposal, made it clear. He said that history has shown that the Congress elected in the presidential year was more co-operative than the one elected at mid-term. For 'co-operative' the Congressmen read 'subservient, more subject to presidential discipline, more easily kicked around'. The measure never even came out of the House committee. But if a different president supported it, the idea just might stand a chance.

A four-year term, with all the members elected in the presidential year, would eliminate the mid-term election for the House. What about the Senate? To eliminate it for the Senate as well would require either lengthening the term of Senators to eight years or reducing it to four. No Senator would support shortening the term, obviously. But they would be reluctant to support lengthening it either. The immediate reaction of most Americans whenever the subject comes up is that eight years is far too long for an elective office, and senators would not want to risk the public reaction. It is therefore likely that any amendment seriously considered would be limited to the four-year House term. That would, of course, negate the fundamental purpose, as I see it, because there would still be a mid-term election to distract the Senate, and the President and his whole Administration, if not the House. The fact is, substituting an eight-year term for one of six years would affect the composition of the Senate hardly at all. Very few Senators are retired by the voters after only one term and to give those few an extra two years would make no appreciable difference in the character of that body.

Lengthened terms would give members that necessary breathing spell between elections. It would also lead – or should lead – to a somewhat more orderly legislative process. Now, every piece of legislation must be considered and enacted within the two-year span, or it dies and must be considered fresh from the beginning when the next Congress meets. This results each two years in a great traffic jam as Congress rushes to adjournment. Good bills are lost altogether for want of time, and other measures are passed in an unseemly rush, with members not able to keep up with everything that is going on. A more leisurely four-year process would lead to some additional procrastination, no doubt – applying Parkinson's law – but it would surely also result in a better-considered and better-drafted legislative product.

A third question about the adequacy of our consititutional structure arises from the requirement of a two-thirds vote of the Senate for the approval of treaties. Americans of my post-Second World War generation were brought up to believe that one of the great tragedies of history was the failure of the United States to join the organisation that the world had created as its hope for preventing the Second World War – the League of Nations. That was a flagrant case of minority rule in our country. Our President, Woodrow Wilson, had taken the lead in designing the League; the country from every evidence (in those days before public opinion polls) was for it; and 58 per cent of the Senate voted for it. But that was less than two-thirds of the Senate, and so it lost.

A recalcitrant minority can still defeat a constructive international agreement which a large majority of the country may be ready and eager to accept. It is ironic that it only takes a simple majority of Congress to declare war but a two-thirds majority is required in the Senate to make peace, or to take steps to avert war. This difficulty could be resolved by lowering the two-thirds to, say, 60 per cent, or by permitting treaties to be approved by an absolute majority of both houses. The latter solution has the additional advantage of admitting the House into the approval process.

A fourth question arises from the absence in our system of the kind of safety valve that parliamentary governments have of being able to call a new election whenever and for whatever reason the government in power has lost its ability to lead and govern. We in the United States are so heavily dependent on presidential leadership that one flinches in contemplating all the things that can happen to an individual human being. We do have a safeguard now, in the Twenty-fifth Amendment, when a president becomes physically disabled, as Woodrow Wilson was during the final eighteen months of his term in office when his wife and a couple of cabinet members were running the government. Even that requires a kind of palace coup, with the Cabinet, consisting entirely of the President's own appointees, taking the initiative, and one wonders whether that would have happened even in Wilson's case. And there is also the impeachment process, if the president can be convicted of high crime and misdemeanours.

Impeachment has been carried all the way to a trial only once, when President Andrew Johnson was acquitted by a single vote in 1868. And it was carried, in the case of Richard Nixon, to the point where it forced a president to resign for the firt time in history. Before the resignation, many people were saying, 'We do have a problem here. How do we get rid of the man? But when he resigned, they sighed in relief and said, 'that proves the system does work, after all'.

To my mind, it proved nothing of the sort. The president's resignation did not come until after the famous 'smoking gun' tape was found that implicated the President beyond doubt in an indictable crime. But consider what had to happen before he could be implicated. First, the president had to record his crime on tape. Second, he had to neglect to destroy it. You can be sure that no future president will make those mistakes. He won't record his crimes in the first place, but he'll destroy them if he does. So there won't be any smoking gun lying around in the future.

Moreover, if a President is neither physically incapacitated nor guilty of an indictable crime or some other abuse of power so gross that even his own party is compelled to repudiate him, there is no safeguard whatever in the American system. A President can turn out to be weak, or stubborn, or erratic, or he can develop aberrations under the pressures of his office, have a mental or emotional, as distinct from a physical breakdown, as has happened to top executives in many other organisation, public and private, and nothing can be done about it.

Or the government can be in a state of collapse even if a president is strong and healthy, if he finds himself in a state of hopeless deadlock with Congress. This is always on the verge of happening, and has indeed happened at least two or three times, depending on one's definition, in these recent years of Republican presidents confronting Democratic congresses. In such cases, as in the cases of presidential failure, the United States is in bondage to the calendar. Everybody in office, all the parties to the deadlock, the President and the legislators alike, hang on to their offices as a kind of property right until that November date in the year divisible by four rolls around. We can be without an effective government in a time of crisis; we can be impotent to deal with a collapse of the economy (as we were during the administration of a narrow-visioned president in the early years of the Great Depression) or we could be losing a war, and there is no way to bring fresh leadership to the pinnacle of government, as Winston Churchill was brought in to supplant Neville Chamberlain after Narvik. If a Narvik happened to us, we would just go on losing.

There is a belief in the country that the mid-term election – which we abolished a few minutes ago – is the American solution to the problem of governmental failure. But that is clearly a myth, because the mid-term election does not include the presidency. The people can send a message to the President, as they often do, by voting for the opposition candidates for House and Senate. But strengthening the opposition does not reconstitute the government or break a deadlock, quite the opposite. All it can do is intensify an existing deadlock, if one exists, or create one, if it doesn't.

Just how can a remedy for this endemic weakness be fitted into the American system? My own reflections have led me to conclude that a system for special elections to install fresh leadership is needed when the government has clearly and palpably failed; that it needs to be written in such a way that it will not be invoked casually, for reasons of petty, partisan advantage, and that the best means to that end is to require that all elected office-holders – every member of the House and Senate as well as the President – vacate their seats; that, with this proviso, the special election be called either by the President or a constitutional majority of either house, which would enable either side in a deadlocked government to take the initiative to put the case before the people to decide. After the ordeal of a special election, the newly-elected office-holders should begin complete new terms rather than just finish the unexpired terms.

One problem that has perplexed our committee is how we could hold an election on short notice. In Britain, when the Prime Minister decides to call an election, the question is, shall it be in three weeks' time, or four? In our system, the time span between the selection of the first delegates to the nominating convention, through the conventions, to the election itself, is more than eight months, and most candidates campaign almost full-time at least a year before that. I think our parties could adjust their nominating processes to accommodate those rare cases when special elections would be called. But I am not at all sure that any practising politicians could ever be persuaded to think so.

Questions such as these were considered all over America in the bicentennial year by groups who held meetings and conferences. But the questions are abstract and remote from people's every day concerns, and no groundswell of support for any constitutional change can be detected. Most people feel protective about the ancient document; they resist, and often reject out of hand, suggestions that it be tampered with. Members of Congress, who normally would have to initiate any constitutional amendment, have shown no interest, not even in the proposal to lengthen their own terms.

We can predict with certainly that action on the two most severe problems of our consititutional structure that I have mentioned – divided government, and the lack of a mechanism for reconstituting a failed government – will not occur until the country lives through a crisis in which the govenment collapses utterly, over a sustained period. It would be better, naturally, to repair the structure *before* it does collapse. The necessity to experience governmental failure of crisis proportions, in order to prepare for it, is not a happy prospect. But the overburdened people running our government, who would have to initiate any change, have all they can do to solve today's pressing problems, without worrying about tomorrow's. Unfortunately, but inevitably, that is the way of politicians and of people generally. That nothing happens short of crisis has been the case with all fundamental constitutional reform, in every country and throughout history.

12

The President, Congress, and foreign policy

KENNETH W. THOMPSON
University of Virginia

Two viewpoints have characterised discussion by the American public during the Iran-contra hearings and in the post-mortems that have followed. The one that called to mind the Watergate hearings involved the search for answers to the question: who knew what and when did he know? For those who held to this view the hearings were simply a repetition of the questioning in the Watergate hearings: did President Nixon know about the Watergate break-in and when did he know? This time the questions were: did the President know about the sale of arms to Iran for hostages and did he know about the diversion of funds to the contras? If so, when did he know?

The other viewpoint set off the Iran-contra hearings from Watergate. According to this, the real issue was the collapse of constitutionalism in the foreign decision-making process. For various reasons, the Founding Fathers gave power to both the President and Congress in foreign policy. On the one hand, the President is the Commander-in-Chief. He sends and receives diplomats. He delivers diplomatic messages on behalf of the United States. He negotiates treaties. Thomas Jefferson wrote of 'the transaction of business with foreign nations' being 'executive altogether'. Balanced against this, it is agreed that there is no open-ended grant of Executive power in the Constitution. Whereas some debate the phrase used by Dean Rusk in the 1960s, 'the president *makes* foreign policy', few debate that primary responsibility for the *conduct* of US foreign relations rests with the President. Because it is agreed that a committee has difficulty executing foreign policy and because foreign policy requires flexibility of response, the Executive must take on the task of negotiating and implementing policy.

At the same time, congressional responsibilities in foreign policy are substantial. Article I not only catalogued the powers of Congress making clear that it had, at least so some of the founders thought, primacy in foreign policy. Nearly half of the enumerated congressional powers are in the area of foreign policy. Many things the President undertakes in the conduct of American foreign relations require legislation or appropriations or both. For example, treaties require the advice and consent of the Senate and important appointments require confirmation. Undergirding the success or failure of every foreign policy is the need for consensus, beginning with Congress but extending to the public at large. A national consensus came into being after the Second World War, thanks in large part to bipartisan support for the Truman Doctrine, the Marshall Plan and NATO. Much has changed since the halcyon days of the late 1940s, including the number and perhaps the intent of players in Congress. However, failure in policies for Vietnam and aid to the Nicaraguan contras are significantly a result of the lack of a lasting consensus. If partnership and communication between the President and Congress was important in simpler days it is still more vital today.

What is unfortunate about the fragmentation of American thinking reflected in the two prevailing viewpoints regarding the Iran-contra dispute is that it is difficult to see how and when such differences can be reconciled. Linked with the former is the assumption that the President alone is responsible for foreign policy and with the latter that the ever greater involvement of Congressmen and Senators is a prescription for failure. Carried to extremes, the powers of each branch bring about continuing confrontation, unresolved disputes and, ultimately, a stalemate. The risk is the greater when one party controls the Executive and the other the legislative branch of government. Historically, the party that controls the Executive claims exclusive responsibilities for the President in foreign policy while the party that prevails in Congress is more likely to remember that Congress and the President share overlapping powers.

In an address delivered on 3 October 1985 at the University of Virginia, former Secretary of State Dean Rust observed:

> The separation of powers in the conduct of our foreign relations, whatever theorists may have to say about it, is real. It is a fundamental part of our constitutional system and it gives rise to constitutional tensions throughout the day on every working day throughout the year.
>
> Chief Justice Earl Warren shortly before his death reminded us that if each branch of the federal government were to pursue its own constitutional powers to the end of the trail our system simply could not function. In effect he was saying that it would freeze up like an engine without oil. Impasse is the overhanging threat in our constitutional system, deliberately made complicated by our Founding Fathers in order to place restraints upon the exercise of the raw power of government.[1]

The thrust of Secretary Rusk's argument was that participants in foreign policy-making who in the American system follow one another in rapid succession must, first, recognise that both the President and Congress have responsibilities for foreign policy. Those who watched the televised hearings in Summer 1987 remember the look of utter disbelief on the faces of both Lieutenant-Colonel Oliver North and Admiral John Poindexter when questioners referred to constitutional provisions regarding Congress. The two presidential aides were apparently convinced that they were carrying out the will of the President and that he alone had a mandate in foreign policy.

The other point that both Secretary Rusk and Chief Justice Warren seem to be making is that even recognising the dual responsibility of the President and Congress, each has sufficiently great obligations so that any administration or congress which fully carries them out can bring the process of foreign policy-making to a halt. In fact when Congress refused to appropriate funds for certain aspects of American policy in Vietnam and refused to assist what Secretary Kissinger and President Ford defined as essential in Vietnam it was in effect saying that successive presidents had gone too far in Vietnam. The War Powers Resolution of 1973 passed over President Nixon's veto was a further response to alleged excess of Executive power, especially with regard to war-making powers. It requires the President: (1) to consult with Congress 'in every possible instance' before US armed forces enter hostilities or situations of imminent hostilities; (2) to report to Congress within forty-eight hours when forces are so consulted; and (3) to terminate the engagement within sixty days if Congress has not declared war or specifically authorised continued use of armed forces. Lastly, it permits Congress within those sixty days to direct the President to withdraw US forces by a concurrent resolution passed by both houses, but not requiring the President's signature. It may be worth noting that individual Senators, including Senator Thomas Eagleton, were sufficiently ambivalent about the resolution as it emerged from their deliberations to support it reluctantly; Eagleton actually voted against it. Senator Ives of New York, however, considered it the most important piece of legislation in his long and distinguished career as a legislator.

In practice, the War Powers Resolution has proved extraordinarily difficult to apply. In the present Persian Gulf crisis, numerous legislators have expressed concern that American policy is leading to a situation of 'imminent hostilities'. Yet when Congress had an opportunity to oppose the reflagging of Kuwaiti tankers, they in effect did not do so. Congress was unhappy with the Executive's policy but had no alternatives to suggest. The present situation is reminiscent of an event in the Kennedy administration that emphasised the limits of Congress's role in foreign policy in a crisis. About two hours before his celebrated speech to the nation on the Cuban missile crisis, President Kennedy met with some thirty members of the Senate and House. Many listened in shock to what was for them a first reporting of the presence of the missiles. None of them questioned whether the President had the constitutional authority to take the steps he told them he was about to take, even though they recognised the risks involved. Instead their mood was reflected in the statement of one senator to Secretary Rusk as they left the meeting. He said: 'Thank God I'm not the President of the United States'.

CONSTITUTIONALISM, BALANCE AND MORALITY

If we turn from the present to the past, the philosophy and values that led to the constitutional provisions on foreign policy become apparent. Realism about values and politics was manifested from the founding within the American constitutional system. The Founders saw constitutionalism as offering a political order based on checks and balances. They wrote of the interplay of 'opposite and rival interests'. Constitutionalism was intended to remedy man's 'defect of better motives'. While Hamilton defended the concept of an energetic Executive and was not unsympathetic to the monarchical idea, his views were set aside for what James Sterling Young has called the idea of the leaderless state. The majority preferred a government in which authority rested in laws, not persons. For at least some of the Founders, that government was best that governed least. Government was cast in a framework of utilitarianism; it was conceived as an instrument to ensure those conditions under which individuals could follow their chosen lives and liberties and the pursuit of happiness.

Not only a monarchy but a hierarchical structure of government was rejected. The Founders displayed a mistrust of political power. As John Adams put it in a classic statement:

> Power always thinks it has a great soul and vast views beyond the comprehension of the weak and that it is doing God's service when it is violating all His laws. Our passions, ambitions, love and resentment, etc., possess so much metaphysical subtlety and so much overpowering eloquence that they insinuate themselves into the understanding and the conscience and convert both to their party.

During much of early national period Thomas Jefferson and John Adams were respectful adversaries. Jefferson balanced his unquenchable faith in the people with a clear-eyed recognition of the place of checks and balances. In 1798, speaking on the Virginia Resolutions, he wrote:

> Confidence in the men of our choice . . . is . . . the parent of despotism: free government is founded in jealousy and not in confidence: it is jealousy and not confidence which prescribes limited constitutions to bind down those whom we are obliged to trust with power . . . In questions of power then let no more be heard of confidence in man, but bind him down from mischief by the claims of the Constitution.

The exercise of power and the imposing of the will of an individual or group on others was 'of all known causes the greatest promoter of corruption'. However much the Enlightenment may have shaped the thought of early Americans, their views of power reflected a sturdy recognition of the promise, the hazards and the reality of power. This was the same Jefferson who wrote: 'Before the establishment of the American States, nothing was known to history but the man of the old world crowding within limits either small or overcharged and steeped in vices which the situation generates.'²

The separation of powers in the Constitution was a particular expression of the Founders' concept of checks and balances. The division of powers among the Executive, legislative and judicial branches of government imposed limitations on the exercise of power. The doctrine of separation of powers was intended to provide a check against what James Madison in *Federalist* 51 called 'a gradual concentration of the several powers in the same department'. It was tyranny that the Founders feared most and the best safeguard for Madison would be realised by 'contriving the interior structure of the government as that its several constituent parts may, by their mutual relations, be the means of keeping each other in their proper places'. They went back to classical writers in searching for the intellectual basis for their politics.

Underlying the divergent perspectives on the morality of a system of separation of powers and determining its shape and character are two competing views of human nature. The one is based on a conception of man which stresses the duality of human nature. It affirms that man is both good and evil, rational and irrational, altruistic and selfish. It maintains that human nature has not changed fundamentally over the centuries. If men were angels, the Founders had written, government would not be necessary. If men were devils, government would not be possible. Because men possess both a spark of the divine and a trace of the demonic, government is necessary to channel virtue and hold selfishness in check.

An opposing view of human nature prophesies with confidence the emergence of the new man. For Marxists, the new man awaits only the creation of a genuine socialist order. For children of the Enlightenment,

reason will triumph with the universal spread of democracy and education. The rivalries and conflict of earlier periods in political history are
no more than a stage in man's evolution. The struggle for power of rival
and opposite interests in politics, to the extent it persists, represents a
cultural lag in mankind's march from a primitive to a modern scientific
age. Privately, man is honest and ethical; publicly he covers his acts with
rationalisations, lies and deception. Early in man's evolution, his conduct
in private affairs was corrupted by strife and violence. Through Reason,
he has progressed from conflict to co-operation in personal relations and
in organised domestic politics. The same conception of ethics which
determines the conduct of individuals in interpersonal relations is
capable of shaping the way nations behave in a universal world community. The forward march of history is raising nations from the level of
primitive rivalries into new and enlightened standards of relations when
private norms will become public rules.

Viewed from the perspective of a realist view of human nature, such
beliefs in the transformation of human nature are erroneous and mis-
placed. Man's ambition for influence and power, hence the enduring
character of competition with his fellow man is inherent in the human
condition. Because of a Hobbesian fear, nations in their quest for
security achieve power and influence at the price of security in other
groups. Tragically, there is no alternative to the morally hazardous quest
for security through power. This principle is expressed in each generation by moral, logical, and sentimental arguments which acquire the
authority of doctrine. The early founding American statesmen were
imbued with political and historical insight concerning political power
and the balancing of power.

From the standpoint of the realists' conception of human nature and
politics, the separate units in all societies composed of autonomous members owe their existence primarily to the success of the balance of power
and a system of checks and balances. Unless one component unit is prevented from gaining ascendancy over the others, the overall political
system will ultimately be shattered or destroyed. It is common to human
existence and to animal life in general that when any member or group
seeks to increase its influence and power beyond the point where equilibrium with its rivals can be preserved, either the rivals will give way and
disappear or else, by combining, will keep the expansionist force in its
place. With animal life, the process is often unconscious and automatic,
but in politics and diplomacy effectiveness depends on those sharp discriminations and informed calculations by which statesmen perceive
crucial changes in the equilibrium of power. A steady view of human

nature, the recurrent patterns of political rivalries and the necessity to keep political competition in check, all point to the perennial need for balances of power and checks and balances in politics.

Lord Bryce saw this clearly, writing: 'The Constitution was avowedly created as an instrument of checks and balances'. However, he added: 'Each branch . . . has striven to extend its range and its powers; each has advanced in certain directions but in others has been restrained by the equal or stronger powers of other branches.'[3]

Finally, because of the nature of man and of politics, statesmen and nations never wholly escape the judgement of elementary ethical standards. The history of politics makes plain that no people have ever completely divorced politics from ethics. Political actors justify themselves in moral terms in most societies and cultures. They pay tribute to some kind of moral order with consequences both in words and deeds. In politics, a striking dialectical movement occurs between expediency and morality. Practical political moves are articulated with an eye to moral principles. In however limited and fragmentary a way, acts of political expediency are seen to carry forward aims of justice and the common good. Thus the statesmen who would link expedience with ethics are forced to choose political measures so that the practical and moral march hand in hand.

Certain basic assumptions underpin checks and balances in American constitutionalism and balance or equilibrium in world politics. One assumption is that the maintenance of a pluralistic society is preferable, for the present at least, to its destruction. Another is that some type of orderly change through the workings of a particular political process is more desirable than radical and disruptive change. To the extent that the individual is considered to be of primary importance in politics, individual rights are more likely to be safeguarded. Harking back to the Greeks, balance and moderation rather than domination and extremism, are defined as political virtues. Not only the individual but minorities will be protected by checks and balances. The author (Hamilton or Madison, according to different historians) of *Federalist* 51 recommended: 'comprehending in the society so many separate descriptions of citizens as will render an unjust combination of a majority of the whole very improbable, if not impracticable . . . The society itself will be broken into so many parts, interests, and classes of citizens, that the rights of individuals, or of the minority, will be in little danger from interested combinations of the majority'.

John Stuart Mill set forth the ethical basis of such a system in more explicit terms:

In a state of society thus composed, if the representative system could be made ideally perfect, and if it were possible to maintain it in a state, its organization must be such that these two classes, manual laborers and their affinities on one side, employers of labor and their affinities on the other, should be, in the arrangement of the representative system, equally balanced, each influencing about an equal number of votes in Parliament; since, assuming that the majority of each class, in any difference between them, would be mainly governed by their class interest, there would be a minority of each in whom the consideration would be subordinate to reason, justice, and the good of the whole; and this minority of either, joining with the whole of the other, would turn the scale against any demands of their own majority which were not such as ought to prevail.[4]

If Mill's optimism regarding minorities reflected the spirit of his age, his statement remains a further elaboration of the ethics of equilibrium and divided power. In the world of politics, the most that men can hope for is some type of distributive justice. Robert Frost wrote that 'good fences make good neighbors'. In all of the more contentious arenas of life, the principle of the fence dividing those struggling to advance their own interests remains a symbol of proximate justice. In every human community, lines of demarcation are drawn to designate areas of authority and jurisdiction that each party claims. If distributive justice falls short of the higher and nobler formulations of abstract justice, it has at least the virtue of endeavouring 'to give each man his due'.

The system of checks and balances in the American Constitution and the structure of the international balance of power both rest on common intellectual and political foundations. The same motive forces in politics gave rise to both systems. Each undertakes to provide some measure of order and stability and to safeguard the independence of their component parts. Both go back to the same theory of human nature. Both are subject to the same dynamic process of change. In each, the political actors achieve equilibrium, are threatened by disequilibrium, and search for new balances of power in response to new social forces. Both are deserving of study and reflection not as outmoded forms of political order but as perennial realities of politics.

THE CONSTITUTION: THEORIES AND PRACTICE

From the time of the Constitutional Convention in 1787 to the present, Americans have offered three answers to the question 'who makes foreign policy?' Alexander Hamilton and his followers are in general spokesmen for the supremacy of the Executive. In *Federalist* 6, Hamilton asked,

'Are not popular assemblies frequently subject to the impulses of rage, resentment, jealousy, avarice, and of other irregular and violent propensities?' Opposed to Hamilton, others insist that Congress is dominant in foreign policy in part because it is accountable to the people: it holds the 'power of the purse' and the authority to declare war and to approve the ratification of treaties. The third view is the doctrine of shared responsibility and overlapping powers, the idea of 'a balanced Constitution'. Underlying the Constitution, as we have seen, is a philosophy of government providing for checks and balances and restraining the 'lesser motives' of human nature. One consequence of shared responsibility is what some have called 'an invitation to struggle' accentuated by a vagueness in the definition of overlapping powers. The Founders were ambivalent and uncertain about who should make foreign policy and their uncertainty is reflected in the Constitution.

Three streams of experience came together in shaping the views of the Founders. One was the British experience, with its blending of foreign policy powers and with fluctuating periods of royal and executive and legislative dominance. Parliament sought to increase power at the King's expense. The treatment of the American colonies added to the concern over unchecked Executive power. However, the British lesson for Americans was not one of legislative supremacy but overlapping powers.

A second stream was the colonial experience. Its effect was again to produce mixed feelings toward the legislature and the Executive. In the prerevolutionary period, the dominant feeling was hostility towards the Executive, whether the King or his governors. Early in the Revolution, of the eight states with written constitutions, only New York opted for executive supremacy. However, weak executives brought uncontrolled disorders like Shay's Rebellion and anxiety and frustration. Only New York under a strong governor was spared.

The third stream was manifest under the Articles of Confederation. During the Revolution, George Washington suffered from lack of resources and a Congress powerless to act. A weak Congress without taxing powers and checked by state legislatures and the failings of a 'token' Executive dramatised the need for a stronger national government. Following the war, the shortcomings of the system were once more apparent in a Continental Congress that could not make treaties, form alliances, or even maintain order.

When the delegates to the Constitutional Convention met in 1787, lessons from the past were fresh in their minds. The majority favoured a stronger national government as indicated in their vote for the Virginia Plan. The debate centred on the powers and interrelationships of the branches of government. Congress was given the dominant place and was assumed to be a key actor in foreign policy. Its powers were related to policy-making while the Executive's were linked with policy administration highlighted in Jefferson's later phrase that 'the transaction of business with foreign nations is executive altogether'. Controlling money, approving treaties and declaring war were congressional powers. Of the eighteen powers assigned to Congress in Article 1, Section 8, seven related directly to foreign policy.

The drift towards the primacy of Congress was tempered by the memory of Washington's frustrations in the Revolutionary War. The Founders not only rejected legislative election of the President but gave explicit powers to his office including those of the commander-in-chief and the power to negotiate treaties, receive ambassadors, nominate and remove officers, and veto legislation. By amending the power of Congress from to 'make' to to 'declare' war, the delegates recognised the necessary power of the Executive to repel sudden attacks and to carry on actual warfare once it began. Both houses of Congress were to be involved; they were to 'raise and support armies', 'provide and maintain a navy', and regulate the armed services. At the same, time, the Founders accepted the President's need for substantial leeway to conduct a war.

The debate over constitutional powers was resolved then through the sharing of responsibility for foreign policy; two vigorous and active branches with overlapping roles were envisaged. Abraham D. Sofaer writes: 'The President was to manage diplomatic intercourse and negotiations, and to conduct all authorised military operations. But Congress, and especially the Senate, would be able to approve or reject foreign policy in exercising their powers over treaties, appointments, and appropriations.' As the Founders saw it, Congress was to have ultimate authority but a vigorous and independent Executive was essential for a balanced and effective foreign policy.

In the years that followed, it was not the written but the living Constitution that determined the powers of the two branches. A less vigorous President than Washington might have meant a different pattern of relationships. While acknowledging the role of Congress, Washington expanded the role of the President. In treaty negotiations and in the declaration of neutrality in the war between France and England, he established the power of the Executive. Having unsuccessfully sought the advice of the Senate in person in 1789 before beginning negotiations with Creek Indians, he decided with a sense of disgust never to return to the Senate but to consult them in writing. He resisted attempts by the House to influence not only treaty-making but the naming of negotiators and through appropriations, the implementation of treaties. Washington asserted and the House retreated. Through his eight years, he sought recognition by Congress of the Executive's broad powers in foreign policy while accepting Congress's prerogatives to balance his authority.

After Washington several successors expanded the President's role in war-making. Thomas Jefferson sent American forces to check piracy along the Barbary Coast, James Madison to initiate military action against Spain in Florida, and John Adams, in his proclamation, approved by the Supreme Court, declared 'qualified hostility'. Later presidents sought greater control over foreign policy and war powers. James Polk sent soldiers into disputed land between Texas and Mexico and called on Congress to recognise a state of war. And the same Abraham Lincoln who had criticised Polk later claimed unprecedented presidential powers during the Civil War.

Throughout the nineteenth and twentieth centuries, presidents and congresses had to strike compromises and co-operate with one another – as, for example, Franklin Roosevelt on Lend–Lease and the Selective Service Acts, and Harry Truman on the Marshall Plan. In some instances, Congress prevailed, as with the Senate's rejection of Woodrow Wilson's League of Nations and the Treaty of Versailles. The trend, however, was towards expanding presidential powers. From the 1940s to the mid-1960s, the foreign policy consensus between presidents and Congress reinforced the trend. By the 1970s, however, consensus had broken down with dissension over Vietnam. The change occurred within the framework of the Constitution as the Founders conceived it. Indeed, Professor Norman J. Ornstein has argued that the sharing of responsibility in foreign policy during this period 'is much closer to that envisioned by the founding Fathers than what preceded it'.

Another change is worth noting. Vietnam brought the demise of the 'closed' system which had enhanced the foreign policy consensus. In the 1940s and 1950s, reward and sanctions affected Congressmen within the boundaries of the policy process. The media presence was limited, and struggles between committee chairmen and maverick junior legislators went largely unnoticed. A newcomer seeking fame and notoriety was unlikely to find it outside the power structure of Congress. With the loss of the authority of committee chairmen and the decline of political parties, the 'closed' system changed. Authority was dispersed. The result was a Congress opened up to far greater participation by individual legislators outside the dominant power structure. A freshman legislator, for example, with a budget of a third of a million dollars, could now hire up to twenty-two staff people. Open voting, open committee hearings and open mark-ups, combined with greater media presence, provided new incentives for legislators to go on the record. One route to national prominence was withholding co-operation from legislative or Executive branch leaders or outright defiance of them. The ability of party leaders to influence such members diminished. Interest groups, including those with limited resources, found it easier to bring influence to bear on congressional decision-making, as with the coalition to stop the B-1 bomber and the various ethnic and nationality lobbying groups. As Congress's influence expanded, the number of lobbyists on Capitol Hill increased.

Furthermore, the composition of Congress underwent significant changes which have been referred to as the 'juniorization' of the Capitol. A post-Second-World War membership was replaced by a post-Vietnam and post-Watergate membership. Three-quarters of the members of Congress are new since Richard Nixon's presidency. Accompanying this goup of young Congressmen are enlarged and activist staffs matched by similarly enlarged White House staffs. Thus both Congress and the Executive have found theselves with a growing number of participants in the foreign policy process, all of whom are accessible to the media.

In the mid-1980s, some observers see evidence of a levelling-out of this trend. Staff growth has stopped, sub-committees giving younger Congressmen a springboard for popular attention have declined slightly in number, and significance and committee recommendations have tended once again to carry more weight. Presidential leadership has also regained a greater degree of credibility. Nevertheless, Congress continues to play the more forceful role it has claimed for itself over the past fifteen years.

The living-Constitution, built on the written Constitution, has allowed for strong executive action when necessary. At the same time, it has provided elaborate sets of congressional checks and balances. Because the Constitution left open certain grey areas, strong presidents were even able to cite them as grounds for more additions to presidential power.

Inevitably, Congress with its inherent powers and its role among the branches as 'first among equals' from time to time sought to restore the balance. In reasserting its power in foreign policy during the last two decades, congressional acts were in harmony with the Constitution. Nevertheless, recent presidents, when they have been able to convince the public of the merit of their policies, have gained congressional support as with Jimmy Carter and the Panama Canal Treaty and with Ronald Reagan and Grenada, and perhaps Libya. Indeed, despite a resurgent Congress, it can be argued that President Reagan has been denied few major foreign policy requests.

THE LIVING CONSTITUTION V. CONSTITUTIONAL REFORM

The 1980s are apparently another of the decades in American history when we are witnessing calls for constitutional reform. President Reagan has repeatedly urged constitutional amendments, requiring a balanced budget and granting him authority to veto line items in the budget. Voluntary groups made up of private citizens have also called for constitutional amendments, including a single six-year presidential term.

The philosophy that underpins the American political system may be as important as its laws and institutions. It is a philosophy that puts its emphasis on liberty and equality and the search for justice. Liberty means communication and discourse carried on within a long-established constitutional framework. Liberty is both an end and a means to the achievement of national purposes. It pays tribute in this sense both to continuity and change, to the preservation as well as the alteration of its institutions.

Associated with this philosophy of governance is the tradition of constitutional reform. Each generation, Jefferson is quoted as saying, should re-examine and perhaps change the Constitution. This prompts certain contemporary leaders and thinkers to call for fundamental changes in our system of governance.

Americans are witnessing in the 1980s a period of reflection on and re-examination of the structure and functioning of government. A prominent American has written a provocative essay on the founding or creating of a government (Lloyd Cutler, 'To form a government'). Recent experiences with divided counsels and responsibilities in government have led some to question whether the United States can survive deadlock in government. Even public figures and observers who earlier applauded the wisdom of a government of divided powers have expressed discontent with present trends in governance. The state of thinking and support for the American political system can be described as controversial and unsettled.

What we may be experiencing nationally is the resurgence of the view that manifested itself in the 1960s and early 1970s with respect to the international scene. Then it was dissatisfaction with governance internationally that drove the reformers. The United Nations in which men of goodwill had placed their faith was seen as deadlocked first by the conflicts of the Cold War involving East and West and thereafter by the growing differences between the industrial and the developing or Third-World nations, between North and South. Significantly, the same intellectual and business leaders who rather generously financed inquiries and proposals intended to promote a new structure of international relations are now in the forefront of those who urge constitutional reform within the nation. In short, the same Americans who sponsored world order movements are leading the movement for constitutional change nationally in the present decade.

In both the international and national political arenas, the question worth asking is what changes in governance are possible and what may be the consequences of focusing so much attention on creating new patterns as against preserving older patterns of governance. What should be the balance between creating and preserving government? Specifically, have efforts at building new structures of world order strengthened or weakened the United Nations? Will constitutional reform strengthen or weaken the existing constitutional system? Such are the issues that must be addressed.

In the field of Executive–legislative relations, the question may be whether communications between the branches of government can be improved or whether constitutional amendments are required. To consider constitutional reform is, in one sense, beside the point. The Constitution is a living instrument and is continuously demonstrating its ability to adapt to changing times. The living Constitution is, on many issues, more important than the text in Articles 1 and 2 as interpreted by the Founders. Personalities and events play a decisive role, as we have seen with George Washington and the Creek Indian treaties, Jefferson and the Barbary pirates or Franklin D. Roosevelt and Executive agreements. Because of the weight of personalities and events the living Constitution is constantly changing and this includes the framework for making and implementing foreign policy. It is fashionable for constitutional reformers to lecture one another about the need for constitutional changes. Foundations and wealthy individuals appear more willing to finance such endeavours than they do, for example, to aid studies of how a viable foreign policy can be forged and defended in dealing with authoritarian and totalitarian regimes, something that historically each administration confronts but find itself unable to justify to public opinion. From Wilson to Reagan almost every administration, rather than acknowledge the need to cope with non-democratic regimes, has offered the people its own version of the Reagan Doctrine. Each has pointed to some new route for changing the political map of the world from what is to what we would like it to be. Wilson offered non-recognition, Dulles liberation, Carter human rights and Reagan the Institute of Democracy and the Reagan Doctrine.

Setting aside crusades of this kind, the other question that constitutional reformers have to confront is the type of constitutional process they envisage as capable of bringing about their hoped-for constitutional change. It is difficult to imagine a constitutional convention called to change the President's term of office that would restrict itself to that question. With ideological politics dominating the debate and with a proliferation of single-interest groups demanding prayer in the schools or the outlawry of abortion, a constitutional convention would probably become a raucous and emotional confrontation between nearly irreconcilable organised political forces. To suppose it would limit itself to, say the issue of the single six-year presidential term is illusory in the extreme.

The other argument against constitutional reform is its tendency to make of the US Constitution what state constitutions have become. Many of them are voluminous collections of minutae and details that ought rather to be left to the legislative process. To clutter up the US Constitution with excessive detail would assure that it would soon take on the jungle-like character of most state constitutions. The Constitution not only leaves to the political process certain important acts of governance such as maintaining restraints on the budget, it also avoids the hyprocrisy which might lead to the erosion of trust and respect for it. For if Congress were to pass a balanced budget amendment, it almost certainly would attach an escape clause that provided 'except in times of emergency', declared by the President and Congress. Thus the President and Congress would put forward the fiction that they were prepared to balance the budget, while following the escape clause whenever it pleased them. In all likelihood the practice of Congress, unless they saw the necessity for restraint, would make a mockery of the Constitution, even if the amendment were to pass, which is highly unlikely.

By contrast, improving communication between the branches is a viable alternative to constitutional reform and one for which definable steps might be taken. It might be argued that better communication is also needed *within* each of the branches. Within Congress, the number of sub-committee chairmen has increased exponentially. Recent years have seen a several hundred per cent increase in both committee staffs and the staffs of individual Congressmen and Senators. The profile of staff is of bright, ambitious, upwardly mobile young people all with a capacity for 'quick study'. By their presence they set in motion the presumption that each can demonstrate that their jobs are important and that they are earning their pay. They seek alliances with the White House staff and the bureaucracy with whom their associations are often closer than with colleagues on congressional staffs.

Such factors (and many more) make for the decentralisation of Congress's role in foreign policy. They encourage Congress to seek to micromanage the conduct of foreign policy. The net effect of such decentralisation is that the centres of authority that formerly existed with leadership in key committees no longer exist. No single centre in Congress exists for weighing and assessing foreign policy as a whole. Friends abroad express confusion over where the decision-making power is lodged at any given time. One possible change, short of restoring power to the two committees that earlier had responsibility, would be to give the Senate Committee on Foreign Relations and the House Committee on Foreign Affairs power to call up any question pending before any other committee in the Congress in order to comment on the main issues from the standpoint of foreign policy as a whole. Yet the present arrangement of committees and the distribution of power in Congress makes this an unlikely solution. Unfortunately the prestige and political attractiveness of appointments to the two major committees has declined. Senators like Charles Percy discovered they had more to lose than to gain from such membership. Yet if communication within Congress is to occur, some such innovation is needed.

As to communication within the Executive branch, what everyone has known was clearly confirmed by the Iran–contra hearings. Issues of communication involve the CIA, Treasury and a multitude of departments with briefs for certain forms of international relations. The central focus of the problem, however, is the National Security Commission (NSC). Part of the problem may be the absence of sufficient continuity and lack of institutional memory. The quintessential Washington figure, Clark Clifford, has proposed several changes to promote improved communication and introduce controls on its members. To achieve the former, Clifford would install in the White House a small, permanent staff of career civil servants who were experienced, non-partisan and non-ideological. They would bring vision and the longer view. Clifford would also add a permanent assistant staff director to serve uninterruptedly from administration to administration and become a primary source of institutional continuity.

To further discipline and control, and protect against Executive branch abuse, Clifford proposes the strengthening of statutes that might deter presidents and their subordinates from running amok and getting out of control. Clifford, incidentally, is convinced that in recent events no less than five laws were broken, including the Boland Amendment, various requirements for notification to intelligence committees of covert activities and two statutes governing the sale of American military equipment to foreign countries. If these laws had been obeyed, there would have been no scandal, he asserts. Staff penalties would have assured internal discipline. He constructs an imaginary dialogue concerning a proposed action that has come before the NSC. Someone warns that the action would violate the law. Colonel North asks 'What is the penalty?' The answer is there is no penalty. Having heard this, North decides to go full-stream ahead. A penalty, Clifford suggests, might just have given North pause. In one other respect, Clifford urges a change. He would promote the chairman of the Joint Chiefs to full membership in the NSC on the theory that he might have exercised restraint if not excluded from the Iran–contra deliberations. Further, Clifford would add the Secretary of the Treasury as a full member so that he could contribute advice when public funds were at issue.[5]

The other sphere in which communication is vital is of course communications between the Executive and legislative Branches. If either assumes it has the final answer to or responsibility for a problem, no communications at all or evasive communications at most will be the result. The state of mind of the actors will be more important than any number of constitutional provisions. Those who understand what the Constitution provides will accept the importance of communication. In Dean Rusk's words: 'If the separation of powers is a fundamental notion of our constitutional system, as I believe it to be, the other side of the same coin is the constitutional necessity for comity between the branches, for cooperation between the branches, and for due regard for the responsibilities of another branch. That requires communication.'[6]

The most time-honoured form of communication between the Executive and legislature is congressional testimony by high officials. It is a time-consuming and often frustrating experience but an utterly essential one. Officials who have excelled in such communications offer a few dos and don'ts, such as: never lose your temper before a congressional committee, never deceive a committee, never filibuster a committee, and never try to make a Senator or Congressman look bad to the people who are his constituents. On Congress's side, it needs to discipline itself. The traditional demands by committees with long-standing interests in foreign policy are numerous in themselves. Not only must an official appear before the two main committees in the Senate and House, but, on policies requiring appropriations he must testify twice each year at authorisation hearings and twice at appropriation hearings. Secretary Rusk estimated he testified thirty-two times in eight years on foreign aid alone. Each committee hearing requires at least two days of preparation.

A further burden is that on foreign relations questions, each committee requires that the Secretary of State lead off the testimony. Reacting to this, Secretary of State George Shultz has attempted to limit his apearance to hearings of the main foreign relations committees.

Increasingly, members of the Executive branch have been asking themselves if other forms of communications are possible. A few secretaries of state have joined Senators or Congressmen in radio or television shows produced on Capitol Hill and sent back to the legislators' states and districts. More attention has been paid to congressional mail and, in the Rusk era, the administration set itself a three day turnaround time and gave their responses the highest priority.

The decentralisation and dispersion of leadership in the Congress has vastly complicated the communications process. In the 1950s and early 1960s, it was enough to discuss policy with four senators: Senator Richard Russell of Georgia who, it was said, could deliver twenty-five votes on any subject; Senator Robert Kerr of Oklahoma; Senator Hubert Humphrey of Minnesota; and Senator Everett Dirksen of Illinois. In the House, Sam Rayburn was able to control what Congress would or would not do. Lyndon Johnson referred to this group as the whales in Congress and, while philosophically democrats with a small 'd' found this offensive, one of them quipped that the situation was better than 535 minnows swimming around in a bucket.

Two other areas of possible improvement in communications are worth mentioning in conclusion. The one is the presence of extraordinary bipartisan leaders who possess the moral stature and recognise possible political gains from co-operation with the other branch. Some presidents have considered it their special responsibility to become the driving force for bipartisanship in foreign policy. Harry Truman joined Senator Arthur H. Vandenberg in the Republican Eighteenth Congress, as did President Dwight D. Eisenhower with Senate Majority Leader Lyndon B. Johnson. In the Kennedy and Johnson administrations, it was Senator Everett Dirksen who played the role and in the process, as Senator Birch Bayh and others have shown, enhanced his political standing. It is noteworthy that Senators like Richard Lugar and Charles Percy, who in certain respects followed in this tradition, lost out electorally or in committee assignments in the Reagan and Carter administrations (the parallel, especially with Lugar, is obviously inexact). Given the rise of ideological politics, bipartisanship is more complex if not impossible.

The other area of more promising communications is with respect to the executive sessions of the major congressional committees. The source for studying these sessions is becoming available as the Senate Foreign Relations Committee publishes edited texts, beginning in the Truman administration. As more such materials are released, especially for the period where televised sessions of open hearings have been held, the more fruitful communications that exist in executive sessions should become apparent. An extension of such sessions whenever possible should provide another means of improved communications.

Dean Rusk has given advice to future presidents in the following proposition: 'I recommend that any administration proceed the basis that partnership between the executive and legislative branch is utterly essential in our constitutional system.'[7] That recommendation is a fitting point on which to end this discussion. Apparently not all administrations take it to heart. Failing to do so causes a collapse of constitutional processes and a whole series of consequences which no one can afford in the nuclear age.

NOTES

1 Dean Rusk, 'Foreign policy and the separation of powers', in *Perceptions of Policymakers,* ed. Kenneth W. Thompson, Lanham, Md., 1987, vol. VI, p. 4.
2 Thomas Jefferson to John Adams, 28 October 1813, in Thomas Jefferson, *Writings,* Washington DC, 1904, XIII, p. 401.
3 Lord Bryce, *The American Commonwealth,* New York, 1891, vol. I, 390.
4 John Stuart Mill, *Considerations on Representative Government,* New York, 1822, p. 142.
5 Philip Geylin, 'The Clark Clifford remedy', *Washington Post,* 16 August 1987, p. D7.
6 Dean Rusk, 'Foreign policy and the separation of powers', p. 8.
7 *Ibid.,* p. 15.

13

What is still vital in the political thought of the Founders?

J. R. POLE
St Catherine's College, Oxford

Rhetorical questions do not always deserve rhetorical answers. But the question to which I have promised to address myself is not merely rehetorical; it would serve no better purpose to gather here to praise the wisdom of the Founders than to reiterate the Ten Commandments. The question, 'What is still *vital* in the political thought of the Founders?' is worth asking when we recognise that it is another way of putting the slightly more ominous question, 'what do we still agree with in their political thought?'

This little act of reconstruction may be a useful – if slightly uncomfortable – exercise, if only because it reminds us of two things: first, that we are under no *obligation* to agree with the Founders; and secondly, that in many respects we find it impossible. After all, in many important matters they themselves disagreed with each other; how then, can we agree with them all? If we are to do justice to the Founders of the Constitution, we are under no less an obligation to try to understand the true nature of the connections which tie us to them. We do not, after all, owe more understanding to them than to ourselves. This occasion, more than most centennial celebrations, is an appropriate moment for pausing to ask what it is that we do owe to the past. As I remarked many years ago, they cannot hear us; they are not listening.[1] But – as I do not remember remarking at the time – we can hear them, if we listen attentively, and if we subject ourselves to the difficult exercise of screening out the mass of information that separates us from them. It seems to me that we owe to the Founders a deep measure of respect: not veneration, but the respect that requires a serious attempt to understand them and their work within their own terms of reference.

We can make up our own minds about the Founders; they cannot tell us what they would have thought of us. People sometimes ask what Mr Jefferson would have said about some aspect of public policy if he were alive today, usually meaning that he would have disapproved of something the government is doing. The point that this type of applied historical judgement overlooks is that if Mr Jefferson were alive today he would be 244 years old, and that persons of that age are seldom in complete possession of their faculties. I have invoked Jefferson, although he was not technically a Founder of the Constitution, because his name seems to be more susceptible than most to this sort of treatment. My point is a serious one. Times have not only changed; they have changed out of all recognition. It is a very remarkable fact that the United States Constitution, the oldest written constitution in the world, should have survived in documentary form. But the Constitution we have today is not the one that the Founders made, and the first course of wisdom is to recognise that it is a constitution which they could not have foreseen. What they might have thought if they had been able to experience the immense changes between their times and ours can only be a matter for speculation. Some of them would undoubtedly have held up their hands and said, 'Thank God we didn't live to see that!' What we are decidedly not entitled to do is to decide the question for them, and to deduce from some position held only in the most vaguely analogous situation 200 years ago that a strict line of reasoning would have dictated one rather than another conclusion to one of our own contemporary problems, or for that matter any of the intervening constitutional problems of national history.

In certain fairly specific cases I believe this sort of reasoning is still possible. I do not want to rule out of court all possibility of linear connections, and I am safeguarding that position because I have one or two to suggest myself. But the mere fact that justices of the Supreme Court are very seldom in unanimous agreement is alone enough to indicate that clear and unmistakable lines simply cannot be drawn from the text of the Constitution to the solution of later disputes. Let me suggest a comparatively non-contentious example. In the 1880s the Supreme Court began to adopt the view that a corporation had all the rights and protections of an individual person, and a prolonged controversy followed as to whether this reading was intended by the makers of the Fourteenth Amendment. The Founders had no knowledge of the Fourteenth Amendment, which none of them could have foreseen and which many of them would not have approved; but the line drawn by the Court connected these rights with the principle of due process of law, of which all the Founders undoubtedly did approve. Even so, I venture to doubt that any of them could have anticipated the line of reasoning or could, so to speak, have been relied on to predict the view that corporate rights were constitutionally identical with personal rights; they could hardly have foreseen the impending existence of corporations, of whose benefits to the public some of them might have been sceptical. And one could say very much the same for any number of issues arising both under the original Constitution and under its subsequent amendments.

To test the problem of linear interpretation, I would like to suggest an intellectual exercise which might be well worth trying out in two different settings – a law school class and a history graduate seminar. Let the teacher take certain well-known judgements – Marshall on Interstate Commerce, Taney on the Charles River Bridge case, Holmes on clear and present danger, Frankfurter on flag salutes, Warren on apportionment, for a start perhaps – ask the class to extract the constitutional essence of these opinions, and then set them down for debate in the middle of the Philadelphia Convention. How would Rufus King, Gouverneur Morris, James Madison, Charles Pinckney (a difficult case to predict!) or Luther Martin have spoken, in 1787, on these questions? I am not offering to write these speeches for them; I do not, with a few exceptions, feel any confidence that we can know what they would have said. One feature of the exercise that I would find instructive would be the different conclusions offered by the lawyers and the historians. But there would be other forms of instruction, whose benefits could extend to politicians.

The historians might be the first to remind us of a distinction which used to be drawn between 'strict construction' of the Constitution and 'loose construction'. The lawyers would tell us that in more modern, and therefore more sophisticated times we need to distinguish between 'interpretivism' and 'anti-interpretivism'. Now it seems to me that in the matter of 'original intent' these distinctions need to be marked off by a broad line of common sense. If Congress passed and the President signed a law abolishing the office of President of the United States, or permitting New York and California to send three members to the Senate, it would be relatively easy to gather a majority for the opinion that this law would be unconstitutional. That would not just be strict construction: it would be common-sense construction. But strict construction, transmuted into 'anti-interpretivism', usually means that a certain act of congress expressly contravenes the words of the Constitution. Invariably the person announcing this opinion disapproves of the act. The truth, however, is that the Constitution does not address most of the problems of modern life, and which therefore arise from modern litigation, in any direct sense. But more than that, the Constitution does not anticipate the circumstances in which they arise. The question as to whether state legislatures have the lawful power to compel schoolchildren to salute the flag, on which Felix Frankfurter maintained an opinion now generally considered to be nationalistic, does not receive much light from the period when the Constitution was drawn up, when state-sponsored school systems did not exist and there could hardly be said to be a national flag.[2] Though Frankfurter's opinion may in the climate of the times have seemed conservative – and more so perhaps in the climate of ours – it can hardly be called strict-constructionist. It represented a very free interpretation of legislative power. I doubt very much whether any 'strict-constructionist' before the Civil War would have assented to Frankfurter's views. Of the clutch of well-known opinions I mentioned, we may suspect that Marshall's use of interstate commerce as an instrument of nationalisation of power would have been unlikely to command the assent of a fair number of the signers of the original Constitution, although his argument was a legitimate and clear reading of the text. On the other hand, the highly 'interventionist' opinions of Chief Justice Warren which established the constitutional principle of one person, one vote, would in my opinion have seemed to most of the framers an absolutely indisputable application of their own political rules. In their day representation did bear a broad relation to the actual distribution of the population; and the terms of the Constitution's provisions on apportionment do not merely permit the rule of equality but require it as an exclusive principle for the House of Representatives and of course for the Electoral College. This is a case in which straight-line reasoning does apply to the duties of the Court. I shall return to this point before I close.

The political impulse behind the drive for direct application of original intent is political. But this political aim gains some of its strength from a psychology which is widespread in the United States and has a great deal in common with the also widespread phenomenon of religious fundamentalism. It may be that the survival of religious fundamentalism into the age of the microchip, of super-conductors, space flight and genetic engineering, is attributable to a yearning for two lost values: certainty and simplicity. No doubt it would also be comforting if we could be certain of the meaning of the Constitution, and its meaning could be simple.

It is partly for this reason that people in many walks of life, including the Executive department, with the deep political nostalgia which is so readily susceptible to certain kinds of exploitation, regard the more subtle advances of constitutional theory as sinister. But the point I am arguing is neither difficult nor sinister. It is simply that interpretation is inevitable. The question is, not whether or not there is to be interpretation, but what the interpretation is to be? The distinguished legal thinker, Professor Guido Calabresi of the Yale Law School, is rather fond of using a topographical image; he writes of 'the legal landscape' into which new decisions must somehow fit, but which in turn they do something to alter.[3] I wonder whether we may develop this visual imagery. Suppose the federal judges to be artists painting this landscape. Since each came by a different route and set up his easel in the place of his own choice, each viewpoint will be slightly different from that of the others. Now every artist knows that he is not taking a photograph. The picture he paints represents his own interpretation of what he sees. Some colours will have to be accentuated, others reduced, from time to time a feature will be omitted, not in order to distort the landscape but in order to impress all the more strongly its dominant features and to establish a dominant mood. One thing that is really essential is a thematic consistency. The artist may seem to be making it up, but watch and you will see that he has to keep looking at the 'real' landscape before him. It is curious, this necessity, because the painter is perfectly free to invent anything he wants; but what he is trying to do is to paint *that* landscape, the one he sees before him and which he will want you to see when you look at his finished work. In this sense, if you will allow me the flight of fancy, the judge is an artist. He must begin by looking at the landscape as a whole; he must paint in a way that is consistent with what he sees; and what he paints must have a consistency of its own. Differences of opinion in matters of art resolve themselves into questions of taste; in matters of judicial opinion they tend to resolve themselves into differences of social philosophy.

The disagreements among the Founders, even among those who remained to sign the draft Constitution, and those who ratified it, are clear and often loud on the record of their work. They disagreed about the amount of power to be conferred on the federal government and on the basic structure through which power was to be exercised. When Madison, King, and the other nationalists asked for a break – it was on 17 July – to give them time to consider the implications of the report of the grand committee which had proposed the so-called Connecticut Compromise, they sensed crisis. The idea of retaining state equality in the Senate did not seem a happy solution to them. They thought it was a disaster which might make the whole scheme so enfeebled as to be unworkable. They accepted it because the only alternative at that stage was to abandon the entire project. Agreement here was at a lowest common denominator of consent. It is even rather touching that men who were dissatisfied with this compromise as Hamilton and Madison should have joined forces soon afterwards to write so energetically in the Constitution's favour.

The basic disagreement which nearly broke up the Convention was about the location of power. Although the terms of reference have changed profoundly, this disagreement is certainly not without relevance for our own society. But we can make the ideas, even the antagonisms, of the founding generation work for ourselves only, I think, if we begin by recognising that the aims of society have themselves changed. Since we all, whatever our political persuasions, want our society to do very much more for us than anyone did in the eighteenth century, we must all want a more powerful government than was envisaged even by Alexander Hamilton. In that case, James Madison would no doubt warn us, you must have even more effective safeguards against abuses of that power. The forms have changed, he would say, but the essence has not. For his generation long anticipated Lord Acton's famous aphorism, 'Power tends to corrupt; and absolute power corrupts absolutely.' And the post-Watergate generation might reply, 'Yes. We know. We learnt that for ourselves.' But is this a lesson that each generation has to learn for itself? And in the light of the revelations of the Tower Commission and related enquiries still in progress, we also ask now whether people wielding irresponsible power will ever learn it. For *all* power, as Madison warned his contemporaries in *Federalist* 51, must somewhere be called to account. Here on this occasion is something we can surely learn from history, and not least from the Founders, for it is a lesson they definitely intended to hand down to their successors.

The immense and ramifying power that the modern state machine inevitably wields sometimes makes it more difficult to remember, and still more difficult to apply, the related Common Law principle that was well understood by eighteenth-century Whigs whether British or American: that no officer of state is above the law. It was at the core of the famous General Warrants cases in England in the mid-1760s. Let me recall the circumstances in which they arose. In the opinion of the British Secretary of State, the Earl of Halifax, John Wilkes was guilty of publishing seditious libel, and he sent his agent Robert Wood to arrest Wilkes and search his house under a general warrant. This meant that no item was specified as the object of the search and anything could be seized. This was obviously a very dangerous power to place in the hands of an agent of the Crown. Within two weeks Wilkes appeared to sue Wood for damages in the Court of Common Pleas before Chief Justice Sir Charles Pratt, who found for the plaintiff and awarded Wilkes £1,000 damages. I think it is worth quoting the language used by the Chief

Justice because its relevance can hardly escape us at the present day: 'If such a power is truly invested in a Secretary of State, and he can delegate this power,' he declared, 'it may certainly affect the person and property of every man in this kingdom, and is totally subversive of the liberty of the subject.' This, you may think, is strong language from the bench to the executive, but more was to follow when John Entick, a publisher, sued Nathan Carrington, a Crown agent, in a related case arising from a similar warrant. The year was now 1765 and Pratt had been elevated to the peerage in the title by which he is known to history, as Lord Camden. He laid down firmly that the key to the rights of Englishmen lay in Common Law. 'If it be law, it will be found in our books. If it is not to be found there, it is not law.' But could the Crown plead a higher law, what we might now call *'raison d'état'*? Not a bit of it. 'And with respect to the argument of state necessity, or of a distinction that has been aimed at between state offences and others, the common law does not understand that kind of reasoning, nor do our books take notice of any such distinctions.'[4]

Colonial Americans had no doubts about their own status as British subjects entitled to common-law protections. Much else happened between these pronouncements from the English Court of Common Pleas and the passage of the American Bill of Rights, but I would nevertheless claim a direct line of descent. The Fourth Amendment, with its specific prohibition of 'unreasonable searches and seizures', is clearly indebted to Lord Chief Justice Camden's enunciation of the common-law rights of British subjects.

I have claimed that we ought to bear these principles in mind. That is not to say that it is always easy to apply them as clearly and firmly as Lord Camden did. One reason for the difficulty is that crime has become immensely more complex and more pervasive than it was in the eighteenth century. If police officers with a warrant to search for specified stolen goods unexpectedly discover a cache of heroin, should they not seize it on the spot? Common sense suggests that they should. But it is obvious that modern conditions have introduced complexities which require very careful consideration. However we may stand on these matters, and on the closely related questions of the right of a person under suspicion to legal representation, the very nature of the problem gives us another example of the case I have been trying to make, at the risk of being repetitious and even obvious: the constitutional principles we are working with, laid down in the eighteenth century, protect the liberty and property of the individual. But they do not tell us exactly what to do on any one occasion. To get it right for our own times we have to apply our minds to our own circumstances.

In this exercise in distinguishing what we can still find of value in the political thought of the Founders, it is becoming clear that we – or most of us, I assume – will agree with some of them more than with others. But the greatest issue that divided them in their day is also the issue which most deeply divides us from them. Slavery was known and felt to be a wrong; men and women who had fought for their own liberty were not unmindful of the paradox. In fact they had often used the very word 'slavery' to express the worst that they feared from the Britain of George III. Yet even those who most deeply deplored the existence of slavery were willing in the end to compromise with those who wanted to maintain it. The Constitution may not have mentioned the institution by name, but it did more than that in affording protection to the owners of runaway slaves. The Union was a voluntary association between the peoples of states with many different types of society, but nothing was more profound than this division between the states which depended on slavery for their labour force and those that did not.

This is not the place to review the whole corpus of social thought that has accompanied the long and arduous struggle for racial and other forms of ethnic equality in America's history. But we cannot ignore this truth: that political thought is thought about the relationship between politics and social order. Injustice is always a form of disorder. So that a society which prides itself on its ability to maintain a just political order can never be satisfied with its own achievement if the political order fails to reflect, or represses, the legitimate aspirations of substantial parts of its own people.

The early Republic did not witness the end of this problem. I doubt if we have witnessed it yet. For the residue of slavery is racial prejudice. But we are certainly not the first to become aware of it; the Founders, to whom we owe a constitution which protected human slavery, were also aware of the dilemma and many of them both hoped and believed that slavery would wither away under that same consititution. That was one way of dealing with the problem of slavery – to pass it on to their successors with the prayer, 'Give us peace in our time, O Lord, give us peace in our time.' That was the response of many contemporaries, including Thomas Jefferson; even Noah Webster's denunciation of slavery advocated a very gradualist plan of emancipation.

At the level of theory, by which I suppose one means in this sort of context an intellectually coherent explanation for keeping things as they are, the South dealt with this difficulty in an intelligible way. What the South said was that the black population could have no 'legitimate aspirations' within the context of American society because blacks were not members of the society. The racial line itself was quite arbitrary. State legislatures had to decide what proportion of 'Negro blood' made a person black rather than white; and there were exceptions and inconsistencies – in North Carolina, for example, free blacks could actually vote until 1835, and I know of no kind of reasoning under which voters can be non-members of political society. But this was an exception. On the whole the South effectively maintained that all slaves were outside the pale of society and therefore deprived of its benefits and protections; and then extended this exclusion to free blacks – whose numbers had increased very considerably as a direct result of the War of Independence.

The Northern way of dealing with all this was less conspicuous but it was also less tidy and comprehensive. To put it briefly, blacks were more freely involved in many aspects of society but they were almost as effectively excluded from its politics and its system of justice. This involved almost as many contradictions and confusions as the Southern way, but it enabled Northerners to take a more high-minded tone when talking about the South.

The Founders did not solve these problems. As we know, they differed deeply on them – and the defenders of black slavery were able at least to maintain their consistency by denying that a problem existed. The Founders did not hand down guidelines for the solution of these problems either, since they were not in agreement about the solutions required, if any were. But it is not fair to accuse them of too many inconsistencies: the inner consistency of the Constitution is far more pervasive, and I believe one of these consistencies operates forcefully through time. The Founders did give America a constitution which operated directly on individuals. I want to make this point here, though I shall need to come back to it later, because it belongs here if we are later to understand its full implications.

Suppose, as an alternative, that the Constitution had actually designated Americans by specified groups, and had laid down that different groups were to be treated differently for purposes of social policy. It could, for example, have said that all Roman Catholics were to be confined within limited residential areas; or that all non-Christians were to have the letter 'I' for Infidel branded on their foreheads. The latter suggestion may seem a little far-fetched, but several of the state constitutions included religious qualifications for public office. Most of them treated persons of African descent as inferiors, and none of them treated American Indians as equals. Obviously, moreover, they all excluded women from political society, although this exclusion was mitigated by the fact that women had certain legal protections and had recourse to law. What I am doing here is to postulate a constitution, under which the people on whom it operated were actually described by group, and which then prescribed different treatment for different groups. Such an arrangement is by no means difficult to conceive. We actually do more of this sort of thing as a matter of policy under modern social conditions than anybody thought of doing in the eighteenth century, if mainly because the imperatives of modern society call for a far greater measure of social legislation. But a constitution which divided people in these ways and then acted on them according to these divisions would be consistent in principle with the Supreme Court of 1896, when it handed down the decision in *Plessy* v. *Ferguson* which wrote the doctrine of 'equal but separate' into the Constitution of the United States.[5]

But the Constitution does not do this. It leaves to the individual states the power to impose suffrage and religious qualifications for public office; but the states are the only internal political entities known to the Constitution. In itself it is a constitution for individuals. That fact, I believe, has some bearing on public policy in our own times.

We have been talking all this time about the Founders, while recognising that they did not form a homogeneous group. We ought to say a word for their opponents, the Antifederalists, because they too were included under the aegis of the Constitution, they used the same language and cleaved to the same rights. My main point here is to emphasise that the Antifederalists shared with their opponents the classical fear of power. They too believed that power tends to corrupt. But they mightily feared that the power under the new form of government would get into the wrong hands – those which were making the Constitution in their own interests. It was for this reason that they could agree so readily to the principle of the separation of powers, which, translated into practice, was expected to make it almost impossible for any one faction to get control of the government. Some of them complained that the branches of government had not been kept separate *enough*.

When we look beyond these institutions, the main thrust of Antifederalist objections came to centre in the failure of the framers to include a bill of rights. If the first ten amendments to the Constitution, or perhaps only some of them, had been set at the head of the original document, there would have been much less difficulty about ratification.

No doubt many of the Antifederalists felt themselves to be at a disadvantage because they were economically vulnerable, and in that sense they belonged to identifiable social groups. But the rights they were determined to protect were *individual* rights. They were even more determined than their opponents to safeguard these rights because they did not expect to control the great institutions of law and policy.

To this considerable extent, then, in an intense emphasis on the individual in his political and legal capacity – and generally speaking, it must be added, as a member of the male sex – the Antifederalists of the Constitution-making era shared the convictions of the Federalists. And I think this point has an importance that can be overlooked, for the Constitution has certainly not always united the American people. It does mean, however, that with the adoption of the Bill of Rights, the Constitution begins its life with a fair measure of general approval; although it met vigorous opposition, that opposition was to a large extent reconciled, and the process did not leave the United States, like some countries, with a bitter and unreconciled opposition seeking to overthrow the government, if necessary by violence, at the first opportunity. We tend to take these things for granted, and we are fortunate in being able to do so; but they were not certain or obvious at the time. Perhaps it is worth reminding you on this occasion that the presidential election of 1800 represented the first occasion in modern history when a government changed hands, fully, as the immediate result of a free election. No one could be absolutely sure that the system would work until it did.

Momentous historical events sometimes pass by a sort of default. They are taken for granted by history because the alternative did not happen. So let me draw your minds for a moment to the alternative that did not happen. No-one, not even Alexander Hamilton, who was the most militaristic of opposition leaders, even contemplated the possibility of a coup; in fact Hamilton's principal concern had been to facilitate the process of making an acceptable choice between Jefferson and Burr, who had drawn equal electoral votes – and in this potentially dangerous situation, Hamilton recognised, grudgingly, the superior quality of his personal rival, Jefferson. The prescribed formalities were observed, the electoral votes counted, the election was thrown into the House of Representatives, and Thomas Jefferson of Virginia was duly declared the elected President of the United States.

When John Adams rode away, averting his presence from the inauguration of his successor, he signalled his recognition of the process of free elections. There was no alternative, and if there had been he would not have wished to take it. Now I am not trying to assert that the United States was the only country in which elections freely took place. In Britain, to go no further into Europe, elections took place in conditions of occasionally almost riotous freedom and had profound political consequences. What I am arguing is that there were other elements in the system, other considerations and powers, which had to affect the actual outcome of even a general election in Britain: it was for the monarch to make his choice of ministers, and ministers had to be able to work with the monarch as well as with Parliament. In the United States, the electorate, fulfilling its constitutional role in the several states, had changed the administration as well as changing the composition of Congress.

This meant something for constitutional history which is easy to overlook but important to grasp. It meant, as Richard Hofstadter argued in one of his most important books, *The Idea of Party System*, that a separation had silently taken place between the Constitution and the government of the day, between the politics of the Constitution and the politics of party.[6] The fundamental principle which is of such profound importance to democratic government and which emerges from these events is that of legitimate opposition. The Federalists, during their twelve-year tenure of power, had not seemed to grasp this principle either clearly or willingly; there are many indications that both Washington and Adams tended to regard opposition as a form of disloyalty not far removed from sedition. But the invention of the political party mediated the process by which an opposition could actually become the government without in any way threatening the constitutional system. Washington, as he showed in his Farewell Address, had very grave doubts as to whether the Constitution could survive. Twice, in successive sentences, he called it an 'experiment'.[7] Moreover we should remember that the Founders did not anticipate the rise of political parties and had hoped that the system would actually prevent that type of politics from emerging. While they accepted the need for some species of informal political grouping, it can be said that in general they disapproved of the idea of parties and would have been dismayed to have been told that the Constitution they had created would give rise to party government.

It is thus a further irony of this early, vital phase in the development of the Republic that Washington specifically doubted whether the system could survive the creation of political parties. He was referring to parties that drew their loyalties from geographical sections, and he was right in his perception that that was where the real danger lurked; but the political party as such seemed to him to threaten the stability and intentions of the system. Yet, as we can see, and he might have seen if he had lived a little longer, the party was actually the mechanism which made the system work, the mechanism for choosing suitable candidates and for harmonising the very widely ranging operations of the political process in different parts of the country. It is almost impossible to imagine the United States operating as an entity without political parties. And I am inclined to think that the elections of 1986 and the presidential election of 1988 will prove the party system to have greater powers of endurance than the Political Action Committees (PACS) and the medley of special interest groups which many people, notably ex-President Carter, believe have weakened it. It is too early to say what the long-term balance will be between the forms of the nationally organised party and the multiplicity of interest groups, which Madison might have called factions. The parties have a capacity for assimilating these groups, and to the extent that this happens it will provide one resounding answer to the question at the start of this essay, because the concept of a stable system of mutually balancing interests was expounded by James Madison in *Federalist* 10 as the operative and in a sense the legitimating principle of the new legislative structure of the United States.

The lesson we can draw from this experience is that the Founders were themselves learning from experience. Most of the men who participated in the operation of government in federal politics in those early years had been involved at some level in the processes which had brought the government into existence only a few years earlier. When we speak of the political ideas of the Founders, then, we ought to bear very carefully in mind that these ideas, firmly held in 1787 and 1788, were capable of changing when the government itself came into action, and when, as inevitably very soon happened, it was presented with difficult situations in which men differed from each other as to the right choice of policy. Veneration for the work of the Founders should not obscure these lessons. They were engaged in the craft of politics; many of them were committed partisans. The system they had created itself changed under their management. It has been changing ever since and it is changing still. Being faithful to their principles of government does not mean refusing to accept any interpretation of the Constitution that they would not themselves have accepted. That would be literally impossible, since they were at odds with each other over this very question within a few years; there can be no 'authoritative' view of what the Constitution meant in their day. It follows of necessity that there can be no final view of what it means in ours.

Just over 100 years ago, in 1884, James Bryce (later Lord Bryce) delivered two lectures in Oxford which were subsequently published as one, under the title 'Flexible and rigid constitutions'.[8] This essay is virtually the point of departure for the modern comparative study of constitutions. Part of the significance of Bryce's famous lectures was that they represented the first attempt to break from the formalistic distinction that used to be drawn between written and unwritten constitutions. People were in the habit of thinking that written constitutions were incapable of change, while the advantage – or danger, depending on your point of view – of the British type of constitution was its adaptability.

I do not myself think that Bryce's reformulation was cast in the happiest of language. The word 'rigid' is hardly an improvement on 'written', and still conveys the notion of complete inflexibility – an impression accentuated by his contrast with 'flexible' constitutions. But the point Bryce made, and which he certainly did convey to many generations of constitutional scholars, is clear enough. 'There is', he observed, 'an element of unwritten usage in all written constitutions.' In the United States, Bryce went on to observe, a large body of parasitic legislation, usage and interpretation grows up round the documents that form the Constitution. In all written constitutions these secondary growths develop to fill up 'the vacant spaces' left by the formal words.

Bryce might perhaps have chosen instead to speak of 'formal' and 'informal' constitutions. But he used the word 'rigid' to force home another theme, that when constitutions are really unbendable, they tend to break. Under the pressure of the crises produced by slavery and sectional conflict, the American Constitution had not been able to adapt: it had broken.

Now I want to take up Bryce's argument in order to make two points which help to advance my own general theme in this essay. The first is that the crisis of Southern secession, and of the social conflicts which caused it, did break the Constitution: the Constitution we have now is not the Constitution the Founders wrote, debated and finally agreed on. And we can say with complete confidence that it would have been quite impossible in the historical circumstances of 1787 or 1788 to command agreement for the Constitution that was re-made by the Thirteenth, Fourteenth, and Fifteenth Amendments. The armies of Grant and Sherman, the iron will of Abraham Lincoln, though he did not live to see the day, had more to do with the ultimate powers of the Federal government than did Madison and his contemporaries. Bryce would have regarded this point as obvious at the date he wrote and it is obvious to us now.

But my second point is one he did not specifically make, though I think it follows and I think he would have agreed. It is that the Constitution not only changed through the addition of the Reconstruction amendments but that, in subtle but significant respects, it became a different *kind* of constitution as a result. There had of course been a great

deal of interpretation under Marshall and Taney. The character and subject matter of this intepretation, however, underwent significant changes
in the nineteenth century. Before the Civil War, and especially under
Marshall, the most consequential of interpretations had to do with structural relations: Marshall's chief accomplishment was to define the
relationship between federal and state governments in a sense that established federal superiority in cases of conflict. In certain cases, however,
the Court began to find itself engaged in determining values rather than
structures. In the *Dartmouth College* case (1819) and in the *Charles
River Bridge* case (1837) it entered into adjudicating the social values
involved in conflicts between competing interests; in the latter case, for
the first time, the issue involved party politics. Both these cases had to
be decided on the basis of what the Constitution said about violation of
contract. The *Dred Scott* case (1857) dealt with race, citizenship and
civil liberty. But the balance shifted decisively after the Civil War, partly
as a direct result of the Reconstruction amendments, partly because of
the changing American economy. The judiciary became more frequently
and more intricately involved in issues of administration and through
them of policy. The primary emphasis on structure and considerations
dependent on power gave way to a primary emphasis on values and considerations dependent on policy.

The great body of interpretation that developed under the aegis of the
Supreme Court and in the form of judicial review has been directed to
the amendments, particulary the Fourteenth Amendment, rather than
to the formal frame of the Constitution. This is a fact of some importance
when we are trying to look at the history of the Constitution, which is so
often seen as an accumulation of case law similar to that of the English
Common Law. Before the Civil War, the Supreme Court interposed
itself only twice between the Congress and the Constitution – in
Marbury v. *Madison* (1803) and in the *Dred Scott* case (1857). In the
generation after the Civil War, judicial review became much more frequent, with the inevitable result that the Court came to resemble a political arm of the government. During the Progressive era, and certainly
again during the New Deal, there were many who would no longer have
agreed with Hamilton's assertion that the judiciary was 'the least dangerous branch' of the government.[9] It is hardly an exaggeration to say that
there were times in the adjudication of railroad cases in the later
nineteenth century when the Court converted itself into a board of
accountants; and in describing the contours of school districts, not to
mention legislative district boundaries, the judiciary has sometimes
resembled a body of mathematically-inclined sociologists.

I am not here to argue the merits of these controversies. The case I am making is that the actual character of the Constitution has to some extent changed with the changes in the very nature of the society which it has to interpret. The compromises agreed by the Framers were not only compromises, they were *provisional* compromises: their practical meaning remained to be worked out in practice, and as I remarked earlier, history started to work on the Constitution as soon as the actual government went into action. But the history that intervened in later years was far more earth-shaking, its inevitable effects more transforming.

The Civil War negated one of the most fundamental of all tenets that seemed to control the thinking of the Founders. This was the idea that political society itself was voluntary – the result of the free action of independent wills. The formation of the Union came close to replicating this idea. It is true that the newly formed Constitution contained no procedure for its own dissolution; it is true that when the states acceded to it, they actually yielded vital portions of their much-proclaimed sovereignty, and that political theory offers no way of reclaiming such powers once they have been voluntarily given away. But it also seems likely that some of the state delegations could do this because they thought they were securing the better protection of their own vital interests, and they would not have ratified the constitution if they had been able to foresee the Civil War. It seems to me that in spite of the heroic imitation of voluntary consent which resulted in the ratification of the Fourteenth Amendment, the events of 1861-69 strike fatal blows at the sincere if naive voluntarism of the political thought of the founding generation.

In little more than a generation after the Civil War, monopoly capitalism transformed the American economy and in the process brought transforming effects to many aspects of American society. In a very strong sense, the economic structure of the United States was nationalised before the national government had time to catch up; and the drive that followed, to expand the powers and reach of the Federal government, was a consequence of the growth of the corporations and the trusts.

One of the differences between the Progressive response to these developments – which were very widely regarded as threatening to important American values – and that of the New Deal was bureaucratic rather than ideological. The Progressives passed acts. The Interstate Commerce Commission had been in existence since 1886, but on the whole it cannot be said that the political will of the Progressive era was embodied in any great elaboration of governmental agencies. The New

Deal on the other hand carved out great areas of public policy, in industry, in agriculture, in conservation, in public works, and instead of attributing them to existing departments of government, as would be done in Britain, created semi-autonomous agencies to exercise the kind of powers that the Founders must, I think, have believed belonged to the legislature or to the executive departments.

One result has been the growth of a far more elaborate and esoteric legal language than ever existed in the days of the Founders or indeed for a century aferwards. The concept of Legal Realism as it developed in the earlier years of this century was not only a method of analysis; before that it might be described as an attempt to cope with the ever increasing complexity of the material to be interpreted. When you read the writings of the Founders you do not find that they write about constitutional law or jurisprudence in a private language; their language is intelligible to anyone interested in public affairs. The more recent development of concepts such as Legal Realism, Constructivism, and so forth is part of the process of professionalisation which has overtaken the law just as it has overtaken other specialisms such as economics and medicine – even I am afraid, political science.

No doubt the Founders would have found some of this confusing, but that is because, like many of us, they were laymen, not specialists. I do not think this means that there has been any fundamental breach of principle, any course that they could not have followed had they been presented with the implications of their own creation. I do think, however, that they might have been surprised at something else that has happened, and happened in relatively recent years. I am thinking of what I would call a standardisation of values. Throughout the United States, the same principles are made to apply to different situations that have about them a certain generic similarity. In this sense the United States has become one nation, and it is a sense which I do not think the Founders envisaged; I do think, however, that in a sense they would not not have expected, it follows from their handiwork. It was Lincoln who said that the nation could not survive half-slave and half-free. The Founders either thought it could, or decided that if they wanted to have a Union at all, they would have to leave that question to the future. But here is the nub of the question: how badly do you want to have a Union? In 1861 a great majority – and some of them certainly were in the South, though unable to have their way – wanted to have a Union even at the cost of imposing that unity by force.

It is a fact we ought to face that although the Founders were divided about slavery they were, on the whole, in much greater agreement with each other about race. None, or hardly any of them, envisaged a genuinely multi-ethnic society of equal individuals. Those are values that I believe most of us have left behind; the looseness, the formlessness of early American society, the vast distances and accepted differences, all made it possible to envisage a variety of social orders vaguely conforming to the formula of a republican form of government. The deeper paradox is that, as I have suggested, certain essential elements of the Constitution do mandate equal treatment and equal protection of individuals.

This is the kind of problem that most of the Founders preferred to leave to the discretion of the states. And yet I have a surprise for them. (History is full of surprises, except, of course, for historians, who always know what is going to happen.) It is arguable, I think, that some of the principles which would have seemed least likely to be adopted by the Founders' generation are implicit in their own work. Let me draw attention to Section 2 of Article Four of the Constitution itself. It is known as the Comity Clause, and is very brief – a masterly condensation, in fact, of a much more complicated statement of the same point in the old Articles of Confederation – and says simply: 'The citizens of each State shall be entitled to all the privileges and immunities of citizens in the several states.'

The Comity Clause has always been treated very cautiously by the Supreme Court, which has rejected the idea that a citizen on his travels through several states carries with him all the rights he may enjoy as a citizen of his own state.[10] But it has more extensive possibilities, as was twice indicated by dissenting justices in the nineteenth century with specific reference to racial matters. The first occurred when Justice Curtis invoked it in defence of Dred Scott's claims to freedom in 1857. Since only the Federal government could make citizens, it followed that all state citizens must have been taken up into national citizenship when the Constitution came into force. If Scott became free during his residence in free territory, he became a claimant to the rights of citizenship.[11] Fifty years later, Justice Harlan, in his famous dissent in *Plessy* v. *Ferguson*, again invoked the Comity Clause in a much more substantial claim for equality of treatment between blacks and whites.

It would be unhistorical to press twentieth-century conclusions on the eighteenth century. But I do suggest that it is possible to extract from the eighteenth-century concept of comity among citizens of different states a strand that will lead to substantive equality when you have a much more highly unified nation–state – a condition that certainly applied after the adoption of the Fourteenth and Fifteenth Amendments.

This thesis becomes all the more plausible when we take account of the general principles on which most of the Founders were agreed – with their own private reservations and interpretations, no doubt, but agreed in principle. The most important of these general principles were liberty and equality. We know that both these high-sounding words were and still are fraught with complexities, ambiguities and even internal contradictions: the research and indeed the public policy dilemmas of recent years have made that plain as never before. But the liberty in which the Founders believed was liberty of citizens enjoying equal rights under the law. That is why it was possible for Lincoln to conjoin these ideas when he described the nation as 'conceived in liberty and dedicated to the proposition that all men are created equal'. There existed at the time of the founding of the Constitution no American principle under which any one man could have claimed a right to differential treatment as a political individual or in the processes of law by virtue of social rank, title or descent. In fact the Constitution outlawed the notion of titles of nobility. I said 'man' and I said it advisedly. Men are in fact descended from women, but the world did not recognise women as political or even as legal equals in the eighteenth century. We know that there were people around who already regarded this situation as an anomaly, but they were exceptions, whose views would be appreciated only by later generations.

Ideas of equality need favourable ground in which to flourish. The United States provided that ground in varying degrees during later years, ground more favourable for some than for others. For our purposes the important point is that when the ground was friendly, the ideas were already there, powerfully enforced by the ideology of the Founders.

The Founders were also convinced of the truth of a view of politics which characterised the thought of the Enlightenment and was stated expressly by David Hume – the view that 'all government is founded on opinion'.[12] That opinion had in a sense to be voluntary – if it were coerced, the foundation of the state was insecure, and might even be illegitimate. There is an element of legal fiction about this when translated into politics, and the Founders were probably more convinced of it than we are. They certainly thought that the opinion in question ought to be that of free adults of the male sex and generally of the white race, but given those limitations, they saw these individuals as equals in political consent.

This brings me back to the point I made earlier, to which I promised to return. When Chief Justice Warren gave the judgement of the Supreme Court in *Reynolds* v. *Sims* in 1964, the first of the definitive apportionment cases, he laid down that 'Legislators represent people, not trees or acres. Legislators are elected by voters, not farms or cities or economic interests."[3] Representation was not perfectly equal in 1787; the equal representation of the states in the Senate even wrote a formal inequality into the Constitution. But representation was certainly meant to be based on a general principle of equality, and a long debate took place in the Convention on the number of persons for each legislative constituency. The inequalities that existed in representation in the states were unsatisfactory more from a theoretical point of view than from any serious injustice that flowed from them.

The situation changed in later generations but it did not change from any alteration in the governing principle. It changed because the distribution of population changed and legislators consciously subverted the principles on which the state had been founded. I therefore affirm my belief – whether you happen to believe in the principle itself is another matter – that Warren's strong words would have met with the approval of the Founders in the circumstances of their own time. There is irony in the fact that the most discerning of them, Madison, very soon saw that the circumstances of the time might change and that these changes might call for changed principles. That was because he wanted the agrarian interest to continue to prevail. Jefferson, despite his dislike of cities, was more content to rest on the judgement of the people.

The Founders gave to their successors a Constitution based on the fundamental principle of the rule of law. That law had to be judged by judges, but given by lawfully elected representatives. Madison gave America the credit for applying the idea of representation to an extended republic. And although the content of the laws has changed to an extent that would have passed beyond the recognition of the Founders, the principles are with us still.

I have left till last a theme that is easily taken for granted but which I believe to be very important. The Constitution contains provisions for its own amendment. These provisions are so cumbersome that political scientists often treat them as meaning that the Framers were in fact very strongly determined to prevent change in the Constitution. That is true to the extent that they did not wish to encourage change for what Jefferson had once called 'light and transient causes'. But the significant thing, within the terms of reference of the eighteenth century, is that they did recognise that social change was inevitable, and a constitution which failed to adapt itself to changes in society would eventually cease to be a constitution for that society.

The question of amendment has acquired new prominence; seldom in its two-hundred-year history has the Constitution been the object of so much concern. Although the operations of the presidency are at the centre of much of this concern, the real problem, as the Commission on the Constitution has rightly discerned, lies in the incongruous relations between executive and legislature.

It is worth recalling that when the Constitution was founded, informed opinion was pretty solidly agreed that in any republican form of government the chief source of power would always be in the legislature. 'In republican government, the legislative power necessarily predominates', said Madison in *Federalist* 51, with little fear of contradiction. This was one of the reasons for a strong and independent Executive: to act as a break on the popular passions that were expected to take possession of the legislature, at least from time to time.

All this has changed out of all recognition. If Attorney-General Meese wishes to be true to his principles, he might begin by advising the President to dismantle many of the powers of his office. Apart from the clause permitting the President to make annual recommendations to Congress, the Executive department was not expected to become a major source of policy. But as we all know, policy has long been worked out in Executive Bureaux when it does not emanate from the White House itself. The trouble is that there are really two *systems* of government, presidential and legislative, operating side by side. And they are too often pursuing different policies – even opposed ones.

The United States can no more afford the deadlocks and blockages that arise from the struggles, hostilities, and jealousies between the White House and the Hill than it can afford the excesses of a runaway presidency. It is not a particularly good method of government to render the executive powerless when you have no effective alternative method of forming and executing policy. Painful though it may be, the real need is to make the President accountable to Congress – which means giving Congress power to dismiss a president in whom it has lost confidence, and who has consequently lost his power to govern.

It has been said that 'continuity with the past is not a duty, it is only a necessity'.[4] The corollary to that is that adaptation to change is a necessity and therefore a duty. Failing that adaptability, you run the risk implied by Bryce's description of rigid constitutions. The actual direction and content of change is always a matter for debate. That is why you have political representation, parties and the rule of law – and a method, two methods in fact, of amending the Constitution.

NOTES

1 J. R. Pole, 'The American Past: is it still usable?', in *Paths to the American Past*, New York, 1979, originally published 1967.
2 *Minersville School District* v. *Gobitis*, 310 U.S. 586. 1940.
3 Guido Calabresi, *A Common Law for the Age of Statutes*, Cambridge, Mass., 1982, p. 18.
4 T. B. Howell (ed.), *State Trials*, London, 1816, XIX, pp., 1159 ff.
5 163 U.S. 537, 1896.
6 *The Idea of a Party System: the Rise of Legitimate Opposition in the United States, 1780-1840*, Berkeley, Ca., 1969.
7 John Marshall, *The Life of George Washington*, New York, 1925, V, pp. 279-306, 287.
8 James Bryce, *Studies in History and Jurisprudence*, 2 vols., New York, 1901, I, pp. 124-215.
9 *Federalist*, 78.
10 *Luther* v. *Borden*, 4 U.S. Howard I, 1849.
11 19 U.S. Howard 393, 1857.
12 'Of the first principles of government', in *Essays Moral, Political and Literary*, ed. T. H. Green and T. H. Grose, 2 vols., London, 1875, I, p. 110.
13 *Reynolds* v. *Sims*, 377 U.S. 533, 1964.
14 I think by C. H. McIlwain, though I have failed to find it.

Constitutional faith and the American people

ARTHUR J. GOLDBERG

Former Associate Justice of the Supreme Court

In America, as in Great Britain, we take justifiable pride in the fact that we are a government of law and not of men. The Magna Carta proclaimed the rule of law; this was its most significant contribution to the evolution of our two democracies.

No clause of the Magna Carta has proved to be of greater historic and contemporary import than Chapter 39, which provides that no freeman shall be imprisoned, dispossessed, banished or destroyed 'except by the legal judgment of his peers or by the law of the land'. This provision is, in effect, the origin of the concept of 'due process of law', the bedrock of the American Constitution.

The rule of the Magna Carta in the formulation of the American Constitution was well expressed by the Supreme Court in the case of *Bank of Columbia* v. *Okley,* 4 Wheat 235, 244, decided in 1819, in these words: 'The great Charter . . . (provides) that no freeman shall be taken, or imprisoned or disseized of his freehold, or liberties of his freehold, or liberties of free customs, nor passed upon, nor condemned, but by lawful judgment of his peers, or by the law of the land.'

Other key documents in Great Britain followed to enforce the promise and protect the liberties established by the Magna Carta: Confirmatio Cartarum, 1297, the Petition of Right, 1628, the Abolition of the Star Chamber, 1641, the Habeas Corpus Act, 1679, the Declaration and Bill of Rights, 1689, and the several colonial charters. Thus the framers of the American Constitution did not write on a clean slate in drafting our great Charter of Freedom and Liberty. It is, therefore, only fitting and proper that, on this occasion and in this setting, due acknowledgement be made of our debt to Great Britain for these great documents. They have contributed immeasurably to American Constitutional provisions and concepts.

A critical question, as the Bicentennial of the American Constitution is celebrated, is: Do the people of the United States have faith in this great Charter of Liberty?

The Constitution is an instrument of practical government: it is also a declaration of faith – in the spirit of freedom, equality and religious tolerance.

As an instrument of government, it has served Americans well for 200 years – a great testimonial to the wisdom and foresight of its Framers and the judicial statesmanship and legal skill of the Constitution's ultimate interpreter, the Supreme Court of the United States.

For the Court's role, we owe a great and lasting debt to Chief Justice Marshall and his historic decision in *Marbury* v. *Madison* asserting the evolutionary character of the Constitution and the right and duty of the judiciary to declare void an act of congress or a state which contravenes the Constitution.

His decision laid the foundation for both the judicial viewpoint and the propositions that all of high or low estate are subject to the rule of law and that constitutional safeguards of fundamental personal liberties are instilled with an innate capacity for growth to enable them to meet new needs.

These concepts were well stated by Associate Justice Joseph McKenna of the Supreme Court, in his opinion in *Weems* v. *United States*, decided in 1910:

Time works changes, brings into existence new conditions and purposes. Therefore a principle to be vital must be capable of wider application than the mischief which gave it birth. This is peculiarly true of constitutions. They are not ephemeral enactments, designed to meet passing occasions. They are, to use the words of Chief Justice Marshall, 'designed to approach immortality as nearly as human institutions can approach it'. The future is their care and provision for events of good and bad tendencies of which no prophecy can be made. In the application of a constitution, therefore, our contemplation cannot be only of what has been but of what may be. Under any other rule a constitution would indeed be as easy of application as it would be deficient in efficacy and power. Its general principles would have little value and be converted by precedent into impotent and lifeless formulas. Rights declared in words might be lost in reality.

These powers of the Court are responsible, in great measure, for the endurance and vitality of this great document.

As a declaration of faith, the Constitution is a testimonial to the commitment of Americans to the great goals of our revolution, liberty, equality and religious freedom. Yet, at the time the Constitution was drafted, liberty and equality were for whites only; the enslavement of blacks was sanctioned even by those who fought for the freedom of the colonies.

The nation's commitment to equality in its fullest sense awaited the passage of the Thirteenth, Fourteenth and Fifteenth Amendments, and the full implementation of these Amendments has not been fully realised to this day.

In addition to the failure to fully eradicate racial discrimination 'root and branch', women have not been accorded by the Court the full protection for all persons. The Court should decide they are so protected, but, if our highest tribunal continues to fail to do so, the Equal Rights Amendment to the Constitution should be enacted. Nevertheless, the Constitution affords the continuing means to remedy injustices and remains the embodiment of America's faith in equality and liberty.

But have the American people kept constitutional faith? The honest answer can only be, on the whole, yes, but on many occasions, no. All too often, we have been disposed to question whether we can accept and afford equality and liberty. I shall cite only a few examples.

An early congress, containing men who either wrote or participated in the ratification of the Constitution and the Bill of Rights, enacted the infamous Alien and Sedition Act. This repressive measure, abridging freedom of speech and of the press, was passed during the term of President Adams. It was enforced by lower federal judges who fined and sentenced to jail non-violent political dissenters, solely for exercising their First Amendment rights.

Fortunately, the statute expired by its terms in 1801; but it took President Jefferson's election to bring about the pardoning of those sentenced under the law, and it was not until half a century later that the fines levied in its prosecutions were repaid by an act of congress, on the ground that the Alien and Sedition Act was unconstitutional.

In *New York Times Company* v. *Sullivan*, decided in the 1960s, Justice Brennan, delivering the opinion of the Supreme Court, aptly observed that 'Although the Sedition Act was never tested in this Court, the attack upon its validity has carried the day in the court of history.'

The Alien and Sedition Act was the first, but by no means the last, law enacted or action taken by Congress abridging the liberties, freedom and equal rights of Americans.

Although invalidating an act of congress was characterised by Justice Holmes to be 'the gravest and most delicate duty that this Court is called upon to perform', the Supreme Court has, nevertheless, deemed it imperative to declare unconstitutional actions of Congress abridging or denying the civil rights and liberties of Americans, on a considerable number of occasions.

The Executive, too, in the past and in recent days, has lapsed in constitutional faith to the great impairment of constitutional provisions. A current illustration is the Iran–Contra scandal. Also, virtually all of the federal statures invalidated by the Supreme Court as abridging constitutional rights and liberties were signed by presidents, rather than vetoed. And to compound Executive failures in this regard, there are notable instances of Executive action, without foundation of law, seeking to deprive persons of their fundamental rights.

To mention only few instances, America's President, Abraham Lincoln, unconstitutionally suspended the great Writ of Habeas Corpus during the War Between the States, thus permitting allegedly disloyal citizens to be arrested and detained in military custody, without due process of law. The Supreme Court later held that the Writ could not be suspended while the civil courts were open and functioning.

President Truman, another great president, ordered the seizure and control of the steel mills, during a time of national emergency, without any statutory authority for doing so, and his action likewise was overturned by the Court.

Other more recent examples of presidential disregard of the Constitution and laws enacted pursuant thereto include the commitment of substantial American combat forces in Vietnam, without a declaration of war by Congress; the continued bombing of Cambodia, despite a congressional enactment cutting off appropriations for this purpose; the unjustified assertion of Executive privilege to frustrate the public's statutory right to information; presidential authorisation of telephone tapping for domestic surveillance without compliance with Fourth Amendment requirements; and, as I have mentioned, the Iran–Contra fiasco.

Thus not only do hard cases make bad law, but times of crisis tempt presidents to jeopardise basic liberties.

It is important to recall, in ths connection, what the Supreme Court said (*ex parte* Milligan) in Civil War days about constitutional protections during times of war:

> The Constitution of the United States is a law for rulers and people, equally in war and in peace, and covers with the shield of its protection all classes of men at all times, and under all circumstances. No doctrine, involving more pernicious consequences, was ever invented by the wit of man than that any of its provisions can be suspended during any of the great exigencies of government.

The Supreme Court itself, I regret to say, has also on occasion proved to be blind to the Constitution's true light.

Dred Scott, overruled by the Thirteenth Amendment, is almost universally recognised as one of the most ill-supported and ill-advised decisions in the Court's history. This decision, refusing to recognise the citizenship of a slave and declaring unconstitutional a federal law banning slavery in the territories, is not only legally unsound but has been characterised by some scholars as motivated by the political and sectional biases of certain members of the Court. It was also largely instrumental in precipitating the Civil War.

Plessy v. *Ferguson* negated the great purpose of the equal protection clause of the Fourteenth Amendment, and although overruled in recent times by *Brown* v. *Board of Education*, its discredited 'separate but equal' doctrine has contributed to the perpetuation of the racial problems which still afflict us.

In *Betts* v. *Brady*, the Court let stand a state court decision that refusal to provide counsel to indigent defendants accused of serious felonies did not violate the Constitution notwithstanding its guarantee to all persons of the right to counsel. Twenty-one years later, the unconstitutionality of that denial was recognised by an unanimous Court in *Gideon* v. *Wainwright* which held that government must provide counsel for those without funds to retain a lawyer.

In the *Gobitis* flag salute case, the Court by an eight-to-one majority rejected the good faith religious objection of Jehovah's Witnesses' schoolchildren by upholding their expulsion from school for refusing to salute the flag, contrary to their sincere religious beliefs. The reversal of this decision three years later hardly undid the injustice of the prior decision for the parties involved.

An egregious example is the Court's decision which allowed Louisiana to proceed with a second electrocution of a convicted felon after the first attempt failed because the flow of electricity to the electric chair, while searing, was not fatal. If the second electrocution is not cruel and unusual in a constitutional sense, it is difficult to conceive a case which is. And this most unfortunate decision has recently been reaffirmed by the Court.

The case of *Korematsu* v. *United States* is another illustration of Executive action, without Congressional sanction, sustained by the Supreme Court which, in my opinion, constituted a horrendous violation of constitutional rights.

By President Roosevelt's Executive Order, at the beginning of the Second World War, the government removed 110,000 persons of Japanese ancestry – 70,000 of whom were American citizens – from their homes in California, Oregon, and Washington and confined them in camps in the Rocky Mountain states. Despite a record devoid of any swing of disloyalty by these persons or a compelling governmental need for the removal or any known instances of American-Japanese aiding the enemy, the Supreme Court bowed to the passions of the time and found the relocation constitutional.

And, I regret to say, the Court has been all too prone to permit breaches in the constitutionally mandated wall of separation between Church and State.

The people, too, our history records, have from time to time failed to heed the warning of Thomas Paine that 'those who expect to reap the blessings of freedom must . . . undergo the fatigue of supporting it'. There are far too many instances where they have either acclaimed or acquiesced in unconstitutional actions abridging fundamental rights and liberties. The popular support for Senator Joseph McCarthy and his trampling on the constitutional right of citizens is a particularly outrageous example. Indeed, substantial segments of the population have often voiced strong disapproval of actions of the Executive, Congress or the Supreme Court protective of constitutional rights and liberties.

If thus far I have emphasised American failures to keep the constitutional faith, it is because of the overriding importance of keeping it. The record would be incomplete and totally distorted, however, were I not to make clear that, despite these transgressions, on the whole our constitutional faith has been kept. Presidents, from the very beginnings of the Republic, have accepted decisions of the Supreme Court totally repugnant to their own conceptions of the Constitution, thereby ensuring that we are a government of laws and not of men. President Eisenhower, for example, did so in the Little Rock civil rights case. Congress has railed against unpopular decisions of the Supreme Court, but, with rare exceptions has not interfered with its role as a 'palladium of liberty'. The Supreme Court itself has overruled prior decisions restrictive of the rights of Americans to liberty and equality and, indeed, enlarged these rights. And the people, to their great credit, despite passing transgressions, have stood by the Constitution and not tampered with it in any significant degree. The Bill of Rights has never been repealed – it remains the great protector of our liberties.

True, the Constitution has been amended sixteen times since the passage of the Bill of Rights, but most of these amendments are designed to improve the functioning of government and the electoral process, and the few that deal with citizens' rights enhance rather than contract them. Currently, high-ranking governmental officials, including Attorney-

General Meese, propose to alter the fundamental balance between the power of government and the autonomy of the individual as established in the Bill of Rights. A rising rate of crime has spawned an outcry that permissive Supreme Court decisions have handcuffed the police and over-protected the criminal at the expense of public safety. The attacks centre on the rights and privileges afforded by the Fourth, Fifth and Sixth Amendments, arguing that if these rights are limited there would be more convictions, and more convictions would mean less crime. Crime is a most serious problem but the nexus between the protection of individual rights and a rising crime rate has never been established. It is easy to point to a suspected criminal and characterise his rights as self-imposed restraints that law-abiding members of society have adopted only out of an exaggerated sense of fair play. Murderers and thieves are seen as 'taking advantage' of constitutional protections that the average citizen rarely has cause to exercise. However, the constitutional rights which are so criticised are the rights essential for all citizens and not merely safeguards for criminals. The Bill of Rights protects all Americans and the timeless wisdom embodied in its protections are essential to liberty and freedom for all and to our democracy.

The words of Winston Churchill, then Home Secretary, in a speech delivered in the House of Commons on 20 July 1910, are worth recalling:

> The mood and temper of the public in regard to the treatment of crime and criminals is one of the most unfailing tests of any country. A calm, dispassionate recognition of the rights of the accused, and even of the convicted criminal against the State – a constant heart-searching by all charged with the duty of punishment – a desire and eagerness to rehabilitate in the world of industry those who have paid their due in the hard courage of punishment; tireless efforts towards the discovery of curative and regenerative processes; unfailing faith that there is a treasure, if you can find it, in the heart of every man. These are the symbols, which, in the treatment of crime and criminal, mark and measure the stored up strength of a nation, and are sign and proof of the living virtue within it.

A most crucial inquiry, in constitutional terms, centres around the nature and extent of the right to personal privacy. Privacy does not exist as an absolute concept, but as a relationship to other entities. One may justifiably entertain a reasonable expectation of privacy in the home, while exposing parts of that home life to the postman, the milkman, the salesman and the casual passer-by. Freedom from governmental observation is similarly incomplete. The government naturally requires various types of information from the individual – the filing of tax returns for example. But the taking of information or the limited intrusion into personal privacy for one purpose does not authorise the use of that information for all purposes; and those intrusions must be sufficiently rare and sufficiently justified that the individual knows that his life is his own and that, at least most of the time, he has the right to remain unnoticed.

How many details of one's life are perfectly legal, honourable, yet personal; how many facts are there about each of us that the state or private institutions may at some point seek, but that we legitimately do not want known or publicly exposed? Modern computerised informational systems and their memory banks threaten this justifiable right to anonymity. The collection of personal information through tax forms, credit records, hospital data, and personnel files, for use in other areas, creates a potential for repression that can chill the exercise of guaranteed freedoms. And the subjects of electronic surveillance may never know their conversations have been overheard which leads to a temptation for exploratory eavesdropping with frightening implications.

Constitutional and statutory protections exist to safeguard the individual from such intrusions, provided the Executive respects these safeguards and Courts courageously enforce them.

The right to be free from unreasonable searches and seizures is guaranteed to all by the Fourth Amendment. By my reading of this Amendment, each and every time the government singles out an individual and directs an investigation against him, in any matter of domestic concern, not involving national security, the warrant procedure is required to obtain a disinterested judicial determination that the potential invasion of privacy is justified, except in the most exigent circumstances.

There are myriad other aspects to the right of personal privacy which are not specifically mentioned in the Bill of Rights, but which a majority of justices of the Supreme Court have found in the penumbras and emanations of those rights. As I indicated in my concurrence in *Griswold* v. *Connecticut*, the Connecticut birth control case, I was and am of the view that the marital chamber should be free from governmental intrusion under the Ninth Amendment. More important than scholastic differences over the particular location of this right, whether in the First, Fourth, Fifth, Ninth or Fourteenth Amendments or, in a combination of them, is the fact that the Supreme Court agrees that the right to personal privacy exists and protects interests not specifically enumerated in the Constitution. The abortion decision (*Roe* v. *Wade*) confirmed the holding in *Griswold*.

I venture the hope that the Court will continue to protect this 'right to be left alone' – eloquently described by Justice Brandeis as 'the most comprehensive of rights and the right most valued by civilized men'. The increased recognition of the right to personal privacy by the Court mirrors the increased public awareness of the importance of individual rights and liberties.

It would appear that, notwithstanding passing aberrations, the American people seem increasingly to realize that free speech, a free press, freedom of religion, due process of law, equal protection of personal privacy are potent weapons against governmental lawbreaking or overreaching. It is, I think, right to conclude that, in constitutional totality, the lamp of liberty may have dimmed in the United States on occasion, but it has never been extinguished.

It is encouraging that the American people at large, as the bicentennial celebrations demonstrated, are expressing renewed confidence in the principles of the Constitution. No steadier guide could be found by which the nation should chart its future course. As a nation, we have risked our all on this constitutional faith, as Judge Learned Hand once reminded us. The Constitution has not failed us; let not the American people fail it. After all, the source of the Constitution is – We the People. And it is the People who have, in explicit terms, mandated the Constitution to be the Supreme law of the Land.

Index

[This index includes footnote citations of court cases]